COMMUNAL SOCIETIES IN AMERICA
AN AMS REPRINT SERIES

CAESAR'S COLUMN

AMS PRESS
NEW YORK

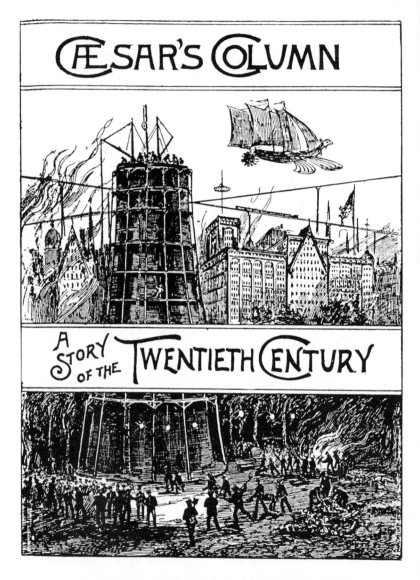

FROM THE ORIGINAL FRONT COVER

CÆSAR'S COLUMN.

A Story of the Twentieth Century.

BY

EDMUND BOISGILBERT, M. D.

"The true poet is only a masked father-confessor, whose special function it is to exhibit what is dangerous in sentiment and pernicious in action by a vivid picture of their consequences."—Goethe.

CHICAGO:
F. J. SCHULTE & COMPANY,
PUBLISHERS.

Library of Congress Cataloging in Publication Data

Donnelly, Ignatius, 1831–1901.
  Caesar's column.

  (Communal Societies in America)
  Reprint. Originally published: Chicago: F. J. Schulte,
c1890.
  I. Title.   II. Series.
PS1545.D55C4   1981   813'.4   76-42811
ISBN 0-404-60060-3   AACR2

Reprinted from the edition of 1890, Chicago, from an original in
the Cleveland Public Library. Trim size and text area have been
altered (original trim: 13.3 × 19.2 cm; original text area: 9 × 15
cm.)

MANUFACTURED
IN THE UNITED STATES OF AMERICA

TO THE PUBLIC.

. . .

It is to you, O thoughtful and considerate public, that I dedicate this book. May it, under the providence of God, do good to this generation and posterity!

I earnestly hope my meaning, in the writing thereof, may not be misapprehended.

It must not be thought, because I am constrained to describe the overthrow of civilization, that I desire it. The prophet is not responsible for the event he foretells. He may contemplate it with profoundest sorrow. Christ wept over the doom of Jerusalem.

Neither am I an anarchist: for I paint a dreadful picture of the world-wreck which successful anarchism would produce.

I seek to preach into the ears of the able and rich and powerful the great truth that neglect of the sufferings of their fellows, indifference to the great bond of brotherhood which lies at the base of Christianity, and blind, brutal and degrading worship of mere wealth, must—given time and pressure enough —eventuate in the overthrow of society and the destruction of civilization.

I come to the churches with my heart filled with the profoundest respect for the essentials of religion; I seek to show them why they have lost their hold

3

upon the poor,— upon that vast multitude, the best-beloved of God's kingdom,— and I point out to them how they may regain it. I tell them that if Religion is to reassume her ancient station, as crowned mistress of the souls of men, she must stand, in shining armor bright, with the serpent beneath her feet, the champion and defender of mankind against all its oppressors.

The world, to-day, clamors for deeds, not creeds; for bread, not dogma; for charity, not ceremony; for love, not intellect.

Some will say the events herein described are absurdly impossible.

Who is it that is satisfied with the present unhappy condition of society? It is conceded that life is a dark and wretched failure for the great mass of mankind. The many are plundered to enrich the few. Vast combinations depress the price of labor and increase the cost of the necessaries of existence. The rich, as a rule, despise the poor; and the poor are coming to hate the rich. The face of labor grows sullen; the old tender Christian love is gone; standing armies are formed on one side, and great communistic organizations on the other; society divides itself into two hostile camps; no white flags pass from the one to the other. They wait only for the drum-beat and the trumpet to summon them to armed conflict.

These conditions have come about in less than a century; most of them in a quarter of a century. Multiply them by the years of another century, and who shall say that the events I depict are impossible? There is an acceleration of movement in human affairs even as there is in the operations of gravity. The dead missile out of space at last blazes, and the very air takes fire. The masses grow more intelligent as they grow more wretched; and more capable of co-operation as they become more desperate. The labor organizations of to-day would have been impossible fifty years ago. And what is to arrest the flow of effect from cause? What is to prevent the coming of the night if the earth continues to revolve on its axis? The fool may cry out: "There shall be no night!" But the feet of the hours march unrelentingly toward the darkness.

Some may think that, even if all this be true, "*Cæsar's Column*" should not have been published. Will it arrest the moving evil to ignore its presence? What would be thought of the surgeon who, seeing upon his patient's lip the first nodule of the cancer, tells him there is no danger, and laughs him into security while the roots of the monster eat their way toward the great arteries? If my message be true it should be spoken; and the world should hear it. The cancer should be cut out while there is yet time. Any other course

> " Will but skin and film the ulcerous place,
>   While rank corruption, mining all beneath,
>   Infects unseen."

Believing, as I do, that I read the future aright, it would be criminal in me to remain silent. I plead for higher and nobler thoughts in the souls of men; for wider love and ampler charity in their hearts; for a renewal of the bond of brotherhood between the classes; for a reign of justice on earth that shall obliterate the cruel hates and passions which now divide the world.

If God notices anything so insignificant as this poor book, I pray that he may use it as an instrumentality of good for mankind; for he knows I love his human creatures, and would help them if I had the power.

CONTENTS.

CÆSAR'S COLUMN.

· . ·

CHAPTER I.

THE GREAT CITY.

[This book is a series of letters, from Gabriel Weltstein, in New York, to his brother, Heinrich Weltstein, in the State of Uganda, Africa.]

NEW YORK, Sept. 10, 1988.

MY DEAR BROTHER:

Here I am, at last, in the great city. My eyes are weary with gazing, and my mouth speechless with admiration; but in my brain rings perpetually the thought: Wonderful!—wonderful!—most wonderful!

What an infinite thing is man, as revealed in the tremendous civilization he has built up! These swarming, laborious, all-capable ants seem great enough to attack heaven itself, if they could but find a resting-place for their ladders. Who can fix a limit to the intelligence or the achievements of our species?

But our admiration may be here, and our hearts elsewhere. And so from all this glory and splendor I turn back to the old homestead, amid the high mountain valleys of Africa; to the primitive, simple shepherd-life; to my beloved mother, to you and to all our dear ones. This gorgeous, gilded room fades away, and I see the leaning hills, the trickling streams, the deep gorges where our woolly thousands graze;

9

and I hear once more the echoing Swiss horns of our
herdsmen reverberating from the snow-tipped mountains.

But my dream is gone. The roar of the mighty
city rises around me like the bellow of many cataracts.

New York contains now ten million inhabitants;
it is the largest city that is, or ever has been, in the
world. It is difficult to say where it begins or ends:
for the villas extend, in almost unbroken succession,
clear to Philadelphia; while east, west and north
noble habitations spread out mile after mile, far beyond the municipal limits.

But the wonderful city! Let me tell you of it.

As we approached it in our air-ship, coming from
the east, we could see, a hundred miles before we
reached the continent, the radiance of its millions of
magnetic lights, reflected on the sky, like the glare of
a great conflagration. These lights are not fed, as in
the old time, from electric *dynamos*, but the magnetism of the planet itself is harnessed for the use of
man. That marvelous earth-force which the Indians
called "the dance of the spirits," and civilized man
designated "the aurora borealis," is now used to
illuminate this great metropolis, with a clear, soft,
white light, like that of the full moon, but many
times brighter. And the force is so cunningly con-
served that it is returned to the earth, without any
loss of magnetic power to the planet. Man has
simply made a temporary loan from nature for which
he pays no interest.

Night and day are all one, for the magnetic light
increases automatically as the day-light wanes; and
the business parts of the city swarm as much at mid-

night as at high noon. In the old times, I am told, part of the streets was reserved for foot-paths for men and women, while the middle was given up to horses and wheeled vehicles; and one could not pass from side to side without danger of being trampled to death by the horses. But as the city grew it was found that the pavements would not hold the mighty, surging multitudes; they were crowded into the streets, and many accidents occurred. The authorities were at length compelled to exclude all horses from the streets, in the business parts of the city, and raise the central parts to a level with the sidewalks, and give them up to the exclusive use of the pedestrians, erecting stone pillars here and there to divide the multitude moving in one direction from those flowing in another. These streets are covered with roofs of glass, which exclude the rain and snow, but not the air. And then the wonder and glory of the shops! They surpass all description. Below all the business streets are subterranean streets, where vast trains are drawn, by smokeless and noiseless electric motors, some carrying passengers, others freight. At every street corner there are electric elevators, by which passengers can ascend or descend to the trains. And high above the house-tops, built on steel pillars, there are other railroads, not like the unsightly elevated trains we saw pictures of in our school books, but crossing diagonally over the city, at a great height, so as to best economize time and distance.

The whole territory between Broadway and the Bowery and Broome Street and Houston Street is occupied by the depot grounds of the great inter-continental air-lines; and it is an astonishing sight to see the ships ascending and descending, like monstrous

birds, black with swarming masses of passengers, to
or from England, Europe, South America, the Pacific
Coast, Australia, China, India and Japan.

These air-lines are of two kinds: the anchored and
the independent. The former are hung, by revolving
wheels, upon great wires suspended in the air; the
wires held in place by metallic balloons, fish-shaped,
made of aluminium, and constructed to turn with
the wind so as to present always the least surface to the air-currents. These balloons, where
the lines cross the oceans, are secured to huge
floating islands of timber, which are in turn anchored
to the bottom of the sea by four immense metallic
cables, extending north, south, east and west, and
powerful enough to resist any storms. These artificial
islands contain dwellings, in which men reside, who
keep up the supply of gas necessary for the balloons.
The independent air-lines are huge cigar-shaped
balloons, unattached to the earth, moving by electric
power, with such tremendous speed and force as to be
as little affected by the winds as a cannon ball. In
fact, unless the wind is directly ahead the sails of the
craft are so set as to take advantage of it like the
sails of a ship; and the balloon rises or falls, as the
birds do, by the angle at which it is placed to the
wind, the stream of air forcing it up, or pressing it
down, as the case may be. And just as the old-
fashioned steam-ships were provided with boats, in
which the passengers were expected to take refuge, if
the ship was about to sink, so the upper decks of
these air-vessels are supplied with parachutes, from
which are suspended boats; and in case of accident
two sailors and ten passengers are assigned to each
parachute; and long practice has taught the bold

craftsmen to descend gently and alight in the sea, even in stormy weather, with as much adroitness as a sea-gull. In fact, a whole population of air-sailors has grown up to manage these ships, never dreamed of by our ancestors. The speed of these aerial vessels is, as you know, very great—thirty-six hours suffices to pass from New York to London, in ordinary weather. The loss of life has been less than on the old-fashioned steam-ships; for, as those which go east move at a greater elevation than those going west, there is no danger of collisions; and they usually fly above the fogs which add so much to the dangers of sea-travel. In case of hurricanes they rise at once to the higher levels, above the storm; and, with our increased scientific knowledge, the coming of a cyclone is known for many days in advance; and even the stratum of air in which it will move can be foretold.

I could spend hours, my dear brother, telling you of the splendor of this hotel, called *The Darwin*, in honor of the great English philosopher of the last century. It occupies an entire block from Fifth Avenue to Madison Avenue, and from Forty-sixth Street to Forty-seventh. The whole structure consists of an infinite series of cunning adjustments, for the delight and gratification of the human creature. One object seems to be to relieve the guests from all necessity for muscular exertion. The ancient elevator, or "lift," as they called it in England, has expanded until now whole rooms, filled with ladies and gentlemen, are bodily carried up from the first story to the roof; a professional musician playing the while on the piano—not the old-fashioned thing our grandmothers used, but a huge instrument capable of giving forth all sounds of harmony from the trill of a

nightingale to the thunders of an orchestra. And
when you reach the roof of the hotel you find yourself
in a glass-covered tropical forest, filled with the perfume of many flowers, and bright with the scintillating
plumage of darting birds; all sounds of sweetness fill
the air, and many glorious, star-eyed maidens, guests
of the hotel, wander half seen amid the foliage, like the
houris in the Mohammedan's heaven.

But as I found myself growing hungry I descended
to the dining-room. It is three hundred feet long: a
vast multitude were there eating in perfect silence. It
is considered bad form here to interrupt digestion with
speech, as such a practice tends to draw the vital powers, it is said, away from the stomach to the head. Our
forefathers were expected to shine in conversation,
and be wise and witty while gulping their food between brilliant passages. I sat down at a table to
which I was marshaled by a grave and reverend seign-
ior in an imposing uniform. As I took my seat my
weight set some machinery in motion. A few feet in
front of me suddenly rose out of the table a large
upright mirror, or such I took it to be; but instantly
there appeared on its surface a grand bill of fare, each
article being numbered. The whole world had been
ransacked to produce the viands named in it; neither
the frozen recesses of the north nor the sweltering
regions of the south had been spared: every form of
food, animal and vegetable, bird, beast, reptile, fish;
the foot of an elephant, the hump of a buffalo, the
edible bird-nests of China; snails, spiders, shell-fish,
the strange and luscious creatures lately found in the
extreme depths of the ocean, and fished for with dynamite; in fact, every form of food pleasant to the palate
of man was there. For, as you know, there are men

who make fortunes now by preserving and breeding the game animals, like the deer, the moose, the elk, the buffalo, the antelope, the mountain sheep and goat, and many others, which but for their care would long since have become extinct. They select barren regions in mild climates, not fit for agriculture, and enclosing large tracts with wire fences, they raise great quantities of these valuable game animals, which they sell to the wealthy gourmands of the great cities, at very high prices.

I was perplexed, and, turning to the great man who stood near me, I began to name a few of the articles I wanted. He smiled complacently at my country ignorance, and called my attention to the fact that the table immediately before me contained hundreds of little knobs or buttons, each one numbered; and he told me that these were connected by electric wires with the kitchen of the hotel, and if I would observe the numbers attached to any articles in the bill of fare which I desired, and would touch the corresponding numbers of the knobs before me, my dinner would be ordered on a similar mirror in the kitchen, and speedily served. I did as he directed. In a little while an electric bell near me rang; the bill of fare disappeared from the mirror; there was a slight clicking sound; the table parted in front of me, the electric knobs moving aside; and up through the opening rose my dinner carefully arranged, as upon a table, which exactly filled the gap caused by the recession of that part of the original table which contained the electric buttons. I need not say I was astonished. I commenced to eat, and immediately the same bell, which had announced the disappearance of the bill of fare, rang again. I looked up, and the mirror now contained the name of every state in the Republic, from Hudson's Bay to the Isthmus of Darien; and the names of all the nations of the world; each name being numbered. My attendant, perceiving my perplexity, called my attention to the fact that the sides of the table which had brought up my dinner contained another set of electric buttons, corresponding with the numbers on the mirror; and he explained to me that if I would select any state or country and touch the corresponding button the news of the day, from that state or country, would appear in the mirror. He called my attention to the fact that every guest in the room had in front of him a similar mirror, and many of them were reading the news of the day as they ate. I touched the knob corresponding with the name of the new state of Uganda, in Africa, and immediately there appeared in the mirror all the doings of the people of that state—its crimes, its accidents, its business, the output of its mines, the markets, the sayings and doings of its prominent men; in fact, the whole life of the community was unrolled before me like a panorama. I then touched the button for another African state, Nyanza; and at once I began to read of new lines of railroad; new steamship fleets upon the great lake; of large colonies of white men, settling new states, upon the higher lands of the interior; of their colleges, books, newspapers; and particularly of a dissertation upon the genius of Chaucer, written by a Zulu professor, which had created considerable interest among the learned societies of the Transvaal. I touched the button for China and read the important news that the Republican Congress of that great and highly civilized nation had decreed that English, the universal language of the rest of the globe, should be hereafter used in the courts of justice and taught in all the schools. Then came the news that a Manchurian professor, an iconoclast, had written a learned work, in English, to prove that George Washington's genius and moral greatness had been much over-rated by the partiality of his countrymen. He was answered by a learned doctor of Japan, who argued that the greatness of all great men consisted simply in opportunity, and that for every illustrious name that shone in the pages of history, associated with important events, a hundred abler men had lived and died unknown. The battle was raging hotly, and all China and Japan were dividing into contending factions upon this great issue.

Our poor ignorant ancestors of a hundred years ago drank alcohol in various forms, in quantities which the system could not consume or assimilate, and it destroyed their organs and shortened their lives. Great agitations arose until the manufacture and sale of alcoholic beverages was prohibited over nearly all the world. At length the scientists observed that the craving was based on a natural want of the system; that alcohol was found in small quantities in nearly every article of food; and that the true course was to so increase the amount of alcohol in the food, without gratifying the palate, as to meet the real necessities of the system, and prevent a decrease of the vital powers.

It is laughable to read of those days when men were drugged with pills, boluses and powders. Now our physic is in our food; and the doctor prescribes a series of articles to be eaten or avoided, as the case may be. One can see at once by consulting his "vital-watch," which shows every change in the magnetic

2

and electric forces of the body, just how his physical strength wanes or increases; and he can modify his diet accordingly; he can select, for instance, a dish highly charged with quinine or iron, and yet perfectly palatable; hence, among the wealthier classes, a man of one hundred is as common now-a-days as a man of seventy was a century ago; and many go far beyond that point, in full possession of all their faculties.

I glanced around the great dining-room and inspected my neighbors. They all carried the appearance of wealth; they were quiet, decorous and courteous. But I could not help noticing that the women, young and old, were much alike in some particulars, as if some general causes had molded them into the same form. Their brows were all fine — broad, square, and deep from the ear forward; and their jaws also were firmly developed, square like a soldier's; while the profiles were classic in their regularity, and marked by great firmness. The most peculiar feature was their eyes. They had none of that soft, gentle, benevolent look which so adorns the expression of my dear mother and other good women whom we know. On the contrary, their looks were bold, penetrating, immodest, if I may so express it, almost to fierceness: they challenged you; they invited you; they held intercourse with your soul.

The chief features in the expression of the men were incredulity, unbelief, cunning, observation, heartlessness. I did not see a *good* face in the whole room: powerful faces there were, I grant you; high noses, resolute mouths, fine brows; all the marks of shrewdness and energy; a forcible and capable race; but that was all. I did not see one, my dear brother, of whom I could say, "That man would sacrifice himself for another; that man loves his fellow man."

I could not but think how universal and irresistible must have been the influences of the age that could mold all these men and women into the same soulless likeness. I pitied them. I pitied mankind, caught in the grip of such wide-spreading tendencies. I said to myself: "Where is it all to end? What are we to expect of a race without heart or honor? What may we look for when the powers of the highest civilization supplement the instincts of tigers and wolves? Can the brain of man flourish when the heart is dead?"

I rose and left the room.

I had observed that the air of the hotel was sweeter, purer and cooler than that of the streets outside. I asked one of the attendants for an explanation. He took me out to where we could command a view of the whole building, and showed me that a great canvas pipe rose high above the hotel, and, tracing it upwards, far as the eye could reach, he pointed out a balloon, anchored by cables, so high up as to be dwarfed to a mere speck against the face of the blue sky. He told me that the great pipe was double; that through one division rose the hot, exhausted air of the hotel, and that the powerful draft so created operated machinery which pumped down the pure, sweet air from a higher region, several miles above the earth; and, the current once established, the weight of the colder atmosphere kept up the movement, and the air was then distributed by pipes to every part of the hotel. He told me also that the hospitals of the city were supplied in the same manner; and the result had been, he said, to diminish the mortality of the sick one-half; for the air so brought to them was perfectly free from bacteria and full of all life-giving properties. A company had been organized to supply the houses of the rich with this cold, pure air for so much a thousand feet, as long ago illuminating gas was furnished.

I could not help but think that there was need that some man should open connection with the upper regions of God's charity, and bring down the pure beneficent spirit of brotherly love to this afflicted earth, that it might spread through all the tainted hospitals of corruption for the healing of the hearts and souls of the people.

This attendant, a sort of upper-servant, I suppose, was quite courteous and polite, and, seeing that I was a stranger, he proceeded to tell me that the whole city was warmed with hot water, drawn from the profound depths of the earth, and distributed as drinking water was distributed a century ago, in pipes, to all the houses, for a fixed and very reasonable charge. This heat-supply is so uniform and so cheap that it has quite driven out all the old forms of fuel—wood, coal, natural gas, etc.

And then he told me something which shocked me greatly. You know that according to our old-fashioned ideas it is unjustifiable for any person to take his own life, and thus rush into the presence of his Maker before he is called. We are of the opinion of Hamlet that God has "fixed his canon 'gainst self-slaughter." Would you believe it, my dear brother, in this city they actually facilitate suicide! A race of philosophers has arisen in the last fifty years who argue that, as man was not consulted about his coming into the world, he has a perfect right to leave it whenever it becomes uncomfortable. These strange arguments were supplemented by the economists, always a powerful body in this utilitarian land, and they urged that, as men could not be prevented from destroying themselves, if they had made up their minds to do so, they might just as well shuffle off the mortal coil in the way that would give least trouble to their surviving fellow-citizens. That, as it was, they polluted the rivers, and even the reservoirs of drinking-water, with their dead bodies, and put the city to great expense and trouble to recover and identify them. Then came the humanitarians, who said that many persons, intent on suicide, but knowing nothing of the best means of effecting their object, tore themselves to pieces with cruel pistol shots or knife wounds, or took corrosive poisons, which subjected them to agonizing tortures for hours before death came to their relief; and they argued that if a man had determined to leave the world it was a matter of humanity to help him out of it by the pleasantest means possible. These views at length prevailed, and now in all the public squares or parks they have erected handsome houses, beautifully furnished, with baths and bed-rooms. If a man has decided to die, he goes there. He is first photographed; then his name, if he sees fit to give it, is recorded, with his residence; and his directions are taken as to the disposition of his body. There are tables at which he can write his farewell letters to his friends. A doctor explains to him the nature and effect of the different poisons, and he selects the kind he prefers. He is expected to bring with him the clothes in which he intends to be cremated. He swallows a little pill, lies down upon a bed, or, if he prefers it, in his coffin; pleasant music is played for him; he goes to sleep, and wakes up on the other side of the great line. Every day hundreds of people, men and women, perish in this way; and they are borne off to the great furnaces for the dead, and consumed. The authorities assert that it is a marked improvement over the old-fashioned methods; but to my mind it is a shocking combination of impiety and mock-philanthropy. The truth is, that, in this vast, over-crowded city, man is a drug,—a superfluity,—and I think many men and women end their lives out of an overwhelming sense of their own insignificance;—in other words, from a mere weariness of feeling that they are nothing, they become nothing.

I must bring this letter to an end, but before retiring I shall make a visit to the grand parlors of the hotel. You suppose I will walk there. Not at all, my dear brother. I shall sit down in a chair; there is an electric magazine in the seat of it. I touch a spring, and away it goes. I guide it with my feet. I drive into one of the great elevators. I descend to the drawing-room floor. I touch the spring again, and in a few moments I am moving around the grand salon, steering myself clear of hundreds of similar chairs, occupied by fine-looking men or the beautiful, keen-eyed, unsympathetic women I have described. The race has grown in power and loveliness—I fear it has lost in lovableness.

Good-by. With love to all, I remain your affectionate brother,

GABRIEL WELTSTEIN.

CHAPTER II.

My Dear Heinrich:

I little supposed when I wrote you yesterday that twenty-four hours could so completely change my circumstances. Then I was a dweller in the palatial Darwin Hotel, luxuriating in all its magnificence. Now I am hiding in a strange house and trembling for my liberty;—but I will tell you all.

Yesterday morning, after I had disposed by sample of our wool, and had called upon the assayer of ores, but without finding him, to show him the specimens of our mineral discoveries, I returned to the hotel, and there, after obtaining directions from one of the clerks at the "Bureau of Information," I took the elevated train to the great Central Park.

I shall not pause to describe at length the splendors of this wonderful place; the wild beasts roaming about among the trees, apparently at dangerous liberty, but really inclosed by fine steel wire fences, almost invisible to the eye; the great lakes full of the different water fowl of the world; the air thick with birds distinguished for the sweetness of their song or the brightness of their plumage; the century-old trees, of great size and artistically grouped; beautiful children playing upon the greensward, accompanied by nurses and male servants; the whole scene constituting a holiday picture. Between the trees everywhere I saw the white and gleaming statues of the many hundreds of great men and women who have adorned the history of this country during the last two hundred years—poets, painters, musicians, soldiers, philanthropists, statesmen.

After feasting my eyes for some time upon this charming picture of rural beauty, I left the Park. Soon after I had passed through the outer gate,— guarded by sentinels to exclude the ragged and wretched multitude, but who at the same time gave courteous admission to streams of splendid carriages, —I was startled by loud cries of "Look out there!" I turned and saw a sight which made my blood run cold. A gray-haired, hump-backed beggar, clothed in rags, was crossing the street in front of a pair of handsome horses, attached to a magnificent open carriage. The burly, ill-looking flunkey who, clad in gorgeous livery, was holding the lines, had uttered the cry of warning, but at the same time had made no effort to check the rapid speed of his powerful horses. In an instant the beggar was down under the hoofs of the steeds. The flunkey laughed! I was but a few feet distant on the side-walk, and, quick as thought, I had the horses by their heads and pushed them back upon their haunches. At this moment the beggar, who had been under the feet of the horses, crawled out close to the front wheels of the carriage; and the driver, indignant that anything so contemptible should arrest the progress of his magnificent equipage, struck him a savage blow with his whip, as he was struggling to his feet. I saw the whip wind around his neck; and, letting go the horses' heads, who were now brought to a stand-still, I sprang forward, and as the whip descended for a second blow I caught it, dragged it from the hand of the miscreant, and with all my power laid it over him. Each blow where it touched his flesh brought the blood, and two long red gashes appeared instantaneously upon his face. He dropped his lines and shrieked in terror, holding his hands up to protect his face. Fortunately a crowd had assembled, and some poorly dressed men had seized the horses' heads, or there would have been a run-away. As I raised my hand to lash the brute again, a feminine shriek reached my ears, and I became aware that there were ladies in the open barouche. My sense of politeness overcame in an instant my rage, and I stepped back, and, taking off my hat, began to apologize and explain the cause of the difficulty. As I did so I observed that the occupants of the carriage were two young ladies, both strikingly handsome, but otherwise very unlike in appearance. The one nearest me, who had uttered the shrieks, was about twenty years of age, I should think, with aquiline features, and black eyes and hair; every detail of the face was perfect, but there was a bold, commonplace look out of the bright eyes. Her companion instantly arrested all my attention. It seemed to me I had never beheld a more beautiful and striking countenance. She was younger, by two or three years, than her companion; her complexion was fairer; her long golden hair fell nearly to her waist, enfolding her like a magnificent, shining garment; her eyes were blue and large and set far apart; and there was in them, and in the whole contour of the face, a look of honesty and dignity, and calm intelligence, rarely witnessed in the countenance of woman. She did not appear to be at all alarmed; and when I told my story of the driver lashing the aged beggar, her face lighted up, and she said, with a look that thrilled me,

and in a soft and gentle voice: "We are much obliged
to you, sir; you did perfectly right."

I was about to reply, when I felt some one tugging
fiercely at my coat, and, turning around, I was surprised to find that the beggar was drawing me away
from the carriage by main force. I was astonished also
at the change in his appearance. The aspect of decrepi-
tude had disappeared, a green patch that I had
noticed covering one of his eyes had fallen off, and
his black eyes shone with a look of command and
power that was in marked contrast with his gray hair,
his crooked back, and his rags.

"Come," he said, in a hoarse whisper, "come
quickly, or you will be arrested and cast into prison."

"What for?" I asked.

"I will tell you hereafter—look!"

I looked around me and saw that a great crowd
had collected as if by magic, for this city of ten millions of people so swarms with inhabitants that the
slightest excitement will assemble a multitude in a
few minutes. I noticed, too, in the midst of the mob,
a uniformed policeman. The driver saw him also, and,
recovering his courage, cried out, "Arrest him—arrest him." The policeman seized me by the collar.
I observed that at that instant the beggar whispered
something in his ear: the officer's hand released its
hold upon my coat. The next moment the beggar cried
out, "Back! Back! Look out! Dynamite!" The crowd
crushed back on each other in great confusion; and
I felt the beggar dragging me off, repeating his cry of
warning—"Dynamite! Dynamite!"—at every step,
until the mob scattered in wild confusion, and I found
myself breathless in a small alley. "Come, come," cried
my companion, "there is no time to lose. Hurry,

hurry!" We rushed along, for the manner of the beggar inspired me with a terror I could not explain, until, after passing through several back streets and small alleys, with which the beggar seemed perfectly familiar, we emerged on a large street and soon took a corner elevator up to one of the railroads in the air which I have described. After traveling for two or three miles we exchanged to another train, and from that to still another, threading our way backward and forward over the top of the great city. At length, as if the beggar thought we had gone far enough to baffle pursuit, we descended upon a bustling business street, and paused at a corner; and the beggar appeared to be looking out for a hack. He permitted a dozen to pass us, however, carefully inspecting the driver of each. At last he hailed one, and we took our seats. He gave some whispered directions to the driver, and we dashed off.

"Throw that out of the window," he said.

I followed the direction of his eyes and saw that I still held in my hand the gold-mounted whip which I had snatched from the hand of the driver. In my excitement I had altogether forgotten its existence, but had instinctively held on to it.

"I will send it back to the owner," I said.

"No, no; throw it away: that is enough to convict you of highway robbery."

I started, and exclaimed:

"Nonsense; highway robbery to whip a blackguard?"

"Yes. You stop the carriage of an aristocrat; you drag a valuable whip out of the hand of his coachman; and you carry it off. If that is not highway robbery, what is it? Throw it away."

His manner was imperative. I dropped the whip out of the window and fell into a brown study. I occasionally stole a glance at my strange companion, who, with the dress of extreme poverty, and the gray hair of old age, had such a manner of authority and such an air of promptitude and decision.

After about a half-hour's ride we stopped at the corner of two streets in front of a plain but respectable-looking house. It seemed to be in the older part of the town. My companion paid the driver and dismissed him, and, opening the door, we entered.

I need not say that I began to think this man was something more than a beggar. But why this disguise? And who was he?

CHAPTER III.

THE BEGGAR'S HOME.

THE HOUSE we entered was furnished with a degree of splendor of which the external appearance gave no prophecy. We passed up the stairs and into a handsome room, hung around with pictures, and adorned with book-cases. The beggar left me.

I sat for some time looking at my surroundings, and wondering over the strange course of events which had brought me there, and still more at the actions of my mysterious companion. I felt assured now that his rags were simply a disguise, for he entered the house with all the air of a master; his language was well chosen and correctly spoken, and possessed those subtle tones and intonations which mark an educated mind. I was thinking over these matters when the door opened and a handsome young gentleman, arrayed in the height of the fashion, entered the room. I rose to my feet and began to apologize for my intrusion and to explain that I had been brought there by a beggar to whom I had rendered some trifling service in the street. The young gentleman listened, with a smiling face, and then, extending his hand, said:

"I am the beggar; and I do now what only the hurry and excitement prevented me from doing before —I thank you for the life you have saved. If you had not come to my rescue I should probably have been trampled to death under the feet of those vicious horses, or sadly beaten at least by that brutal driver."

The expression of my face doubtless showed my extreme astonishment, for he proceeded:

"I see you are surprised; but there are many strange things in this great city. I was disguised for a particular purpose, which I cannot explain to you. But may I not request the name of the gentleman to whom I am under so many obligations? Of course, if you have any reasons for concealing it, consider the question as not asked."

"No," I replied, smiling, "I have no concealments. My name is Gabriel Weltstein; I live in the new state of Uganda, in the African confederation, in the mountains of Africa, near the town of Stanley; and I am engaged in sheep-raising, in the mountains. I belong to a colony of Swiss, from the canton of Uri, who, led by my grandfather, settled there seventy years ago. I came to this city yesterday to see if I could not sell my wool directly to the manufacturers, and thus avoid the extortions of the great Wool Ring, which has not only our country but the whole world in its grasp; but I find the manufacturers are tied hand and foot, and afraid of that powerful combination; they do not dare to deal with me; and thus I shall have to dispose of my product at the old price. It is a shameful state of affairs in a country which calls itself free."

"Pardon me for a moment," said the young gentleman, and left the room. On his return I resumed:

"But now that I have told you who I am, will you be good enough to tell me something about yourself?"

"Certainly," he replied, "and with pleasure. I am

a native of this city; my name is Maximilian Petion; by profession I am an attorney; I live in this house with my mother, to whom I shall soon have the pleasure of introducing you."

"Thank you," I replied, still studying the face of my new acquaintance. His complexion was dark, the eyes and hair almost black; the former very bright and penetrating; his brow was high, broad and square; his nose was prominent, and there was about the mouth an expression of firmness, not unmixed with kindness. Altogether it was a face to inspire respect and confidence. But I made up my mind not to trust too much to appearances. I could not forget the transformation which I had witnessed, from the rags of the ancient beggar to this well-dressed young gentleman. I knew that the criminal class were much given to such disguises. I thought it better therefore to ask some questions that might throw light upon the subject.

"May I inquire," I said, "what were your reasons for hurrying me away so swiftly and mysteriously from the gate of the Park?"

"Because," he replied, "you were in great danger, and you had rendered me a most important service. I could not leave you there to be arrested, and punished with a long period of imprisonment, because, following the impulse of your heart, you had saved my life and scourged the wretch who would have driven his horses over me."

"But why should I be punished with a long term of imprisonment? In my own country the act I performed would have received the applause of every one. Why did you not tell me to throw away that whip on the instant, so as to avoid the appearance of stealing it, and then remain to testify in my behalf if I had been arrested?"

"Then you do not know," he replied, "whose driver it was you horsewhipped?"

"No," I said; "how should I? I arrived here but yesterday."

"That was the carriage of Prince Cabano, the wealthiest and most vindictive man in the city. If you had been taken you would have been consigned to imprisonment for probably many years."

"Many years," I replied; "imprisoned for beating an insolent driver! Impossible. No jury would convict me of such an offense."

"Jury!" he said, with a bitter smile; "it is plain to see you are a stranger and come from a newly settled part of the world, and know nothing of our modern civilization. The jury would do whatever Prince Cabano desired them to do. Our courts, judges and juries are the merest tools of the rich. The image of justice has slipped the bandage from one eye, and now uses her scales to weigh the bribes she receives. An ordinary citizen has no more prospect of fair treatment in our courts, contending with a millionaire, than a new-born infant would have of life in the den of a wolf."

"But," I replied, rather hotly, "I should appeal for justice to the public through the newspapers."

"The newspapers!" he said, and his face darkened as he spoke; "the newspapers are simply the hired mouthpieces of power; the devil's advocates of modern civilization; their influence is always at the service of the highest bidder; it is their duty to suppress or pervert the truth, and they do it thoroughly. They are paid to mislead the people under the guise of defending them. A century ago this thing began, and it has gone on, growing worse and worse, until now the people laugh at the opinions of the press, and doubt the truth even of its reports of occurrences."

"Can this be possible?" I said.

"Let me demonstrate it to you," he replied, and, stepping to the wall, he spoke quietly into a telephone tube, of which there were a number ranged upon the wall, and said:

"Give me the particulars of the whipping of Prince Cabano's coachman, this afternoon, at the south gate of Central Park."

Almost immediately a bell rang, and on the opposite wall, in what I had supposed to be a mirror, appeared these words:

From the Evening Guardian:

A HORRIBLE OUTRAGE!

HIGHWAY ROBBERY!—ONE THOUSAND DOLLARS REWARD!

This afternoon, about three o'clock, an event transpired at the south gate of Central Park which shows the turbulent and vicious spirit of the lower classes, and reinforces the demand we have so often made for repressive measures and a stronger government.

As the carriage of our honored fellow-citizen Prince Cabano, containing two ladies, members of his family, was quietly entering the Park, a tall, powerful ruffian, apparently a stranger, with long yellow hair, reaching to his shoulders, suddenly grasped a valuable gold-mounted whip out of the hands of the driver, and, because he resisted the robbery, beat him across the face, inflicting very severe wounds. The horses became very much terrified, and but for the fact that two worthy men, John Henderson of 5222 Delavan Street, and William Brooks of 7322 Bismarck Street, seized them by the head, a terrible accident would undoubtedly have occurred. Policeman number B 17822 took the villain prisoner, but he knocked the guardian of the law down and escaped, accompanied by a ragged old fellow who seemed to have been his accomplice. It is believed that the purpose of the thieves was to rob the occupants

3

of the carriage, as the taller one approached the ladies, but just then his companion saw the policeman coming and gave him warning, and they fled together. Prince Cabano is naturally very much incensed at this outrage, and has offered a reward of one thousand dollars for the apprehension of either of the ruffians. They have been tracked for a considerable distance by the detectives; but after leaving the elevated cars all trace of them was suddenly and mysteriously lost. The whip was subsequently found on Bomba Street and identified. Neither of the criminals is known to the police. The taller one was quite young and fairly well dressed, and not ill-looking, while his companion had the appearance of a beggar, and seemed to be about seventy years of age. The Chief of Police will pay liberally for any information that may lead to the arrest of the robbers.

"There," said my companion, "what do you think of that?"

I need not say that I was paralyzed with this adroit mingling of fact and falsehood. I realized for the first time the perils of my situation. I was a stranger in the great city, without a friend or acquaintance, and hunted like a felon! While all these thoughts passed through my brain, there came also a pleasing flash of remembrance of that fair face, and that sweet and gentle smile, and that beaming look of gratitude and approval of my action in whipping the brutal driver. But if my new acquaintance was right; if neither courts nor juries nor newspapers nor public opinion could be appealed to for justice or protection, then indeed might I be sent to prison as a malefactor, for a term of years, for performing a most righteous act. If it was true, and I had heard something of the same sort in my far-away African home, that money ruled everything in this great country; and if his offended lordship desired to crush me, he could certainly do so. While I was buried in these reflections I had not failed to notice that an electric bell rang upon the side of the chamber and a small box opened, and the young gentleman advanced and took from the box a sheet of tissue paper, closely written. I recognized it as a telegram. He read it carefully, and I noticed him stealing glances at me, as if comparing the details of my appearance with something written on the paper. When he finished he advanced toward me, with a brighter look on his face, and, holding out his hand, said:

"I have already hailed you as my benefactor, my preserver; permit me now to call you my friend."

"Why do you say so?" I asked.

"Because," he replied, "I now know that every statement you made to me about yourself is literally true; and that in your personal character you deserve the respect and friendship of all men. You look perplexed. Let me explain. You told me some little time since your name and place of residence. I belong to a society which has its ramifications all over the world. When I stepped out of this room I sent an inquiry to the town near which you reside, and asked if such a person as you claimed to be lived there; what was his appearance, standing and character, and present residence. I shall not shock your modesty by reading the reply I have just received. You will pardon this distrust, but we here in the great city are suspicious, and properly so, of strangers, and even more so of each other. I did not know but that you were in the employment of the enemies of our society, and sought to get into my confidence by rendering me a service,—for the tricks to which the detectives resort are infinite. I now trust you implicitly, and you can command me in everything."

I took his hand warmly and thanked him cordially. It was impossible to longer doubt that frank and beaming face.

"But," I said, "are we not in great danger? Will not that hackman, for the sake of the reward, inform the police of our whereabouts?"

"No!" he said; "have no fears upon that score. Did you not observe that I permitted about a dozen hacks to pass me before I hailed the one that brought us here? That man wore on his dress a mark that told me he belonged to our Brotherhood. He knows that if he betrays us he will die within twenty-four hours, and that there is no power on earth could save him; if he fled to the uttermost ends of the earth his doom would overtake him with the certainty of fate. So have no uneasiness. We are as safe here as if a standing army of a hundred thousand of our defenders surrounded this house."

"Is that the explanation," I asked, "of the policeman releasing his grip upon my coat?"

"Yes," he replied, quietly.

"Now," said I, "who is this Prince Cabano, and how does he happen to be called Prince? I thought your Republic eschewed all titles of nobility."

"So it does," he replied, "by law. But we have a great many titles which are used socially, by courtesy. The Prince, for instance, when he comes to sign his name to a legal document, writes it Jacob Isaacs. But his father, when he grew exceedingly rich and ambitious, purchased a princedom in Italy for a large sum, and the government, being hard up for money, conferred the title of Prince with the estate. His son, the present Isaacs, succeeded, of course, to his estates and his title."

"'Isaacs,'" I said, "is a Jewish name?"

"Yes," he replied, "the aristocracy of the world is now almost altogether of Hebrew origin."

"Indeed," I asked, "how does that happen?"

"Well," he replied, "it was the old question of the survival of the fittest. Christianity fell upon the Jews, originally a race of agriculturists and shepherds, and forced them, for many centuries, through the most terrible ordeal of persecution the history of mankind bears any record of. Only the strong of body, the cunning of brain, the long-headed, the persistent, the men with capacity to live where a dog would starve, survived the awful trial. Like breeds like; and now the Christian world is paying, in tears and blood, for the sufferings inflicted by their bigoted and ignorant ancestors upon a noble race. When the time came for liberty and fair play the Jew was master in the contest with the Gentile, who hated and feared him.

"They are the great money-getters of the world. They rose from dealers in old clothes and peddlers of hats to merchants, to bankers, to princes. They were as merciless to the Christian as the Christian had been to them. They said, with Shylock: 'The villainy you teach me I will execute; and it shall go hard but I will better the instruction.' The 'wheel of fortune has come full circle;' and the descendants of the old peddlers now own and inhabit the palaces where their ancestors once begged at the back doors for second-hand clothes; while the posterity of the former lords have been, in many cases, forced down into the swarming misery of the lower classes. This is a sad world, and to contemplate it is enough to make a man a philosopher; but he will scarcely know whether to belong to the laughing or the weeping school—whether to follow the example of Democritus or Heraclitus."

"And may I ask," I said, "what is the nature of your society?"

"I cannot tell you more at this time," he replied, "than that it is a political secret society having a membership of millions, and extending all over the world. Its purposes are the good of mankind. Some day, I hope, you may learn more about it. Come," he added, "let me show you my house, and introduce you to my mother."

Touching a secret spring in the wall, a hidden door flew open, and we entered a small room. I thought I had gotten into the dressing-room of a theater. Around the walls hung a multitude of costumes, male and female, of different sizes, and suited for all conditions of life. On the table were a collection of bottles, holding what I learned were hair dyes of different colors; and there was also an assortment of wigs, beards and mustaches of all hues. I thought I recognized among the former the coarse white hair of the quondam beggar. I pointed it out to him.

"Yes," he said, with a laugh, "I will not be able to wear that for some time to come."

Upon another table there was a formidable array of daggers, pistols and guns; and some singular-looking iron and copper things, which he told me were cartridges of dynamite and other deadly explosives.

I realized that my companion was a conspirator. But of what kind? I could not believe evil of him. There was a manliness and kindliness in his face which forbade such a thought; although the square chin and projecting jaws and firm-set mouth indicated a nature that could be most dangerous; and I noticed sometimes a restless, wild look in his eyes.

I followed him into another room, where he introduced me to a sweet-faced old lady, with the same broad brow and determined, but gentle, mouth which so distinguished her son. It was evident that there was great love between them, although her face wore a troubled and anxious look, at times, as she regarded him. It seemed to me that she knew he was engaged in dangerous enterprises.

She advanced to me with a smile and grasped both my hands with her own, as she said:

"My son has already told me that you have this day rendered him and me an inestimable service. I need not say that I thank you with all my heart."

I made light of the matter and assured her that I was under greater obligations to her son than he was to me. Soon after we sat down to dinner, a sumptuous meal, to which it seemed to me all parts of the world had contributed. We had much pleasant conversation, for both the host and hostess were persons of ripe information. In the old days our ancestors wasted years of valuable time in the study of languages that were no longer spoken on the earth; and civilization was thus cramped by the shadow of the ancient Roman Empire, whose dead but sceptered sovereigns still ruled the spirits of mankind from their urns. Now every hour is considered precious for the accumulation of actual knowledge of facts and things, and for the cultivation of the graces of the mind; so that mankind has become wise in breadth of knowledge, and sweet and gentle in manner. I expressed something of this thought to Maximilian, and he replied:

"Yes; it is the greatest of pities that so noble and beautiful a civilization should have become so hollow and rotten at the core."

"Rotten at the core!" I exclaimed, in astonishment; "what do you mean?"

"What I mean is that our civilization has grown to be a gorgeous shell; a mere mockery; a sham; outwardly fair and lovely, but inwardly full of dead men's bones and all uncleanness. To think that mankind is so capable of good, and now so cultured and polished, and yet all above is cruelty, craft and destruction, and all below is suffering, wretchedness, sin and shame."

"What do you mean?" I asked.

"That civilization is a gross and dreadful failure for seven-tenths of the human family; that seven-tenths of the backs of the world are insufficiently clothed; seven-tenths of the stomachs of the world are insufficiently fed; seven-tenths of the minds of the world are darkened and despairing, and filled with bitterness against the Author of the universe. It is pitiful to think what society is, and then to think what it might have been if our ancestors had not cast away their magnificent opportunities—had not thrown them into the pens of the swine of greed and gluttony."

"But," I replied, "the world does not look to me after that fashion. I have been expressing to my family my delight at viewing the vast triumphs of man over nature, by which the most secret powers of the universe have been captured and harnessed for the good of our race. Why, my friend, this city preaches at every pore, in every street and alley, in every shop and factory, the greatness of humanity, the splendor of civilization!"

"True, my friend," replied Maximilian; "but you see only the surface, the shell, the crust of life in this great metropolis. To-morrow we will go out together, and I shall show you the fruits of our modern civilization. I shall take you, not upon the upper deck of society, where the flags are flying, the breeze blowing, and the music playing, but down into the dark and stuffy depths of the hold of the great vessel, where the sweating gnomes, in the glare of the furnace-heat, furnish the power which drives the mighty ship resplendent through the seas of time. We will visit the *Under-World.*"

But I must close for to night, and subscribe myself affectionately your brother,

GABRIEL.

CHAPTER IV.

MY DEAR HEINRÍCH:

Since I wrote you last night I have been through dreadful scenes. I have traversed death in life. I have looked with my very eyes on Hell. I am sick at heart. My soul sorrows for humanity.

Max (for so I have come to call my new-found friend) woke me very early, and we breakfasted by lamp-light.

Yesterday he had himself dyed my fair locks of a dark brown, almost black hue, and had cut off some of my hair's superfluous length. Then he sent for a tailor, who soon arrayed me in garments of the latest fashion and most perfect fit. Instead of the singular-looking mountaineer of the day before, for whom the police were diligently searching, and on whose head a reward of one thousand dollars had been placed (never before had my head been valued so highly), there was nothing in my appearance to distinguish me from the thousands of other gallant young gentle-men of this great city.

A carriage waited for us at the door. We chatted together as we drove along through the quiet streets.

I asked him:

"Are the degraded, and even the vicious, members of your Brotherhood?"

"No; not the criminal class," he replied, "for there is nothing in their wretched natures on which you can build confidence or trust. Only those who have fiber enough to persist in labor, under conditions which so strongly tend to drive them into crime, can be members of our Brotherhood."

"May I ask the number of your membership?"

"In the whole world they amount to more than one hundred millions."

I started with astonishment.

"But amid such numbers," I said, "there must certainly be some traitors?"

"True, but the great multitude have nothing to tell. They are the limbs and members, as it were, of the organization; the directing intelligence dwells elsewhere. The multitude are like the soldiers of an army; they will obey when the time comes; but they are not taken into the councils of war."

A half hour's ride brought us into the domain of the poor.

An endless procession of men and women with pails and baskets — small-sized pails and smaller baskets — streamed along the streets on their way to work. It was not yet six o'clock. I observed that both men and women were undersized, and that they all very much resembled each other; as if similar circumstances had squeezed them into the same likeness. There was no spring to their steps and no laughter in their eyes; all were spare of frame and stolid or hungry-looking. The faces of the middle-aged men were haggard and wore a hopeless expression. Many of them scowled at us, with a look of hatred, as we passed by them in our carriage. A more joyless, sullen crowd I never beheld. Street after street they unrolled before us; there seemed to be millions of them. They were all poorly clad, and many of them in rags. The women, with the last surviving instinct of the female heart, had tried to decorate themselves; and here and there I could observe a bit of bright color on bonnet or apron; but the bonnets represented the fashions of ten years past, and the aprons were too often frayed and darned, the relics of some former, more opulent owners. There were multitudes of children, but they were without the gambols which character- ize the young of all animals; and there was not even the chirp of a winter bird about them; their faces were prematurely aged and hardened, and their bold eyes revealed that sin had no surprises for them. And every one of these showed that intense look which marks the awful struggle for food and life upon which they had just entered. The multitude seemed, so far as I could judge, to be of all nations com- mingled — the French, German, Irish, English — Hun- garians, Italians, Russians, Jews, Christians, and even Chinese and Japanese; for the slant eyes of many, and their imperfect, Tartar-like features, re- minded me that the laws made by the Republic, in the elder and better days, against the invasion of the Mongolian hordes, had long since become a dead letter.

What struck me most was their incalculable multi- tude and their silence. It seemed to me that I was witnessing the resurrection of the dead; and that these vast, streaming, endless swarms were the con- demned, marching noiselessly as shades to unavoida- ble and everlasting misery. They seemed to me merely automata, in the hands of some ruthless and unrelenting destiny. They lived and moved, but they were without heart or hope. The illusions of the imagination, which beckon all of us forward, even over the roughest paths and through the darkest valleys and shadows of life, had departed from the scope of their vision. They knew that to-morrow could bring them nothing better than to-day—the same shameful, pitiable, contemptible, sordid struggle for a mere existence. If they produced children it was reluctantly or unmeaningly; for they knew the wretches must tread in their footsteps, and enter, like them, that narrow, gloomy, high-walled pathway, out of which they could never climb; which began almost in infancy and ended in a pauper's grave— nay, I am wrong, not even in a pauper's grave; for they might have claimed, perhaps, some sort of ownership over the earth which enfolded them, which touched them and mingled with their dust. But public safety and the demands of science had long ago decreed that they should be whisked off, as soon as dead, a score or two at a time, and swept on iron tram-cars into furnaces heated to such intense white heat that they dissolved, crackling, even as they entered the chamber, and rose in nameless gases through the high chimney. That towering structure was the sole memorial monument of millions of them. Their graveyard was the air. Nature reclaimed her own with such velocity that she seemed to grudge them the very dust she had lent them during their wretched pilgrimage. The busy, toiling, rushing, roaring, groaning universe, big with young, appeared to cry out: "Away with them! Away with them! They have had their hour! They have performed their task. Here are a billion spirits waiting for the substance we loaned them. The spirits are boundless in number; matter is scarce. Away with them!"

I need not tell you, my dear brother, of all the

shops and factories we visited. It was the same story everywhere. Here we saw exemplified, in its full perfection, that "iron law of wages" which the old economists spoke of; that is to say, the reduction, by competition, of the wages of the worker to the least sum that will maintain life and muscular strength enough to do the work required, with such little surplus of vitality as might be necessary to perpetuate the wretched race; so that the world's work should not end with the death of one starved generation. I do not know if there is a hell in the spiritual universe, but if there is not, one should certainly be created for the souls of the men who originated, or justified, or enforced that damnable creed. It is enough, if nothing else, to make one a Christian, when he remembers how diametrically opposite to the teaching of the grand doctrine of brotherly love, enunciated by the gentle Nazarene, is this devil's creed of cruelty and murder, with all its steadily increasing world-horrors, before which to-day the universe stands appalled.

Oh! the pitiable scenes, my brother, that I have witnessed! Room after room; the endless succession of the stooped, silent toilers; old, young; men, women, children. And most pitiable of all, the leering, shameless looks of invitation cast upon us by the women, as they saw two well-dressed men pass by them. It was not love, nor license, nor even lust; it was degradation,—willing to exchange everything for a little more bread. And such rooms—garrets, sheds—dark, foul, gloomy; overcrowded; with such a stench in the thick air as made us gasp when entering it; an atmosphere full of life, hostile to the life of man. Think, my brother, as you sit upon your mountain side; your gentle sheep feeding around you; breathing the exquisite air of those elevated regions; and looking off over the mysterious, ancient world, and the great river valleys leading down to that marvelous Nile-land afar,—land of temples, ruins, pyramids,—cradle of civilization, grave of buried empires,—think, I say, of these millions condemned to live their brief, hopeless span of existence under such awful conditions! See them as they eat their mid-day meal. No delightful pause from pleasant labor; no brightly arrayed table; no laughing and loving faces around a plenteous board, with delicacies from all parts of the world; no agreeable interchange of wisdom and wit and courtesy and merriment. No; none of these. Without stopping in their work, under the eyes of sullen task-masters, they snatch bites out of their hard, dark bread, like wild animals, and devour it ravenously.*

Toil, toil, toil, from early morn until late at night; then home they swarm; tumble into their wretched beds; snatch a few hours of disturbed sleep, battling with vermin, in a polluted atmosphere; and then up again and to work; and so on, and on, in endless, mirthless, hopeless round; until, in a few years, consumed with disease, mere rotten masses of painful wretchedness, they die, and are wheeled off to the great furnaces, and their bodies are eaten up by the flames, even as their lives have been eaten up by society.

I asked one of the foremen what wages these men

---

*The testimony taken before the Parliamentary Commission in 1888 shows that the workers in the "sweating" shops of London worked in this way, even at that time, for fifteen and sixteen hours a day, and ate their meals in the manner described in the text.

and women received. He told me. It seemed impossible that human life could be maintained upon such a pittance. I then asked whether they ever ate meat. "No," he said, "except when they had a rat or mouse." "A rat or mouse!" I exclaimed. "Oh yes," he replied, "the rats and mice were important articles of diet,— just as they had been for centuries in China. The little children, not yet able to work, fished for them in the sewers, with hook and line, precisely as they had done a century ago in Paris, during the great German siege. A dog," he added, "was a great treat. When the authorities killed the vagrant hounds there was a big scramble among the poor for the bodies."

I was shocked at these statements; and then I remembered that some philosopher had argued that cannibalism had survived almost to our own times, in the islands of the Pacific Ocean, because they had contained no animals of large size with which the inhabitants could satisfy the dreadful craving of the system for flesh-food; and hence they devoured their captives.

"Do these people ever marry?" I inquired.

"Marry!" he exclaimed, with a laugh; "why, they could not afford to pay the fee required by law. And why should they marry? There is no virtue among them. No," he said, "they had almost gotten down to the condition of the Australian savages, who, if not prevented by the police, would consummate their animal-like nuptials in the public streets."

Maximilian told me that this man was one of the Brotherhood. I did not wonder at it.

From the shops and mills of honest industry, Maximilian led me—it was still broad daylight—into the criminal quarters. We saw the wild beasts in their lairs; in the iron cages of circumstance which civilization has built around them, from which they too readily break out to desolate their fellow-creatures. But here, too, were the fruits of misgovernment. If it were possible we might trace back from yonder robber and murderer — a human hyena — the long ancestral line of brutality, until we see it starting from some poor peasant of the Middle Ages, trampled into crime under the feet of feudalism. The little seed of weakness or wickedness has been carefully nursed by society, generation after generation, until it has blossomed at last in this destructive monster. Civilization has formulated a new variety of the genus *homo* — and it must inevitably perpetuate its kind.

The few prey on the many; and in turn a few of the many prey upon all. These are the brutal violators of justice, who go to prison, or to the scaffold, for breaking through a code of laws under which peaceful but universal injustice is wrought. If there were enough of these outlaws they might establish a system of jurisprudence for the world under which it would be lawful to rob and murder by the rule of the strong right hand, but criminal to reduce millions to wretchedness by subtle and cunning arts; and, hoity-toity, the prisons would change their tenants, and the brutal plunderers of the few would give place to the cultured spoilers of the many.

And when you come to look at it, my brother, how shall we compare the condition of the well-to-do man, who has been merely robbed of his watch and purse, even at the cost of a broken head, which will heal in a few days, with the awful doom of the poor multitude, who from the cradle to the grave work without joy and live without hope? Who is there that would

4

take back his watch and purse at the cost of changing places with one of these wretches?

And who is there that, if the choice were presented to him, would not prefer instant death, which is but a change of conditions, a flight from world to world, or at worst annihilation, rather than to be hurled into the living tomb which I have depicted, there to grovel and writhe, pressed down by the sordid mass around him, until death comes to his relief?

And so it seems to me that, in the final analysis of reason, the great criminals of the world are not these wild beasts, who break through all laws, whose selfishness takes the form of the bloody knife, the firebrand, or the bludgeon; but those who, equally selfish, corrupt the fountains of government and create laws and conditions by which millions suffer, and out of which these murderers and robbers naturally and unavoidably arise.

But I must bring this long letter to a conclusion, and subscribe myself, with love to all,

Your affectionate brother,
GABRIEL.

CHAPTER V.

ESTELLA WASHINGTON.

My Dear Heinrich:

One morning after breakfast, Max and I were seated in the library, enjoying our matutinal cigars, when, the conversation flagging, I asked Maximilian whether he had noticed the two young ladies who were in the Prince of Cabano's carriage the morning I whipped the driver. He replied that he had not observed them particularly, as he was too much excited and alarmed for my safety to pay especial attention to anything else; but he had seen that there were two young women in the barouche, and his glance had shown him they were both handsome.

"Have you any idea who they were?" I asked after a pause, for I shrank from revealing the interest I took in one of them.

"No," said he, indifferently; "probably a couple of the Prince's mistresses."

The word stung me like an adder; and I half rose from my chair, my face suffused and my eyes indignant.

"Why, what is the matter?" asked Maximilian; "I hope I have said nothing to offend you."

I fell back in my chair, ashamed of the exhibition of feeling into which I had been momentarily betrayed, and replied:

"Oh, no; but I am sure you are wrong. If you had looked, for but a moment, at the younger of the two, you would never have made such a remark."

"I meant no harm," he answered, "but the Prince is a widower; he has a perfect harem in his palace; he has his agents at work everywhere buying up handsome women; and when I saw two such in his carriage, I naturally came to the conclusion that they were of that character."

"Buying up women!" I exclaimed; "what are you talking about? This is free America, and the twentieth century. Do you dream that it is a Mohammedan land?"

"It isn't anything half so good," he retorted; "it is enslaved America; and the older we grow the worse for us. There was a golden age once in America — an age of liberty; of comparatively equal distribution of wealth; of democratic institutions. Now we have but the shell and semblance of all that. We are a Republic only in name; free only in forms. Mohammedanism — and we must do the Arabian prophet the justice to say that he established a religion of temperance and cleanliness, without a single superstition — never knew, in its worst estate, a more complete and abominable despotism than that under which we live. And as it would be worse to starve to death in sight of the most delicious viands than in the midst of a foodless desert, so the very assertions, constantly dinned in our ears by the hireling newspapers, that we are the freest people on earth, serve only to make our slavery more bitter and unbearable. But as to the buying up of women for the harems of the wealthy, that is an old story, my dear friend. More than a century ago the editor of a leading journal in London was imprisoned for exposing it. The virtuous community punished the man who protested against the sin, and took the sinners to its loving bosom. And in this last century matters have grown every day worse and worse. Starvation overrides all moralities; the convictions of the mind give way to the necessities of the body. The poet said long ago:

> "'Women are not
> In their best fortunes strong, but want will perjure
> The ne'er-touched vestal.'

"But he need not have confined this observation to women. The strongest resolves of men melt in the fire of want like figures of wax. It is simply a question of increasing the pressure to find the point where virtue inevitably breaks. Morality, in man or woman, is a magnificent flower which blossoms only in the rich soil of prosperity: impoverish the land and the bloom withers. If there are cases that seem to you otherwise, it is simply because the pressure has not been great enough; sufficient nourishment has not yet been withdrawn from the soil. Dignity, decency, honor, fade away when man or woman is reduced to shabby, shameful, degrading, cruel wretchedness. Before the clamors of the stomach the soul is silent."

"I cannot believe that," I replied; "look at the martyrs who have perished in the flames for an opinion."

"Yes," he said, "it is easy to die in an ecstasy of enthusiasm for a creed, with all the world looking on; to exchange life for eternal glory; but put the virgin, who would face without shrinking the flames or the wild beasts of the arena, into some wretched garret, in some miserable alley, surrounded by the low, the ignorant, the vile; close every avenue and prospect of hope; shut off every ennobling thought or sight or deed; and then subject the emaciated frame to endless toil and hopeless hunger, and the very fibers of the soul will rot under the debasing ordeal; and there is nothing left but the bare animal, that must be fed at whatever sacrifice. And remember, my dear fellow, that chastity is a flower of civilization. Barbarism knows nothing of it. The woman with the least is, among many tribes, most highly esteemed, and sought after by the young men for wedlock."

"My dear Maximilian," I said, "these are debasing views to take of life. Purity is natural to woman. You will see it oftentimes among savages. But, to recur to the subject we were speaking of. I feel very confident that the younger of those two women I saw in that carriage is pure. God never placed such a majestic and noble countenance over a corrupt soul. The face is transparent; the spirit looks out of the great eyes; and it is a spirit of dignity, nobleness, grace and goodness."

"Why," said he, laughing, "the barbed arrow of Master Cupid, my dear Gabriel, has penetrated quite through all the plates of your philosophy."

"I will not confess that," I replied; "but I will admit that I would like to know something more about that young lady, for I never saw a face that interested me half so much."

"Now," said he, "see what it is to have a friend. I can find out for you all that is known about her. We have members of our society in the household of every rich man in New York. I will first find out who she is. I will ask the Master of the Servants, who is a member of our Brotherhood, who were the two ladies out riding at the time of our adventure. I can communicate with him in cipher."

He went to the wall; touched a spring; a door flew open; a receptacle containing pen, ink and paper appeared; he wrote a message, placed it in an interior cavity, which connected with a pneumatic tube, rang a bell, and in a few minutes another bell rang, and he withdrew from a similar cavity a written message. He read out to me the following:

"The elder lady, Miss Frederika Bowers; the younger, Miss Estella Washington; both members of the Prince of Cabano's household."

"Estella Washington," I repeated; "a noble name. Can you tell me anything about her?"

"Certainly," he replied; "we have a Bureau of Inquiry connected with our society, and we possess the most complete information, not only as to our own members, but as to almost every one else in the community of any note. Wait a moment."

He opened the same receptacle in the wall, wrote a few words on a sheet of paper, and dispatched it by the pneumatic tube to the central office of that district, whence it was forwarded at once to its address. It was probably fifteen minutes before the reply arrived. It read as follows:

MISS ESTELLA WASHINGTON.—Aged eighteen. *Appearance:* Person tall and graceful; complexion fair; eyes blue; hair long and golden; face handsome. *Pedigree:* A lineal descendant of Lawrence Washington, brother of the first President of the Republic. *Parents:* William Washington and Sophia, his wife. Father, a graduate of the University of Virginia; professor of Indo-European literature for ten years in Harvard University. Grandfather, Lawrence Washington, a judge of the Supreme Court of the United States for fifteen years. Sophia, mother of Estella, *née* Wainwright, an accomplished Greek and Sanscrit scholar, daughter of Professor Elias Wainwright, who occupied the chair of psychological science in Yale College for twenty years. Families of both parents people of great learning and social position, but not wealthy in any of the branches. *History:* Father died when Estella was eight years old, leaving his family poor. Her mother, after a hard struggle with poverty, died two years later. Estella, then ten years old, was adopted by Maria, widow of George Washington, brother of Estella's father, who had subsequently married one Ezekiel Plunkett, who is also dead. Maria Plunkett is a woman of low origin and sordid nature, with a large share of cunning; she lives at No. 2682 Grand Avenue. She had observed that Estella gave promise of great beauty, and as none of the other relatives put in a claim for the child, she took possession of her, with intent to educate her highly, improve her appearance by all the arts known to such women, and eventually sell her for a large sum to some wealthy aristocrat as a mistress; believing that her honorable descent would increase the price which her personal charms would bring. On the 5th day of last month she sold her, for $5,000, to the Master of the Servants of the so-called Prince of Cabano; and she was taken to his house. Estella, who is quite ignorant of the wickedness of the world, or the true character of her aunt, for whom she entertains a warm feeling of gratitude and affection, believes that she is to serve as lady-companion for Miss Frederika Bowers, the favorite mistress of the Prince, but whom Estella supposes to be his niece.

You can imagine, my dear brother—for you have a kind and sensitive heart, and love your wife—the pangs that shot through me, and distorted my very soul, as I listened to this dreadful narrative. Its calm, dispassionate, official character, while it confirmed its truth, added to the horrors of the awful story of crime! Think of it! a pure, beautiful, cultured, confiding girl, scarcely yet a woman, consigned to a terrible fate, by one whom she loved and trusted. And the lurid light it threw on the state of society in which such a sacrifice could be possible! I forgot every pretense of indifference, which I had been trying to maintain before Maximilian, and, springing up, every fiber quivering, I cried out:

"She must be saved!"

Maximilian, too, although colder-blooded, and hardened by contact with this debased age, was also stirred to his depths; his face was flushed, and he seized me by the hand. He said:

"I will help you, my friend."

"But what can we do?" I asked.

"We should see her at once," he replied, "and, if it is not yet too late, carry her away from that damnable place, that house of hell, and its devilish owner, who preys on innocence and youth. We have one thing in our favor: the Master of the Servants, who bought Estella, is the same person who answered my first message. He belongs, as I told you, to our Brotherhood. He is in my power. He will give us access to the poor girl, and will do whatever is necessary to be done. Come, let us go!"

Those thin, firm lips were more firmly set than ever; the handsome eyes flashed with a fierce light; he hurried for an instant into his secret room.

"Take this magazine pistol," he said, "and this knife," handing me a long bowie-knife covered with a handsome, gold-embossed sheath; "we are going into a den of infamy where everything is possible. Never unsheathe that knife until you are compelled to use it, for a scratch from it is certain and instant death; it is charged with the most deadly poison the art of the chemist has been able to produce; the secret is known only to our Brotherhood; the discoverer is an Italian professor, a member of our society."

CHAPTER VI.

MOUNTING to one of the electrical railroads, we were soon at the house of the Prince. Passing around to the servants' entrance of the palace, Maximilian sent in his card to the Master of the Servants, who soon appeared, bowing deferentially to my friend. We were ushered into his private room. Maximilian first locked the door; he then examined the room carefully, to see if there was any one hidden behind the tapestry or furniture; for the room, like every part of the palace, was furnished in the most lavish and extravagant style. Satisfied with his search, he turned to Rudolph, as the Master of the Servants was called, and handed him the message he had received, which gave the history of Estella.

"Read it," he said.

Rudolph read it with a troubled countenance.

"Yes," he said, "I am familiar with most of the facts here stated, and believe them all to be true. What would you have me do?"

"First," said Maximilian, "we desire to know if Estella is still in ignorance of the purpose for which she was brought here."

"Yes," he replied; "Frederika is jealous of her, as I can see, and has contrived to keep her out of the Prince's sight. She has no desire to be supplanted by a younger and fairer woman."

"God be praised for that jealousy," exclaimed

58

Maximilian. "We must see Estella; can you manage it for us?"

"Yes," he said, "I will bring her here. I know she is in the palace. I saw her but a few moments since. Wait for me."

"Stop," said Maximilian, "have you the receipt for the $5,000 signed by Mrs. Plunkett?"

"No; but I can get it."

"Do so, pray; and when you bring her here introduce me to her as Mr. Martin, and my friend here as Mr. Henry. She may refuse our assistance, and we must provide against the revenge of the Prince."

"I will do as you command," replied Rudolph, who acted throughout as if he felt himself in the presence of a superior officer.

As we sat waiting his return I was in a state of considerable excitement. Delight, to know that she was still the pure angel I had worshiped in my dreams, contended with trepidation as I felt I must soon stand in her presence.

The door opened and Rudolph entered; behind him came the tall form of the beautiful girl I had seen in the carriage: she seemed to me fairer than ever. Her eyes first fell upon me; she started and blushed. It was evident she recognized me; and I fancied the recognition was not unpleasant to her. She then turned to Maximilian and then to Rudolph, who introduced us as we had requested. I offered her a chair. She sat down, evidently astonished at such an interview, and yet entirely mistress of herself. After a moment's pause,—for Maximilian, as he told me afterwards, was too bewildered with her splendid beauty to speak,—she said, in a sweet and gentle voice:

"Mr. Rudolph tells me that you desire to speak to me on matters of importance."

At a sign from Maximilian Rudolph closed and locked the door. She started, and it seemed to me that her eyes turned to me with more confidence than to either of the others.

"Miss Washington," said Maximilian, "it is true we desire to speak with you on matters of the greatest moment to yourself. But we shall say things so surprising to you, so harsh and cruel, so utterly in conflict with your present opinions, that I scarce know how to begin."

She had grown paler during this speech, and I then said:

"Be assured that nothing but the profound respect we feel for you, and the greatest desire to serve you, and save you from ruin, could have induced us to intrude upon you."

Her face showed her increasing alarm; she placed her hand on her heart, as if to still its beatings, and then, with constrained dignity, replied:

"I do not understand you, gentlemen. I do not know what the dangers are to which you allude. Can you not speak plainly?"

"My friend here, Mr. Henry," said Maximilian, looking at me, "you have, I perceive, already recognized."

"Yes," she said, with another blush, "if I am not mistaken, he is the gentleman who saved the life of a poor beggar, some days since, and punished, as he deserved, our insolent driver. Miss Frederika, the Prince's niece, has, at my request, refused since that time to permit him to drive us when we go out together, as we often do. I am glad to thank you again," she said, with a charmingly ingenuous air, for your noble act in saving that poor man's life."

"It was nothing," I said, "but if the service was of any value it has been a thousand times repaid by your kind words."

"You can easily imagine," said Maximilian, "that my friend here, after that interview, was naturally curious to find out something about you."

She blushed and cast down her eyes; and the thought flashed across my mind that perhaps she had been likewise curious to find out something about me.

"I am a member," said Maximilian, "of a secret society. We have a 'Bureau of Inquiry' whose business it is to collect information, for the use of the society, concerning every person of any note. This information is carefully tabulated and preserved, and added to from day to day; so that at any moment it is subject to the call of our officers. When my friend desired to know something about you" (here the blue, wondering eyes were cast down again), "I sent a message to our Bureau of Inquiry, and received a reply which I have here. I fear to show it to you. The shock will be too great to learn in a moment the utter baseness of one in whom you have trusted. I fear you have not the courage to endure such a blow; and at the same time I know of no better way to communicate to your purity and innocence the shocking facts which it is my duty to disclose."

Estella smiled, and reached forth her hand for the paper with the dignity of conscious courage and high blood.

"Let me read it," she said; "I do not think it can tell me anything I cannot endure."

Maximilian delivered the paper into her hand. I watched her face as she read it. At first there was a look of wonder at the minuteness of the knowledge of her family which the paper revealed; then the interest became more intense; then the eyebrows began to rise and the blue eyes to dilate with horror; then an expression of scorn swept over her face; and as she read the last word she flung the paper from her as if it had been a serpent, and rising up, yes, towering, a splendid image of wrath, she turned upon us and cried out:

"This is a base falsehood! A cowardly trick to wound me! A shameful attempt to injure my dear aunt."

And, wheeling around on Rudolph, her eyes blazing, she said:

"Unlock that door! I shall reveal at once to the Prince this attack on his good name and Miss Frederika. How dare you bring these men here with such falsehoods?"

Rudolph, alarmed for himself, hung his head in silence. He was trembling violently.

"Rudolph," said Maximilian, solemnly, "I call upon you, by the oath you have taken, to say to this lady whether or not the contents of that paper are true."

"I believe them to be true," responded Rudolph, in a low tone.

It was wonderful to see the fine indignation, the keen penetration that shone in Estella's eyes, as she looked first at Rudolph and then at Maximilian.

"Rudolph," said Maximilian, "by the oath you have taken, tell Miss Washington whether or not you paid $5,000 to her aunt, Maria Plunkett, for the purchase of her body, as set forth in that paper."

"It is true," replied Rudolph, in the same low tone.

"It is false!" cried Estella,—and yet I thought there was that in her tone which indicated that the hideous doubt had begun to enter her soul.

"Rudolph," said Maximilian, "tell this lady whether you took a receipt from her aunt for the money you paid for her."

"I did," replied Rudolph.

"Miss Washington," said Maximilian, like a lawyer who has reached his crucial question, for he was a trained attorney, "would you recognize your aunt's signature if you saw it?"

"Certainly."

"You have often seen her write?"

"Yes; hundreds of times."

"Have you any reason to distrust this good man, Rudolph? Do you not know that in testifying to the truth he runs the risk of his own destruction?"

"Yes, yes," she said, and there was a wild and worried look in her eyes.

"Read the receipt, Rudolph," said Maximilian.

Rudolph read, in the same low and almost trembling tones, the following:

NEW YORK, August 5th, 1988.—Received of Matthew Rudolph, for the Prince of Cabano, the sum of five thousand dollars, in consideration of which I have delivered to the said Prince of Cabano the body of my niece, Estella Washington; and I hereby agree, as the custodian of the said Estella Washington, never to demand any further payment, from the said Prince of Cabano, on account of my said niece, and never to reclaim her; and I also pledge myself never to reveal to any of the relatives of the said Estella Washington her place of residence.

(Signed)   MARIA PLUNKETT.

As he finished reading Estella seized the receipt quickly out of his hands, and fixed her eyes eagerly upon the signature. In a moment she became deadly pale, and would have fallen on the floor, but that I caught her in my arms — (oh, precious burden!) — and bore her to a sofa. Rudolph brought some water and bathed her face. In a few minutes she recovered consciousness. She looked at us curiously at first, and then, as memory returned to her, an agonized and distraught look passed over her features, and I feared she would faint again. I held some water to her lips. She looked at me with an intense look as I knelt at her side. Then her eyes passed to Maximilian and Rudolph, who stood respectfully a little distance from her. The tears flowed down her face. Then a new thought seemed to strike her, and she rose to a sitting posture.

"It cannot be true. My aunt could not do it. You are strangers to me. It is a conspiracy. I will ask Frederika."

"No! no!" said Rudolph; "not Frederika; it would not be to her interest to tell you the truth. But is there any one of the servants in whom you have more confidence than all the others?"

"Yes," she said, "there is Mary Callaghan, an honest girl, if there is one anywhere. I think she loves me; and I do not believe she would deceive me."

"Then," said Rudolph, "you shall send for her to come here. None of us shall speak to her lest you might think we did so to prompt her. We will hide behind the tapestry. Dry your tears; ring for a servant, and request Mary to come to you, and then ask her such questions as you choose."

This was done, and in a few moments Mary appeared—an honest, stout, rosy-cheeked Irish girl, with the frank blue eyes and kindly smile of her people.

"Mary," said Estella, "you have always been kind to me. Do you love me sufficiently to tell me the truth if I ask you some questions?"

"Sure, and you may do so, my dear," said Mary.

"Then, Mary, tell me, is Frederika the Prince of Cabano's niece?"

"Niver a drop's blood to him," replied Mary.

"What is she doing in his house, then?" asked Estella.

"Sure, it would be as much as my place is worth, ma'am, to answer that question; and hard enough it is for an honest girl to get a place now-a-days. If it hadn't been for Barney McGuiggan, who married my brother's sister-in-law, and who is own cousin to Mr. Flaherty, the butler's second assistant, I couldn't have got the place I have at all, at all. And if I said a word against Miss Frederika, out I would go, and where would I find another place?"

"But, Mary, if you speak the truth no harm shall follow to you. I shall never repeat what you say. I do not ask out of idle curiosity, but much depends on your answer."

"Indeed, ma'am," replied Mary, "if you weren't as innocent as ye're purty, you would have found out the answer to your own question long ago. Faith, an' don't everybody in the house know she's"—here she approached, and whispered solemnly in her ear— "she's the Prince's favorite mistress?"

Estella recoiled. After a pause she said:

"And, Mary, who are the other young ladies we call the Prince's cousins—Miss Lucy, Miss Julia and the rest?"

5

"Ivery one of them's the same. It's just as I told
Hannah, the cook's scullion; I didn't belave ye knew
a word of what was going on in this house. And
didn't I tell her that Miss Frederika was contriving
to kape you out of the Prince's sight; and that was
the rason she took you out riding for hours ivery
day, and made you sleep in a remote part of the
palace; for if the Prince ever clapped his two ougly
eyes upon you it would be all up wid Madame Frederika."

I could see from where I was hidden that Estella
grasped the back of a chair for support, and she said
in a low voice:

"You may go, Mary; I am much obliged to you
for your friendship and honesty."

We found her sitting in the chair, with her hands
over her face, sobbing convulsively. At last she
looked around upon us and cried out:

"Oh, my God! What shall I do? I am sold—
sold—a helpless slave. Oh, it is horrible!"

"You will never be without friends while we live,"
I said, advancing to her side.

"But I must fly," she cried out, "and how —
where?"

"My dear Miss Washington," said Maximilian, in
his kindest tones, "I have a dear mother, who will be
glad to welcome you as her own child; and in our
quiet home you can remain, safe from the power of
the Prince, until you have time to think out your
future course of life; and if you conclude to remain
with us forever you will be only the more welcome.
Here is Rudolph, who will vouch for me that I am an
honorable man, and that you can trust yourself to
me with safety."

"Yes," said Rudolph; "Maximilian Petion is the soul of honor. His simple word is more than the oath of another."

"Then let us fly at once," said Estella.

"No," replied Rudolph, "that would not do; this house is guarded and full of spies. You would be followed and reclaimed."

"What, then, do you advise?" asked Maximilian.

"Let me see," replied the old man, thinking; "this is Thursday. On Monday night next the members of 'the government' have their meeting here. There will be a number of visitors present, and more or less confusion; more guards will be necessary also, and I can contrive to have one of the Brotherhood act as sentinel at the door which opens into a hall which connects with this room; for you see here is a special entrance which leads to a stairway and to the door I speak of. I will procure a gentleman's dress for Miss Estella; she is tall and will readily pass in the dark for a man. I will secure for you a permit for a carriage to enter the grounds. You will bring a close carriage and wait with the rest of the equipages, near at hand. But I must have some one who will accompany Miss Estella from this room to the carriage, for I must not show myself."

I stepped forward and said, "I will be here."

"But there is some danger in the task," said Rudolph, looking at me critically. "If detected, your life would pay the forfeit."

"I would the danger were ten times as great," I replied. Estella blushed and gave me a glance of gratitude.

"There is one difficulty I perceive," said Maximilian.

"What is that?" asked Rudolph.

"I hesitate about leaving Miss Washington exposed to the danger of remaining four days longer in this horrible house."

"I will look after that," replied Rudolph. "She had better pretend ill health, and keep her room during that time. It is on an upper floor, and if she remains there the danger will be very slight that the Prince will see her."

"Miss Washington," I said, handing her the dagger which Max had given me, "take this weapon. It is poisoned with the most deadly virus known to the art of man. A scratch from it is certain death. Use it to defend yourself if assailed."

"I know how I shall use it in the last extremity," she said, meaningly.

"Better," I replied, "purity in death than degradation in life."

She thanked me with her eyes, and took the dagger and hid it in her bosom.

"There is one other matter," said Rudolph to Max; "the meeting next Monday night is to be a very important one, I think, from certain indications. It is called to prepare for an expected outbreak of the people. It would be well that some reliable person should be present, as heretofore, who can report to you all that occurs. If you can send me a discreet man I can hide him where I have before hidden our brethren."

"Why could I not serve the purpose?" I said. "I will be here anyhow; and as I would have to remain until the gathering broke up, I might just as well witness the proceedings."

"He is not one of us," said Rudolph, doubtfully.

"No," replied Max; "but I will vouch for his fidelity with my life."

"Then be it so," said Rudolph. "Let Miss Washington withdraw by the farther door; and after a reasonable delay we will pass through into a communicating series of rooms, and I will then show your friend where he is to be concealed."

CHAPTER VII.

THE HIDING-PLACE.

I HAD seen something of the magnificence of this age, and of the splendor of its lordly habitations; but I was not prepared for the grandeur of the rooms through which Rudolph led me. It would be impossible to adequately describe them. We moved noiselessly over carpets soft and deep as a rich sward, but tinted with colors and designs, from the great looms of the world, beside which the comparison of nature's carpets seemed insignificant. We passed up great winding stairs, over which, it seemed to me, three carriages might have been driven abreast; we were surrounded at every step by exquisite statuary and royal paintings; our course led through great libraries where the softened light fell on the endless arrays of richly-bound books. But they were as dead intelligence under the spell of a magician. No pale students sat at the tables here, availing themselves of the treasures which it had taken generations to assemble, and some of which could scarcely be found elsewhere. Men and women passed and repassed us; for the house was so full of servants that it seemed like a town in itself. Here and there were quiet-looking watchmen, who served the place of police in a great city, and whose duty it was to keep watch and ward over the innumerable articles which everywhere met the eye—costly books, works of art, bronzes, jeweled boxes, musical instruments, small groups of exquisite statuary, engravings, curios, etc., from all quarters of the earth. It represented, in short, the very profligacy and abandon of unbounded wealth. Each room seemed to contain a king's ransom. I could not help but contrast this useless and extravagant luxury, which served no purpose but display and vanity, with the dreadful homes and working-places of the poor I had visited the day before. And it seemed to me as if a voice pierced my heart, crying out through all its recesses, in strident tones, "How long, O Lord, how long?" And then I thought how thin a crust of earth separated all this splendor from that burning hell of misery beneath it. And if the molten mass of horror should break its limitations and overflow the earth! Already it seemed to me the planet trembled; I could hear the volcanic explosions; I could see the sordid flood of wrath and hunger pouring through these halls; cataracts of misery bursting through every door and window, and sweeping away all this splendor into never-ending blackness and ruin. I stood still, lost in these engrossing reflections, when Rudolph touched me on the arm, and led the way through a great hall, covered with ancestral portraits, into a magnificent chamber. In the center stood a large table, and around it about two score chairs, all made of dark tropical wood. It was like the council chamber of some great government, with the throne of the king at one end.

"This," said Rudolph, in a solemn whisper, "this is where they meet. This is the real center of government of the American continent; all the rest is sham and form. The men who meet here determine the condition of all the hundreds of millions who dwell on the great land revealed to the world by Columbus. Here political parties, courts, juries, governors, legislatures, congresses, presidents are made and unmade; and from this spot they are controlled and directed in the discharge of their multiform functions. The decrees formulated here are echoed by a hundred thousand newspapers, and many thousands of orators; and they are enforced by an uncountable army of soldiers, servants, tools, spies, and even assassins. He who stands in the way of the men who assemble here perishes. He who would oppose them takes his life in his hands. You are, young man, as if I had led you to the center of the earth, and I had placed your hand upon the very pivot, the well-oiled axle, upon which, noiselessly, the whole great globe revolves, and from which the awful forces extend which hold it all together."

I felt myself overawed. It was as if mighty spirits even then inhabited that dusky and silent chamber; hostile and evil spirits of whom mankind were at once the subjects and the victims. I followed Rudolph on tiptoe as he advanced to the end of the room.

"Here," he said, entering through a wide arch, "is a conservatory which is constantly kept supplied and renewed, from the hot-houses of the palace, with the most magnificent flowers. The only humanizing trait the Prince seems to possess is an affection for flowers. And he especially loves those strange Mexican and South American plants, the *cactaceæ*, which unite the most exquisite flowers to the most grotesque and repulsive forms, covered with great spear-like spines, and which thrive only in barren lands, and on the poorest soil. I have taken advantage of the presence of these plants to construct the hiding-place about which I spoke to you. Here are some which are fifteen feet high. They touch the ceiling of the room. Around them I have arranged a perfect hedge or breast-work of smaller plants of the same family, growing in large boxes. Nothing could penetrate through this prickly wall; and I have united the boxes by hooks and staples on the inside. There is, however, one which a strong man can move aside; and through the opening thus formed he can crawl to the center of the barricade, and, having replaced the hooks, it would be almost impossible to reach him; while he could not be seen unless one were immediately over him and looked down upon him. Then between him and the council room I have arranged a screen of flowers, which will hide you when you stand up, while between the blossoms you can see everything with little risk of being seen. But in case you should be detected you will observe behind you a window, which, as the weather is warm, I shall leave open. On the outside is a great ivy vine that will bear your weight. You will have to dare the spines of the *cacti* behind you; make a great leap to the window and take your chances of escaping the fusillade of pistol shots, by flying in the darkness, into the garden. I will show you the grounds so that you will not be lost in them, if you get that far. If caught, you will have to pretend to be a burglar who entered at the window for purposes of plunder. It would do you no good to inculpate me, for it would doom us both to instant death as spies; while a supposed burglar would be simply turned over to the law and punished by a term of imprisonment. I give you these instructions although I hope there will be no necessity for them.

This hiding-place has been several times used, and the deepest secrets of the aristocracy revealed to our Brotherhood, without detection; and if you are prudent and careful there will be little to fear. The council will meet at eight o'clock; at half past seven it will be my duty to see that the rooms are in order, and to make sure that there are no spies or intruders on the premises, and to so report in person to the Prince, and deliver him the key of the outer door. I shall cover your dress with the garments of one of the household servants, and take you with me to help make that last examination; and, watching an opportunity, you will slip into the hiding-place; having first taken off the disguise I have lent you, which we will hide among the plants. You must be armed and prepared for every emergency. I will meet you in the garden at half past six; before we part I will furnish you with a key to an outer gate, by which you can enter. As soon as the council has broken up, I will return to the room and again disguise you in the servant's dress. The Prince always entertains his guests with a lunch and champagne before they separate.

"In the meantime I will bring Estella to my room; you can then pass out together and boldly advance to your carriage. You will first have to agree with Maximilian where it will stand; and the guard at the door will show you to it. When once in it, drive like the wind. You must arrange with Maximilian as to what is to be done in case you find you are followed, for in that event it will not do to drive directly to his house. You must enter the house of some one of the Brotherhood and pass rapidly through it, with Miss Washington, to a carriage that will be in waiting in a rear street. And you must be prepared with one or more such subterfuges, for you are dealing with men of terrible power and cunning, whose arms reach everywhere; and on the night of their councils—and in fact upon all other nights—the place abounds with spies. Come with me and I will show you the garden and how to enter it."

I was struck with the intelligence, sagacity and executive capacity of the man; and I said to him:

"How comes it that you, holding such a position of trust and power, where your compensation must be all you can ask, are, at the same time, a member of a society which, if I understand aright, threatens to overturn the existing order of things. You are not driven to rebellion by want or oppression."

"No," he said; "I was educated at Heidelberg; I come of a wealthy family; but in my youth, while an enthusiastic lover of liberty and humanity, I became a member of a German branch of this now universal Brotherhood. I had my dreams, as many have, of reforming the world. But my membership, by a strange accident, became known, and I was forced to fly in disgrace, discarded by my relatives, to America. Here I lived in great poverty for a time, until the Brotherhood came to my assistance and secured me a servant's place in this house. I have gradually risen to my present position. While I am not so enthusiastic as I once was, nor so sanguine of the good results of the promised revolution of the *proletariat*, I have nevertheless seen enough within these walls to show me the justice of our cause and the necessity for some kind of reformation. I could not draw back now, if I desired to; and I do not know that I would if I could. We are all moving together on the face of the torrent, and whither it will eventually sweep us no one can tell. But come," he added, "to the garden, or our long conversation may be noticed, and arouse suspicion."

CHAPTER VIII.

THE BROTHERHOOD.

I CANNOT give you, my dear brother, a detailed account of every day's occurrences, although I know that your love for me would make every incident of interest to you. I shall, however, jot down my reflections on sheets, and send them to you as occasion serves.

The more I have seen, and the more I have conversed with Maximilian, the more clearly I perceive that the civilized world is in a desperate extremity. This Brotherhood of Destruction, with its terrible purposes and its vast numbers, is a reality. If the ruling class had to deal only with a brutalized peasantry, they might, as they did in other ages, trample them into animal-like inability to organize and defend themselves. But the public school system, which, with the other forms of the Republic, is still kept up, has made, if not all, at least a very large percentage of the unhappy laboring classes intelligent. In fact, they are wonderfully intelligent; their organizations have been to them clubs, debating societies and legislatures. And you know that all the greatest minds of the earth have come out of the masses, if not directly, at least after one or two removes. The higher aristocracy have contributed but very few to the honored catalogue of men of pre-eminent genius. And therefore you will not be surprised to hear that in these great organizations there have arisen, from among

the very laborers, splendid orators, capable organiz-
ers, profound students of politics and political economy, statesmen and masterly politicians. Nature,
which knows no limit to her capacity for the creation of new varieties, and, dealing with hundreds of
millions, has innumerable elements to mingle in her
combinations, has turned out some marvelous leaders among these poor men. Their hard fortunes have
driven out of their minds all illusions, all imagination, all poetry; and in solemn fashion they have
bent themselves to the grim and silent struggle with
their environment. Without imagination, I say, for
this seems to me to be a world without a song.

And it is to the credit of these great masses that
they are keen enough to recognize the men of ability
that rise up among them, and even out of their poor,
hard-earned resources to relieve them of the necessity for daily toil, that they may devote themselves to the improvement of their minds, and the
execution of the great tasks assigned them. There is
no doubt that if the ruling classes had been willing to
recognize these natural leaders as men of the same
race, blood, tongue and capacity as themselves, and
had reached down to them a helping and kindly hand,
there might have been long since a coming together
of the two great divisions of society; and such a re-
adjustment of the values of labor as would, while it
insured happiness to those below, have not materially
lessened the enjoyments of those above. But the
events which preceded the great war against the aristocracy in 1640, in England; the great revolution of
1789, in France; and the greater civil war of 1861, in
America, all show how impossible it is, by any process
of reasoning, to induce a privileged class to peacefully

yield up a single tittle of its advantages. There is no bigotry so blind or intense as that of caste; and long established wrongs are only to be rooted out by fire and sword. And hence the future looks so black to me. The upper classes might reform the world, but they will not; the lower classes would, but they cannot; and for a generation or more these latter have settled down into a sullen and unanimous conviction that the only remedy is world-wide destruction. We can say, as one said at the opening of the Cromwellian struggle, "God help the land where ruin must reform!" But the proletariat are desperate. They are ready, like the blind Samson, to pull down the pillars of the temple, even though they themselves fall, crushed to death amid the ruins; for

"The grave is brighter than their hearths and homes."

I learn from Maximilian that their organization is most perfect. Every one of their hundred millions is now armed with one of the newest improved magazine rifles. The use of the white powder reduces very much the size of the cartridges; the bullets are also much smaller than they were formerly, but they are each charged with a most deadly and powerful explosive, which tears the body of the victim it strikes to pieces. These small cartridges are stored in the steel stock and barrel of the rifles, which will hold about one hundred of them; and every soldier therefore carries in his hand a weapon almost equal to the old-time Gatling or Armstrong gun.

The mode in which these guns were procured shows the marvelous nature of the organization and its resources. Finding that the cost of the guns was greatly increased by the profits of the manufacturer and

the middleman, and that it was, in fact, very doubt-
ful whether the government would permit them to
purchase them in any large quantities, they resolved to make them for themselves. In the depths
of abandoned coal mines, in the wildest and most
mountainous part of Tennessee, they established,
years ago, their armories and foundries. Here, under
pretense of coal-mining and iron-working, they
brought members of their Brotherhood, workmen
from the national gun-works; and these, teaching
hundreds of others the craft, and working day and
night, in double gangs, have toiled until every
able-bodied man in the whole vast Brotherhood, in
America and Europe, has been supplied with his
weapon and a full accompaniment of ammunition.
The cost of all this was reduced to a minimum, and
has been paid by each member of the Brotherhood
setting aside each week a small percentage of his earnings. But, lest they should break out prematurely,
before the leaders gave the word, these guns have
not been delivered directly to their owners, but to the
"commanders of tens," as they are called; for the
Brotherhood is divided into groups of ten each; and
it is the duty of these commanders to bury the weapons and ammunition in the earth in rubber sacks,
furnished for the purpose, and only to deliver them
when the signal comes to strike. In the meantime the men are trained with sticks in all the evolu-
tions of soldiers. You can see how cunning is all this
system. A traitor cannot betray more than nine of
his fellows, and his own death is certain to follow. If
the commander of a squad goes over to the enemy,
he can but deliver up nine men and ten guns, and perhaps reveal the supposed name of the one man who,

in a disguise, has communicated with him from the parent society. But when the signal is given a hundred million trained soldiers will stand side by side, armed with the most efficient weapons the cunning of man is able to produce, and directed by a central authority of extraordinary ability. Above all this dreadful preparation the merry world goes on, singing and dancing, marrying and giving in marriage, as thoughtless of the impending catastrophe as were the people of Pompeii in those pleasant August days in 79, just before the city was buried in ashes;—and yet the terrible volcano had stood there, in the immediate presence of themselves and their ancestors, for generations, and more than once the rocking earth had given signal tokens of its awful possibilities.

If I believed that this wonderful Brotherhood was capable of anything beyond destruction, I should not look with such terror as I do upon the prospect. But after destruction there must come construction — the erection of law and civilization upon the ruins of the present order of things. Who can believe that these poor brutalized men will be capable, armed to the teeth with deadly weapons, and full of passions, hates and revenges, to recreate the slaughtered society? In civilized life the many must work; and who among these liberated slaves will be ready to lay down their weapons and take up their tasks? When the negroes of San Domingo broke out, in that world-famous and bloody insurrection, they found themselves, when they had triumphed, in a tropical land, where the plentiful bounties of nature hung abundant supplies of food upon every tree and shrub. But in the temperate regions of America and Europe these

6

vast populations can only live by great toil, and if
none will toil all must starve; but before they starve
they will slay each other, and that means universal
conflict, savagery, barbarism, chaos.

I tremble, my brother, I tremble with horror
when I think of what is crawling toward us, with
noiseless steps; couchant, silent, treacherous, pard-
like; scarce rustling the dry leaves as it moves, and
yet with bloodshot, glaring eyes and tense-drawn
limbs of steel, ready for the fatal spring. When
comes it? To-night? To-morrow? A week hence?
Who can say?

And the thought forever presses on me, Can I do
nothing to avert this catastrophe? Is there no hope?
For mankind is in itself so noble, so beautiful, so
full of all graces and capacities; with aspirations
fitted to sing among the angels; with comprehension
fitted to embrace the universe! Consider the exquisite, lithe-limbed figures of the first man and woman,
as they stood forth against the red light of their first
sunset—fresh from the hand of the Mighty One—His
graceful, perfected, magnificent thoughts! What love
shines out of their great eyes; what goodness, like
dawn-awakened flowers, is blooming in their singing
hearts! And all to come to this. To this! A hell of
injustice, ending in a holocaust of slaughter.

God is not at fault. Nature is not to blame. Civilization, signifying increased human power, is not
responsible. But human greed,—blind, insatiable
human greed,—shallow cunning; the basest, stuff-
grabbing, nut-gathering, selfish instincts, these have
done this work! The rats know too much to gnaw
through the sides of the ship that carries them; but
these so-called wise men of the world have eaten away

the walls of society in a thousand places, to the thinness of tissue-paper, and the great ocean is about to pour in at every aperture. And still they hoot and laugh their insolent laugh of safety and triumph above the roar of the greedy and boundless waters, just ready to overwhelm them forever.

Full of these thoughts, which will not permit me to sleep at night, and which haunt my waking hours, I have gone about, for some days, accompanied by Maximilian, and have attended meetings of the workingmen in all parts of the city. The ruling class long since denied them the privilege of free speech, under the pretense that the safety of society required it. In doing so they have screwed down the safety-valve, while the steam continues to generate. Hence the men meet to discuss their wrongs and their remedies in underground cellars, under old ruined breweries and warehouses; and there, in large, low-roofed apartments, lighted by tallow candles, flaring against the dark, damp, smoky walls, the swarming masses assemble, to inflame each other mutually against their oppressors, and to look forward, with many a secret hint and innuendo, to that great day of wrath and revenge which they know to be near at hand —

> "And with pale lips men say,
> To-morrow, perchance to-day,
> Enceladus may arise!"

But as any member is permitted to bring in a friend — for these are not meetings of the Brotherhood itself, but simply voluntary gatherings of workmen, — and as any man may prove a traitor, their utterances are guarded and enigmatical.

More than once I have spoken to them in these dim

halls; and while full of sympathy for their sufferings, and indignant as they themselves can be against their oppressors, I have pleaded with them to stay their hands, to seek not to destroy, but to reform. I preach to them of the glories of civilization; I trace its history backward through a dozen eras and many nations; I show them how slowly it grew, and by what small and gradual accretions; I tell them how radiantly it has burst forth in these latter centuries, with such magnificent effulgence, until to-day man has all nature at his feet, shackled and gyved, his patient logman. I tell them that a ruffian, with one blow of his club, can destroy the life of a man; and that all the doctors and scientists and philosophers of the world, working together for ages, could not restore that which he has so rudely extinguished. And so, I say to them, the civilization which it has taken ten thousand years to create may be swept away in an hour; and there shall be no power in the wit or wisdom of man to re-establish it.

Most of them have listened respectfully; a few have tried to answer me; some have mocked me. But it is as if one came where grouped convicts stood, long imprisoned, who heard—with knives in their hands—the thunderous blows of their friends as they battered down the doors of their prison-house, and he should beg them not to go forth, lest they should do harm to society! They will out, though the heavens and the earth came together! One might as well whisper to Niagara to cease falling, or counsel the resistless cyclone, in its gyrating and terrible advance, to have a care of the rose-bushes.

CHAPTER IX.

THE POISONED KNIFE.

WHEN we returned home, on Sunday evening, Max found the receptacle in the wall which communicated with the pneumatic-tube system standing open. In it he found a long communication in cipher. He read a few lines with a startled look and then said:

"Here is important news, Gabriel. It is written in one of the ciphers of the Brotherhood, which I will translate to you. The number is that of Rudolph — the number it is addressed to is my own. We know each other in the Brotherhood, not by our names, but by the numbers given us when we became members. Listen:

"From number 28,263 M 2, to No. 160,053 P 4. Dated this 7:9, from the house of the condemned, No. 826 B."

"That," said Maximilian, "means the Prince Cabano." He continued to read:

"Startling events have occurred since I saw you. The former favorite mistress of 826 B, who was displaced by Frederika, is a French girl, Celestine d'Aublay. She resented her downfall bitterly, and she hates Frederika with the characteristic vehemence of her race. She learned from the talk of the servants that a new victim — Estella — had been brought into the house, a girl of great beauty; and that Frederika was trying to prevent 826 B from seeing her. A sudden thought took possession of her mind; she would overthrow Frederika just as she herself had been overthrown. Yesterday, Saturday afternoon, she watched for 826 B in the hallways and chambers. The snuffling old wretch has a fashion of prying around in all parts of the house, under the fear that he is being robbed by the servants; and it was not long until Celestine encountered him. She threw herself in his way.

"'Well, little one,' he said, chucking her under the chin, 'how have you been? I have not seen your pretty face for a long time.'

"'Indeed,' said she, 'you care very little now for my pretty face, or that of any one else, since you have your new toy, Estella.'

"'Estella!' he repeated, 'who is Estella?'

"'Come, come,' she said laughing; 'that will not do! Master Rudolph brings into the house a young girl of ravishing beauty, and weeks afterwards you ask me who she is! I am not to be deceived that way. I know you too well.'

"'But really,' he replied, 'I have not seen her. This is the first I have ever heard of her. Who is she?'

"'Her name is Estella Washington,' replied Celestine; 'she is about eighteen years old.'

"'Estella Washington,' he said respectfully; 'that is a great name. What is she like?'

"'I have told you already,' was the reply, 'that she is of magnificent beauty, tall, fair, stately, graceful and innocent.'

"'Indeed, I must see her.'

"He hurried to his library and rang my bell.

"'Rudolph,' he said, when I appeared, 'who is this Estella Washington that you brought into the house some weeks since? Celestine has been telling me about her. How comes it I have never seen her?'

"My heart came into my mouth with a great leap; but I controlled my excitement and replied:

"'My lord, I reported to you the fact of the purchase some time since, and the payment of $5,000 to an aunt of Estella.'

"'True,' he said, 'I remember it now; but I was much occupied at the time. How comes it, however, that she has been in the house and I have never seen her?'

"I determined not to betray Frederika, and so I replied:

"'It must have been by accident, your lordship; and, moreover, Estella is of a very quiet, retiring disposition, and has kept her room a great part of the time since she came here.'

"'Go to her and bring her here,' he said.

"There was no help for it; so I proceeded to Estella's room.

"'Miss Washington,' I said, 'I have bad news for you. The Prince desires to see you?'

"She rose up, very pale.

"'My God,' she said, 'what shall I do?'

"And then she began to fumble in the folds of her dress for the knife your friend gave her.

"'Be calm and patient,' I said; 'do nothing desperate. On the night after next your friend will come for you. We must delay matters all we can. Keep your room, and I will tell the Prince that you are too sick to leave your bed, but hope to be well enough to pay your respects to him to-morrow afternoon. We will thus gain twenty-four hours' delay, and we may be able to use the same device again to-morrow.'

"But she was very much excited, and paced the room with hurried steps, wringing her hands. To calm her I said:

"'You are in no danger. You can lock your door. And see, come here,' I said, and, advancing to one of the window sills, I lifted it up and disclosed, neatly coiled within it, a ladder of cords, with stout bamboo rounds. 'As a last resort,' I continued, 'you can drop this out of the window and fly. All the rooms in this older part of the palace are furnished with similar fire-escapes. You see that yellow path below us; and there beyond the trees you may perceive a part of the wall of the gardens; that path terminates at a little gate, and here is a key that will unlock it. Study the ground well from your windows. Your escape would, however, have to be made by night; but as you would run some risk in crossing the grounds, and, when you passed the gate, would find yourself in the midst of a strange world, without a friend, you must only think of flight as your last resource in the most desperate extremity. We must resort to cunning, until your friends come for you, on Monday night. But be patient and courageous. Remember, I am your friend, and my life is pledged to your service.'

"She turned upon me, and her penetrating eyes seemed to read my very soul.

"'How,' she said, 'can I trust you? You are a stranger to me. Worse than that, you are the hired instrument of that monster — that dealer in flesh and blood. You bought me and brought me here; and who are your friends? They too are strangers to me. Why should I believe in strangers when the one whom I loved, and in whom I placed unquestioning trust, has betrayed me, and sold me to the most dreadful fate?'

"I hung my head.

"'It chances,' I replied, humbly, 'that the instruments of vice may sometimes loathe the work they do. The fearful executioner may, behind his mask, hide the traces of grief and pity. I do not blame you for your suspicions. I once had aspirations, perhaps as high, and purity of soul nearly as great as your own. But what are we? The creatures of fate; the victims of circumstances. We look upon the Medusa-head of destiny, with its serpent curls, and our wills, if not our souls, are turned into stone. God alone, who knows all, can judge the heart of man. But I am pledged, by ties the most awful, to a society which, however terrible its methods may be, is, in its grand conceptions, charitable and just. My life would not be worth a day's purchase if I did not defend you. One of your friends stands high in that society.'

"'Which one is that?' she asked, eagerly.

"'The smaller and darker one,' I replied.

"'Can you tell me anything about the other?' she asked, and a slight blush seemed to mantle her face, as if she were ashamed of the question.

"'Very little,' I replied; 'he is not a member of our Brotherhood; but he is a brave man, and the friend of Mr. Maximilian can not be a bad man.'

"'No,' she said, thoughtfully; 'he is of a good and noble nature, and it is in him I trust.'

"'But,' said I, 'I must leave you, or the Prince will wonder at my long absence.'

"As I took my departure I heard her locking the door behind me. I reported to the Prince that Miss Washington was quite ill, and confined to her bed, but that she hoped to do herself the honor of calling upon him the next day. He looked glum, but assented,

Upon leaving him, I called upon Frederika and requested her to come to my room. In a few moments she appeared. After seating her I said:

"'Miss Frederika, will you pardon me if I ask you a few questions upon matters of importance to both of us?'

"'Certainly,' she replied.

"'In the first place,' I said, 'you regard me as your friend, do you not? Have I not always shown a disposition to serve you?'

"She replied with some pleasant smiles and assurances of friendship.

"'Now let me ask you another question,' I continued. 'Do you entertain friendly sentiments to Miss Estella?'

"'Indeed I do,' she replied; 'she is a sweet-tempered, innocent and gentle girl.'

"'I am glad to hear it,' I said; 'did you know that the Prince has discovered her, and has just sent me for her?'

"Her large black eyes fairly blazed.

"'Who has told him of her?' she asked, fiercely, and her voice rose high and shrill.

"'Your enemy, Miss Celestine,' I replied.

"'I suspected as much,' she said.

"'I need not tell you,' I said, 'that Celestine's motive was to supplant and humble you.'

"'I understand that,' she replied, and her hands twitched nervously, as if she would like to encounter her foe.

"'Now let me ask you another question,' I continued. 'Would you not be glad to see Estella safely out of this house?'

"'Indeed I would,' she replied, eagerly.

"'If I place my life in your hands, will you be true to me?' I asked.

"She took me earnestly by the hand, and replied:

"'Neither in life nor in death will I betray you.'

"'Then,' said I, 'I will tell you that Estella has friends who are as anxious to get her away from this place as you are. They have arranged to come for her on Monday night next. You must help me to protect her from the Prince in the meantime, and to facilitate her escape when the time comes.'

"'I will do so,' she said; 'tell me what I can do now?'

"'Make yourself very entertaining to the Prince,' I replied, 'and keep his thoughts away from the stranger. Estella pleads sickness and keeps her room; and we may be able to protect her in that way until the fateful night arrives. And remember,' I said, touching her upon the breast and looking earnestly into her eyes, for I have little faith in such natures, 'that I am a member of a great secret society, and if any mishap were to happen to me, through your agency, your own life would pay the immediate forfeit.'

"She shrank back affrighted, and assured me again of her good faith. And as she desires to be quit of Estella, I think she will not betray us."

"SUNDAY EVENING, seven o'clock.

"I resume my narrative. I have gone through dreadful scenes since I laid down my pen.

"This afternoon about five o'clock the Prince rang for me.

"'Bring Estella,' he said.

"I went at once to her room. I found her looking

paler than usual. She had the appearance of one that had not slept.

"'Estella,' I said, 'the Prince has again sent for you. I shall return and make the same excuse. Do not worry—all will be well. We are one day nearer your deliverance.'

"I returned and told the Prince that Estella was even worse than the day before; that she had a high fever; and that she apologized for not obeying his summons; but that she hoped by to-morrow to be well enough to pay her respects to him.

"He was in one of his sullen fits. I think Frederika had been overdoing her blandishments, and he had become suspicious; for he is one of the most cunning of men.

"'Frederika is behind this business,' he said.

"'Behind what business, my lord?' I asked.

"'This sickness of Estella. Bring her to me, ill or well,' he replied; 'I want to see her.'

"He was in no humor to be trifled with; and so I returned to my room to think it over. I saw that Estella would have to barricade herself in her room. How could she support life in the meantime? The first requisite was, therefore, food. I went at once to Michael, the cook's assistant, who is a trusty friend of mine, and secured from him, secretly and under a pledge of silence, food enough to last until the next night. I hurried to Estella, told her of her danger, and gave her the basket of provisions. I instructed her to lock her door.

"'If they break it in,' I said, 'use your knife on the first man that touches you. If they send you food or drink, do not use them. If they attempt to chloroform you, stop up the pipe with soap. If the worst

comes to the worst, use the rope-ladder. If you manage to get outside the garden gate, call a hack and
drive to that address.' Here I gave her your direction on a small piece of tissue paper. 'If you are
about to be seized, chew up the paper and swallow it.
Do not in any event destroy yourself,' I added, 'until
the last desperate extremity is reached; for you
have a powerful organization behind you, and even if
recaptured you will be rescued. Good-by.'

"She thanked me warmly, and as I left the room
I heard her again lock the door.

"I returned to the Prince, and told him that Estella had said she was too ill to leave her room, and
that she refused to obey his summons. Unaccus-
tomed to contradiction, especially in his own house,
he grew furious.

"'Call the servants,' he shouted; 'we will see who is
master here!'

"A few of the men came running; Frederika entered with them; some of the women followed. We
proceeded up stairs to Estella's door. The Prince
shook it violently.

"'Open the door,' he cried, 'or I will break it
down.'

"I began to hope that he would rush to the doom
he has so long deserved.

"The calm, steady voice of Estella was now heard
from within the room; speaking in a high and ringing
tone:

"'I appeal to my country. I demand the right to
leave this house. I am an American citizen. The
Constitution of the United States forbids human
slavery. My fathers helped to found this government.
No one has the right to sell me into the most hideous

bondage. I come of a great and noble race. I demand my release.'

"'Come, come, open the door,' cried the Prince, flinging himself against it until it quivered.

"The voice of Estella was heard again, in solemn tones:

"'The man who enters here dies!'

"The cowardly brute recoiled at once, with terror on every feature of his face.

"'Who will break down that door,' he asked, 'and bring out that woman?'

"There was a dead silence for a moment; then Joachim, a broad-shouldered, superserviceable knave, who had always tried to ingratiate himself with the Prince by spying upon the rest of the servants and tattling, stepped forward, with an air of bravado, and said, 'I will bring her out.'

"'Go ahead,' said the Prince, sullenly.

"Joachim made a rush at the door; it trembled and creaked, but did not yield; he moved farther back, drew his breath hard, and,—strong as a bull,—went at it with a furious rush; the lock gave way, the door flew open and Joachim sprawled upon the floor. I could see Estella standing back near the window, her right arm was raised, and I caught the glitter of something in her hand. In an instant Joachim was on his feet and approached her; I saw him grasp her; there was a slight scuffle, and the next moment Joachim rushed out of the room, pale as death, with his hand to his breast, crying out:

"'Oh! my God! she has stabbed me.'

"He tore open his shirt bosom, and there upon his hairy breast was a bloody spot; but the knife had struck the breast-bone and inflicted only a shallow flesh-wound. Joachim laughed, replaced his shirt, and said:

"'Ah! I might have known a girl's hand could not strike a deadly blow. I will bring her out, my lord. Get me a rope.'

"He turned toward me, as he spoke; but on the instant I saw a sharp spasm contract his features; he clapped his hand to his heart; a look of surprise and then of terror came over his face.

"'Oh, my God!' he cried, 'I am poisoned.'

"The most awful shrieks I ever heard broke from him; and the next moment his limbs seemed to lose their strength, and he fell in a heap on the floor; then he rolled over and over; mighty convulsions swept through him; he groaned, cried, shrieked, foamed at the mouth; there was a sudden snorting sound, and he stiffened out and was dead.

"We fell back appalled. Then in the doorway appeared the figure of Estella, her blue eyes bright as stars, her long golden hair falling like a cloak to her waist, the red-tipped knife in her hand; she looked like a Gothic priestess — a Vala of Odin — with the reeking human sacrifice already at her feet. The blood of a long line of heroic ancestors thrilled in her veins. Stepping over the dead body, already beginning to swell and grow spotted with many colors, like a snake, she advanced toward the Prince, who stood in his dressing-gown, trembling, and nearly as bloated, pale and hideous as the wretched Joachim.

"'Is it you,' she said — 'you, the dealer in human flesh and blood, that has bought me? Come to me, and take possession of your bond-woman!'

"With a cry of terror the Prince turned his back and fled as fast as his legs would carry him, while all the rest of us followed pell-mell. At the end of the hall is a large iron door, used for protection in case of fire.

" 'Quick,' shrieked the Prince, 'lock the door! lock the door!'

"This was done, and he stopped to pant and blow in safety. When he had recovered his breath, he cried out:

" 'Send for the police! We will have her chloroformed.'

"I touched Frederika on the arm;—she followed me into an open room.

" 'Tell him,' I whispered to her, quickly, 'tell him that if he calls in the police there will have to be an inquest over the dead body of Joachim; there may be questions asked that will be hard to answer. The girl will have to be taken off to be tried for murder, and he will lose her. If he attempts to use chloroform she will stab herself with the poisoned knife. Tell him you will drug her food with narcotics; that hunger will eventually compel her to eat; and that when she sleeps she may be made a prisoner, and the knife taken away from her.'

"The quick-witted girl saw the force of these suggestions, and ran after her paramour. She succeeded in her mission. He fears the coming outbreak, whispers of which are now heard everywhere. He has recalled the order for the police. He stipulates, however—for he is suspicious of Frederika, and fears treachery—that he is to drug the food himself and see it placed in the room; and he has stationed two trusty guards at the door of Estella's chamber, who are to be changed every eight hours, and who are instructed that, whenever they think she is asleep, one of them is to notify him; and carpenters will then quietly cut the door from its hinges, and they will enter, disarm her and make her a prisoner. Estella, I find, has barricaded her door with her bedstead and the rest of the furniture. If she sleeps she will wake with any attempt to enter the room; but she is not likely, in her present state of high-wrought excitement, to sleep at all; and she will not touch the drugged food sent in to her. I have arranged with Frederika, who has great authority in the house, that on Monday night the two watchmen shall be furnished with some refreshment containing morphine; and when they are sound asleep, and the Prince busy with his guests, she or I will go to the room, carrying Estella's masculine disguise, and then bring her to my room, where she will join your friend.

"I do not think she is in any present danger. The poisoned knife is her safeguard. The whole household, after witnessing its terrible potency, fear it as they would the fangs of a rattlesnake. It was a lucky thought that left it with her.

"If your friend does not fail us, all will be well.

"Farewell.   28,263 M 2."

I need not tell you, my dear Heinrich, that we both followed this narrative with the most rapt attention and the most intense feeling.

"Brave girl!" I cried, when Maximilian stopped reading, "she is worth dying for."

"Or living for," said he, "which is better still. How she rose to the occasion!"

"Yes," I said, "that was *blood*."

"There is as good stuff in the ranks," he replied, "as ever came out of them. The law of heredity is

7

almost as unreliable as the law of variation. Everything rises out of the mud, and everything goes back into it."

"Do you think," I asked, after a pause, "that she will be safe until to-morrow night? Should I not go to her at once? Could I not see Rudolph and have her descend the rope-ladder, and I meet her and bring her here?"

"No," he replied, "it is now too late for that; it is midnight. You can place full faith in Rudolph; his penetration and foresight are extraordinary. He will not sleep until Estella is out of that house; and his busy brain will be full of schemes in the meantime. The best thing we can do now is to go to bed and prepare, by a good long sleep, for the excitements and dangers of to-morrow night. Do not fear for Estella. She has ceased to be a child. In an hour she has risen to the full majesty of her womanhood."

CHAPTER X.

THE next morning I found Maximilian in conference with a stranger; a heavily-built, large-jawed, uncommunicative man. As I was about to withdraw my friend insisted that I should sit down.

"We have been making the necessary arrangements for next Monday night," he said. "The probabilities are great that we may be followed when we leave the house, and traced. It will not do to go, as Rudolph suggested, to the residence of any friend, and pass through it to another carriage. The Oligarchy would visit a terrible vengeance on the head of the man who so helped us to escape. I have instructed this gentleman to secure us, through an agent, three empty houses in different parts of the city, and he has done so; they stand in the center of blocks, and have rear exits, opening upon other streets or alleys, at right angles with the streets on which the houses stand. Then in these back streets he is to have covered carriages with the fleetest horses he can obtain. Our pursuers, thinking we are safely housed, may return to report our whereabouts to their masters. Estella being missed the next day, the police will visit the house, but they will find no one there to punish; nothing but curtains over the windows."

"But," said I, "will they not follow the carriage that brought us there, and thus identify its owner and driver, and force them to tell who employed them?"

"Of course; I have thought of that, and provided for it. There are members of the Brotherhood who have been brought from other cities in disguise, and three of these will have another carriage, which, leaving the Prince's grounds soon after we do, will pursue our pursuers. They will be well armed and equipped with hand-grenades of dynamite. If they perceive that the spies cannot be shaken off, or that they propose to follow any of our carriages to their stables, it will be their duty to swiftly overtake the pursuers, and, as they pass them, fling the explosives under the horses' feet, disabling or killing them. It will take the police some time to obtain other horses, and before they can do so, all traces of us will be lost. If necessary, our friends will not hesitate to blow up the spies as well as the horses."

"But," I suggested, "will they not identify the man who rented the houses?"

Maximilian laughed.

"Why," said he, "my dear Gabriel, you would make a conspirator yourself. We will have to get you into the Brotherhood. We are too old to be caught that way. The man who rented the houses has been brought here from a city hundreds of miles distant; he was thoroughly disguised. As soon as he engaged the buildings, and paid one month's rent in advance for each, he left the city; and before to-morrow night he will be home again, and without his disguise; and he could never be suspected or identified as the same man. And," he added, "I do not propose that you shall go into that lion's den unsupported. We will have twenty of the Brotherhood, under Rudolph's management, scattered through the household, as servants; and three hundred more will be armed to the teeth and near at hand in the neighborhood; and if it becomes necessary they will storm the house and burn it over the villains' heads, rather than that you or Estella shall come to harm."

I pressed his hand warmly, and thanked him for his care of me, and of one so dear to me.

He laughed. "That is all right," he said; "good and unselfish men are so scarce in this world that one cannot do too much for them. We must be careful lest, like the dodo and the great auk, the breed becomes extinct."

"But," said I, "may not the Oligarchy find you out, even here?"

"No," he replied, "my identity is lost. Here I live, in my real appearance, under a false name. But I have a house elsewhere, in which I dwell disguised, but under my real name, and with an unreal character. Here I am a serious, plotting conspirator; there I am a dissipated, reckless, foolish spendthrift, of whom no man need be afraid. It chanced that after certain events had occurred, of which I may tell you some day, I did not return home for several years; and then I came for revenge, with ample preparations for my own safety. I resumed my old place in society with a new appearance and a new character. That personage is constantly watched by spies; but he spends his time in drunkenness and deeds of folly; and his enemies laugh and say, 'He will never trouble us; he will be dead soon.' And so, with the real name and the unreal appearance and character in one place, and a false name, but the real appearance and character, in another, I lead a dual life and thwart the cunning of my enemies, and prepare for the day of my vengeance."

His eyes glowed with a baleful light as he spoke, and I could see that some great injustice, "like eager droppings into milk," had soured an otherwise loving and affectionate nature. I put my hand on his and said:

"My dear Max, your enemies are my enemies and your cause my cause, from henceforth forever."

His face beamed with delight, as he replied:

"I may some day, my dear Gabriel, hold you to that pledge."

"Agreed," I responded; "at all times I am ready."

He gave his agent a roll of money, and with mutual courtesies they separated.

CHAPTER XI.

WE were uneasy, restless, longing for the night to come. To while away the time we conversed upon subjects that were near our hearts.

I said to Maximilian while he paced the room:

"How did this dreadful state of affairs, in which the world now finds itself, arise? Were there no warnings uttered by any intelligent men? Did the world drift blindly and unconsciously into this condition?"

"No," said Maximilian, going to his library; "no; even a hundred years ago the air was full of prophecies. Here," he said, laying his hand upon a book, is *The Century Magazine*, of February, 1889; and on page 622 we read:

For my own part, I must confess my fears that, unless some important change is made in the constitution of our voting population, *the breaking strain upon our political system will come within half a century.* Is it not evident that our present tendencies are in the wrong direction? The rapidly increasing use of money in elections, for the undisguised purchase of votes, and the growing disposition to tamper with the ballot and the tally-sheet, are some of the symptoms. . . . Do you think that you will convince the average election officer that it is a great crime to cheat in the return of votes, when he knows that a good share of those votes have been purchased with money? No; the machinery of the election will not be kept free from fraud while the atmosphere about the polls reeks with bribery. *The system will all go down together.* In a constituency which can be bribed all the forms of law tend swiftly to decay.

"And here," he said, picking up another volume, "is a reprint of the choicest gems of *The North American Review.* In the number for March, 1889, Gen. L. S. Bryce, a member of Congress, said:

We live in a commercial age—not in a military age; and the shadow that is stealing over the American landscape partakes of a commercial character. In short, *the shadow is of an unbridled plutocracy,* caused, created and cemented in no slight degree by legislative, aldermanic and congressional action; *a plutocracy that is far more wealthy than any aristocracy that has ever crossed the horizon of the world's history, and one that has been produced in a shorter consecutive period;* the names of whose members are emblazoned, not on the pages of their nation's glory, but of its peculations; who represent no struggle for their country's liberties, but for its boodle; no contests for Magna Charta, but railroad charters; and whose octopus-grip is extending over every branch of industry; a plutocracy which controls the price of the bread that we eat, the price of the sugar that sweetens our cup, the price of the oil that lights us on our way, the price of the very coffins in which we are finally buried; a plutocracy which encourages no kindly relation between landlord and tenant, which has so little sense of its political duties as even to abstain from voting, and which, in short, by its effrontery, is already causing the unthinking masses to seek relief in communism, in single-taxism, and in every other ism, which, if ever enforced, would infallibly make their second state worse than the first.

"And here are hundreds of warnings of the same kind. Even the President of the United States, in that same year, 1889, uttered this significant language:

Those who use unlawful methods, if moved by no higher motive than the selfishness that prompted them, may well stop and inquire, *What is to be the end of this?*

"Bishop Potter, of New York, in the national ceremonies, held April 30, 1889, which marked the centennial anniversary of the first inauguration of

George Washington, spoke of the plutocracy, which had already reached alarming proportions, and expressed his doubts whether the Republic would ever celebrate another centennial. Afterwards, in explaining his remarks, he said:

When I speak of this as the era of the plutocrats, nobody can misunderstand me. Everybody has recognized the rise of the money power. Its growth not merely stifles the independence of the people, but the blind believers in this omnipotent power of money assert that its liberal use condones every offense. The pulpit does not speak out as it should. These plutocrats are the enemies of religion, as they are of the state. And, not to mince matters, I will say that, while I had the politicians in mind prominently, there "are others." I tell you I have heard the corrupt use of money in elections and the sale of the sacred right of the ballot openly defended by ministers of the gospel. I may find it necessary to put such men of the sacred office in the public pillory.

"And Bishop Spalding, of Peoria, Illinois, about the same time, said:

Mark my words, the saloon in America has become a public nuisance. The liquor trade, by meddling with politics and corrupting politics, has become a menace and a danger. Those who think and those who love America and those who love liberty are going to bring this moral question into politics more and more; also this question of bribery, this question of lobbying, this question of getting measures through state and national legislatures by corrupt means. They are going to be taken hold of. Our press, which has done so much to enlighten our people, which represents so much that is good in our civilization, must also be reformed. It must cease to pander to such an extent to the low and sensual appetites of man. My God, man is animal enough! You don't want to pander to his pruriency! You don't want to pander to the beast that is in him. . . . Our rich men—and they are numerous, and their wealth is great—their number and their wealth will increase—but our rich men *must do their duty or perish.* I tell you, in America, we will not tolerate vast wealth in the hands of men who do nothing for the people.

"And here is a still more remarkable article, by Dr. William Barry, in *The Forum* for April, 1889. He speaks of—

The concrete system of capitalism, which in its present shape is not much more than a century old, and goes back to Arkwright's introduction of the spinning-jenny in 1776—that notable year—as to its hegira or divine epoch of creation.

"And again he says:

This it is that justifies Von Hartmann's description of the nineteenth century as "the most irreligious that has ever been seen;" this and not the assault upon dogma or the decline of the churches. There is a depth below atheism, below anti-religion, and into that the age has fallen. It is the callous indifference to everything which does not make for wealth. . . . What is eloquently described as " the progress of civilization," as "material prosperity," and "unexampled wealth," or, more modestly, as "the rise of the industrial middle class," becomes, when we look into it with eyes purged from economic delusions, the creation of a "lower and lowest" class, without land of their own, without homes, tools or property beyond the strength of their hands; whose lot is more helplessly wretched than any poet of the Inferno has yet imagined. Sunk in the mire of ignorance, want and immorality, they seem to have for their only gospel the emphatic words attributed to Mr. Ruskin: "If there is a next world they *will* be damned ; and if there is none, they are damned already." . . . Have all these things come to pass that the keeper of a whisky-shop in California may grow rich on the spoils of drunken miners, and great financiers dictate peace and war to venerable European monarchies? The most degraded superstition that ever called itself religion has not preached such a dogma as this. It falls below fetichism. The worship of the almighty dollar, incarnate in the self-made capitalist, is a deification at which Vespasian himself, with his "*Ut puto, deus fio*," would stare and gasp.

"And this remarkable article concludes with these words of prophecy:

The agrarian difficulties of Russia, France, Italy, Ireland, and of wealthy England, show us that ere long the urban and the rural populations will be standing in the same camp. They will be demanding the abolition of that great and scandalous paradox whereby, though production has increased three or four times as much as the mouths it should fill, those mouths are empty. The backs it should clothe are naked; the heads it should shelter, homeless; the brains it should feed, dull or criminal, and. the souls it should help to save, brutish. Surely it is time that science, morality and religion should speak out. A great change is coming. It is even now at our doors. Ought not men of good will to consider how they shall receive it, so that its coming may be peaceable?

"And here," Max added, "is the great work of Prof. Scheligan, in which he quotes from *The Forum*, of December, 1889, p. 464, a terrible story of the robberies practiced on the farmers by railroad companies and money-lenders. The railroads in 1882 took, he tells us, one-half of the entire wheat crop of Kansas to carry the other half to market! In the thirty-eight years following 1850 the railroad interest of the United States increased 1580 per cent.; the banking interest 918 per cent., and the farming interest only 252 per cent. A man named Thomas G. Shearman showed, in 1889, that 100,000 persons in the United States would, in thirty years, at the rate at which wealth was being concentrated in the hands of the few, own *three-fifths of all the property of the entire country*. The *American Economist* asserted, in 1889, that in twenty-five years the number of people in the United States who owned their own homes had fallen from five-eighths to three-eighths. A paper called *The Progress*, of Boston, in 1889, gave the following significant and prophetic figures:

The eloquent Patrick Henry said: "We can only judge the future by the past."

Look at the past:

When Egypt went down 2 per cent. of her population owned 97 per cent. of her wealth. The people were starved to death.

When Babylon went down 2 per cent. of her population owned all the wealth. The people were starved to death.

When Persia went down 1 per cent. of her population owned the land.

When Rome went down 1,800 men owned all the known world.

There are about 40,000,000 people in England, Ireland and Wales, and 100,000 people own all the land in the United Kingdom.

For the past twenty years the United States has rapidly followed in the steps of these old nations. Here are the figures:

In 1850 capitalists owned 37½ per cent. of the nation's wealth.

In 1870 they owned 63 per cent.

"In 1889, out of 1,500,000 people living in New York City, 1,100,000 dwelt in tenement-houses.

"At the same time farm-lands, east and west, had fallen, in twenty-five years, to one-third or one-half their cost. State Assessor Wood, of New York, declared, in 1889, that, in his opinion, 'in a few decades *there will be none but tenant farmers in this State.*' *

"In 1889 the farm mortgages in the Western States amounted to *three billion four hundred and twenty-two million dollars.*"

"Did these wonderful utterances and most significant statistics," I asked, "produce no effect on that age?"

"None at all," he replied. "'Wisdom cries in the streets, and no man regards her.' The small voice of Philosophy was unheard amid the blare of the trumpets that heralded successful knavery; the rabble ran headlong to the devil after gauds and tinsel."

* See Popular Science Monthly, November, 1889, p. 28.

"Have there been," I asked, "no later notes of warning of the coming catastrophe?"

"Oh, yes," he replied; "ten thousand. All through the past century the best and noblest of each generation, wherever and whenever they could find newspapers or magazines that dared to publish their utterances, poured forth, in the same earnest tones, similar prophecies and appeals. But in vain. Each generation found the condition of things more desperate and hopeless: every year multiplied the calamities of the world. The fools could not see that a great cause must continue to operate until checked by some higher power. And here there was no higher power that desired to check it. As the domination and arrogance of the ruling class increased, the capacity of the lower classes to resist, within the limits of law and constitution, decreased. Every avenue, in fact, was blocked by corruption. Juries, courts, legislatures, congresses, they were as if they were not. The people were walled in by impassable barriers. Nothing was left them but the primal, brute instincts of the animal man, and upon these they fell back, and the Brotherhood of Destruction arose. But no words can tell the sufferings that have been endured by the good men, here and there, who, during the past century, tried to save mankind. Some were simply ostracised from social intercourse with their caste; others were deprived of their means of living and forced down into the ranks of the wretched; and still others"—and here, I observed, his face grew ashy pale, and the muscles about his mouth twitched nervously—"still others had their liberty sworn away by purchased perjury, and were consigned to prisons, where they still languish, dressed in the hideous garb

of ignominy, and performing the vile tasks of felons."
After a pause, for I saw he was strangely disturbed,
I said to him:

"How comes it that the people have so long sub-
mitted to these great wrongs? Did they not resist?"

"They did," he replied; "but the fruit of the tree
of evil was not yet ripe. At the close of the nineteenth
century, in all the great cities of America, there was
a terrible outbreak of the workingmen; they destroyed much property and many lives, and held
possession of the cities for several days. But the
national government called for volunteers, and hundreds of thousands of warlike young men, sons of
farmers, sprang to arms: and, after several terrible
battles, they suppressed the revolution, with the
slaughter of tens of thousands of those who took
part in it; while afterwards the revengeful Oligarchy
sent thousands of others to the gallows. And since
then, in Europe and America, there have been other
outbreaks, but all of them terminated in the same
way. The condition of the world has, however,
steadily grown worse and worse; the laboring classes
have become more and more desperate. The farmers'
sons could, for generations, be counted upon to fight
the workmen; but the fruit has been steadily ripen-
ing. Now the yeomanry have lost possession of their
lands; their farms have been sold under their feet;
cunning laws transferred the fruit of their industry
into the pockets of great combinations, who loaned
it back to them again, secured by mortgages; and,
as the pressure of the same robbery still continued,
they at last lost their homes by means of the very
wealth they had themselves produced. Now a single
nabob owns a whole county; and a state is divided

between a few great loan associations; and the men
who once tilled the fields, as their owners, are driven
to the cities to swell the cohorts of the miserable, or
remain on the land a wretched peasantry, to
contend for the means of life with vile hordes of Mongolian coolies. And all this in sight of the ruins of
the handsome homes their ancestors once occupied!
Hence the materials for armies have disappeared.
Human greed has eaten away the very foundations
on which it stood. And of the farmers who still remain nearly all are now members of our Brotherhood. When the Great Day comes, and the nation
sends forth its call for volunteers, as in the past,
that cry will echo in desolate places; or it will ring
through the triumphant hearts of savage and desperate men who are hastening to the banquet of
blood and destruction. And the wretched, yellow,
under-fed coolies, with women's garments over their
effeminate limbs, will not have the courage or the
desire or the capacity to make soldiers and defend
their oppressors."

"But have not the Oligarchy standing armies?"
I asked.

"Yes. In Europe, however, they have been constrained, by inability to wring more taxes from
the impoverished people, to gradually diminish their
numbers. There, you know, the real government is
now a coterie of bankers, mostly Israelites; and the
kings and queens, and so-called presidents, are mere
toys and puppets in their hands. All idea of national
glory, all chivalry, all pride, all battles for territory or supremacy have long since ceased. Europe
is a banking association conducted exclusively for
the benefit of the bankers. Bonds take the place

of national aspirations. To squeeze the wretched is
the great end of government; to toil and submit, the
destiny of the peoples.

"The task which Hannibal attempted, so disas-
trously, to subject the Latin and mixed-Gothic races
of Europe to the domination of the Semitic blood, as
represented in the merchant-city of Carthage, has
been successfully accomplished in these latter days
by the cousins of the Phœnicians, the Israelites. The
nomadic children of Abraham have fought and
schemed their way, through infinite depths of persecution, from their tents on the plains of Palestine,
to a power higher than the thrones of Europe. The
world is to-day Semitized. The children of Japhet
lie prostrate slaves at the feet of the children of
Shem; and the sons of Ham bow humbly before
their august dominion.

"The standing armies of Europe are now simply
armed police; for, as all the nations are owned by one
power—the money power—there is no longer any
danger of their assaulting each other. But in the
greed of the sordid commercial spirit which domi-
nates the continent they have reduced, not only the
numbers, but the pay of the soldiers, until it is little
better than the compensation earned by the wretched
peasantry and the mechanics; while years of peace
and plunder have made the rulers careless and secure.
Hence our powerful association has spread among
these people like wild-fire: the very armies are honey-
combed with our ideas, and many of the soldiers
belong to the Brotherhood.

"Here, in America, they have been wise enough to
pay the soldiers of their standing army better salaries; and hence they do not so readily sympathize

with our purposes. But we outnumber them ten to one, and do not fear them. There is, however, one great obstacle which we have not yet seen the way to overcome. More than a century ago, you know, dirigible air-ships were invented. The Oligarchy have a large force of several thousands of these, sheathed with that light but strong metal, aluminium; in popular speech they are known as *The Demons*. Sailing over a hostile force, they drop into its midst great bombs, loaded with the most deadly explosives, mixed with bullets; and, where one of these strikes the ground, it looks like the crater of an extinct volcano; while leveled rows of dead are strewed in every direction around it. But this is not all. Some years since a French chemist discovered a dreadful preparation, a subtle poison, which, falling upon the ground, being heavier than the air and yet expansive, rolls, 'like a slow blot that spreads,' steadily over the earth in all directions, bringing sudden death to those that breathe it. The Frenchman sold the secret of its preparation to the Oligarchy for a large sum; but he did not long enjoy his ill-gotten wealth. He was found dead in his bed the next day, poisoned by the air from a few drops of his own invention; killed, it is supposed, by the governments, so that they would possess forever the exclusive monopoly of this terrible instrument of slaughter. It is upon this that they principally rely for defense from the uprisings of the oppressed people. These air-ships, 'the Demons,' are furnished with bombs, loaded with this powerful poison; and, when an outbreak occurs, they sail, like great, foul birds, dark-winged and terrible, over the insurgents; they let fall a single bomb, which inspires such terror in the multitude that those not

8

instantaneously killed by the poison fly with the utmost speed; and the contest is at an end. We have long labored to bring the men who arm these air-ships, and who manufacture this poison, into our organization, but so far without success. The Oligarchy knows their value, and pays them well. We have, however, bribed one or two of their men, not themselves in the secret, but who have inspired the others to make demand after demand upon the government for increased pay, knowing that they held everything in their power. The Oligarchy has been constrained to yield to these demands, which have only led, under our inspiration, to still greater claims; and it is our hope that before long the rulers will refuse to go farther in that direction; and then, in the discontent that will inevitably follow, the men will yield to our approaches. It will be the old story over again—the army that was called in to defend effete Rome at last took possession of the empire and elected the emperors. This is the fate that cruelty and injustice ultimately bring upon their own heads—they are devoured by their instruments. As Manfred says:

> "'The spirits I have raised abandon me;
> The spells that I had recked of torture me.'"

"You are right," I replied; "there is nothing that will insure permanent peace but universal justice: that is the only soil that grows no poisons. Universal justice means equal opportunities for all men and a repression by law of those gigantic abnormal selfishnesses which ruin millions for the benefit of thousands. In the old days selfishness took the form of conquest, and the people were reduced to serfs. Then, in a later age, it assumed the shape of individual robbery and murder. Laws were made against these crimes. Then it broke forth in the shape of subtle combinations, 'rings,' or 'trusts,' as they called them, corporations, and all the other cunning devices of the day, some of which scarcely manifested themselves on the surface, but which transferred the substance of one man into the pockets of another, and reduced the people to slavery as completely and inevitably as ever the robber barons of old did the original owners of the soil of Europe.''

CHAPTER XII.

GABRIEL'S UTOPIA.

"But what would you do, my good Gabriel," said Maximilian, smiling, "if the reformation of the world were placed in your hands? Every man has an Utopia in his head. Give me some idea of yours."

"First," I said, "I should do away with all interest on money. Interest on money is the root and ground of the world's troubles. It puts one man in a position of safety, while another is in a condition of insecurity, and thereby it at once creates a radical distinction in human society."

"How do you make that out?" he asked.

"The lender takes a mortgage on the borrower's land or house, or goods, for, we will say, one-half or one-third their value; the borrower then assumes all the chances of life in his efforts to repay the loan. If he is a farmer, he has to run the risk of the fickle elements. Rains may drown, droughts may burn up his crops. If a merchant, he encounters all the hazards of trade; the bankruptcy of other tradesmen; the hostility of the elements sweeping away agriculture, and so affecting commerce; the tempests that smite his ships, etc. If a mechanic, he is still more dependent upon the success of all above him, and the mutations of commercial prosperity. He may lose employment; he may sicken; he may die. But behind all these risks stands the money-lender, in perfect security. The failure of his customer only enriches him; for he takes for his loan property worth twice or thrice the sum he has advanced upon it. Given a million of men and a hundred years of time, and the slightest advantage possessed by any one class among the million must result, in the long run, in the most startling discrepancies of condition. A little evil grows like a ferment—it never ceases to operate; it is always at work. Suppose I bring before you a handsome, rosy-cheeked young man, full of life and hope and health. I touch his lip with a single *bacillus* of *phthisis pulmonalis*—consumption. It is invisible to the eye; it is too small to be weighed. Judged by all the tests of the senses, it is too insignificant to be thought of; but it has the capacity to multiply itself indefinitely. The youth goes off singing. Months, perhaps years, pass before the deadly disorder begins to manifest itself; but in time the step loses its elasticity; the eyes become dull; the roses fade from the cheeks; the strength departs, and eventually the joyous youth is but a shell—a cadaverous, shrunken form, inclosing a shocking mass of putridity; and death ends the dreadful scene. Give one set of men in a community a financial advantage over the rest, however slight—it may be almost invisible—and at the end of centuries that class so favored will own everything and wreck the country. A penny, they say, put out at interest the day Columbus sailed from Spain, and compounded ever since, would amount now to more than all the assessed value of all the property, real, personal and mixed, on the two continents of North and South America."

"But," said Maximilian, "how would the men get along who wanted to borrow?"

"The necessity to borrow is one of the results of borrowing. The disease produces the symptoms. The men who are enriched by borrowing are infinitely less in number than those who are ruined by it; and every disaster to the middle class swells the number and decreases the opportunities of the helplessly poor. Money in itself is valueless. It becomes valuable only by use—by exchange for things needful for life or comfort. If money could not be loaned, it would have to be put out by the owner of it in business enterprises, which would employ labor; and as the enterprise would not then have to support a double burden—to wit, the man engaged in it and the usurer who sits securely upon his back— but would have to maintain only the former usurer— that is, the present employer—its success would be more certain; the general prosperity of the community would be increased thereby, and there would be therefore more enterprises, more demand for labor, and consequently higher wages. Usury kills off the enterprising members of a community by bankrupting them, and leaves only the very rich and the very poor; for every dollar the employers of labor pay to the lenders of money has to come eventually out of the pockets of the laborers. Usury is therefore the cause of the first aristocracy, and out of this grow all the other aristocracies. Inquire where the money came from that now oppresses mankind, in the shape of great corporations, combinations, etc., and in nine cases out of ten you will trace it back to the fountain of interest on money loaned. The coral island is built out of the bodies of dead coral insects; large fortunes are usually the accumulations of wreckage, and every dollar represents disaster."

"Well," said Maximilian, "having abolished usury, in your Utopia, what would you do next?"

"I would set to work to make a list of all the laws, or parts of laws, or customs, or conditions which, either by commission or omission, gave any man an advantage over any other man; or which tended to concentrate the wealth of the community in the hands of a few. And having found out just what these wrongs or advantages were, I would abolish them *instanter.*"

"Well, let us suppose," said Maximilian, "that you were not immediately murdered by the men whose privileges you had destroyed—even as the Gracchi were of old—what would you do next? Men differ in every detail. Some have more industry, or more strength, or more cunning, or more foresight, or more acquisitiveness than others. How are you to prevent these men from becoming richer than the rest?"

"I should not try to," I said. "These differences in men are fundamental, and not to be abolished by legislation; neither are the instincts you speak of in themselves injurious. Civilization, in fact, rests upon them. It is only in their excess that they become destructive. It is right and wise and proper for men to accumulate sufficient wealth to maintain their age in peace, dignity and plenty, and to be able to start their children into the arena of life sufficiently equipped. A thousand men in a community worth $10,000 or $50,000, or even $100,000 each, may be a benefit, perhaps a blessing; but one man worth fifty or one hundred millions, or, as we have them now-a-days, one thousand millions, is a threat against the safety and happiness of every man in the

world. I should establish a maximum beyond which
no man could own property. I should not stop his
accumulations when he had reached that point, for
with many men accumulation is an instinct; but I
should require him to invest the surplus, under the
direction of a governmental board of management,
in great works for the benefit of the laboring classes.
He should establish schools, colleges, orphan asy-
lums, hospitals, model residences, gardens, parks,
libraries, baths, places of amusement, music-halls,
sea-side excursions in hot weather, fuel societies in
cold weather, etc., etc. I should permit him to secure
immortality by affixing his name to his benevolent
works; and I should honor him still further by placing his statue in a great national gallery set apart
to perpetuate forever the memory of the benefactors
of the race."

"But," said Maximilian, with a smile, "it would
not take long for your rich men, with their surplus
wealth, to establish all those works you speak of.
What would you do with the accumulations of the
rest?"

"Well," said I, "we should find plenty to do. We
would put their money, for instance, into a great
fund and build national railroads, that would bring
the productions of the farmers to the workmen, and
those of the workmen to the farmers, at the least
cost of transportation, and free from the exactions
of speculators and middlemen. Thus both farmers
and workmen would live better, at less expense and
with less toil."

"All very pretty," said he; "but your middlemen
would starve."

"Not at all," I replied; "the cunning never starve.

There would be such a splendid era of universal prosperity that they would simply turn their skill and shrewdness into some new channels, in which, however, they would have to give something of benefit, as an equivalent for the benefits they received. Now they take the cream, and butter, and beef, while some one else has to raise, feed and milk the cow."

"But," said he, "all this would not help our farmers in their present condition—they are blotted off the land."

"True," I replied; "but just as I limited a man's possible wealth, so should I limit the amount of land he could own. I would fix a maximum of, say, 100 or 500 acres, or whatever amount might be deemed just and reasonable. I should abolish all corporations, or turn them back into individual partnerships. Abraham Lincoln, in the great civil war of the last century, gave the Southern insurgents so many days in which to lay down their arms or lose their slaves. In the same way I should grant one or two years' time, in which the great owners of land should sell their estates, in small tracts, to actual occupants, to be paid for in installments, on long time, without interest. And if they did not do so, then, at the end of the period prescribed, I should confiscate the lands and sell them, as the government in the old time sold the public lands, for so much per acre, to actual settlers, and turn the proceeds over to the former owners."

"But, as you had abolished interest on money, there could be no mortgages, and the poor men would starve to death before they could raise a crop."

"Then," I replied, "I should invoke the power of

the nation, as was done in that great civil war of
1861, and issue paper money, receivable for all
taxes, and secured by the guarantee of the faith and
power of five hundred million people; and make
advances to carry these ruined peasants beyond the
first years of distress—that money to be a loan to
them, without interest, and to be repaid as a tax on
their land. Government is only a machine to insure
justice and help the people, and we have not yet
developed half its powers. And we are under no
more necessity to limit ourselves to the governmental precedents of our ancestors than we are to
confine ourselves to the narrow boundaries of their
knowledge, or their inventive skill, or their theological beliefs. The trouble is that so many seem to
regard government as a divine something which has
fallen down upon us out of heaven, and therefore not
to be improved upon or even criticised; while the
truth is, it is simply a human device to secure human
happiness, and in itself has no more sacredness
than a wheelbarrow or a cooking-pot. The end of
everything earthly is the good of man; and there is
nothing sacred on earth but man, because he alone
shares the Divine conscience."

"But," said he, "would not your paper money
have to be redeemed in gold or silver?"

"Not necessarily," I replied. "The adoration of
gold and silver is a superstition of which the bankers are the high priests and mankind the victims.
Those metals are of themselves of little value. What
should make them so?"

"Are they not the rarest and most valuable productions of the world?" said Maximilian.

"By no means," I replied; "there are many

metals that exceed them in rarity and value. While a kilogram of gold is worth about $730 and one of silver about $43.50, the same weight of iridium (the heaviest body known) costs $2,400; one of palladium, $3,075; one of calcium nearly $10,000; one of stibidium, $20,000; while vanadium, the true 'king of metals,' is worth $25,000 per kilogram, as against $730 for gold or $43.50 for silver."

"Why, then, are they used as money?" he asked.

"Who can tell? The practice dates back to pre-historic ages. Man always accepts as right any-thing that is in existence when he is born."

"But are they not more beautiful than other metals? And are they not used as money because acids will not corrode them?"

"No," I replied; "some of the other metals exceed them in beauty. The diamond far surpasses them in both beauty and value, and glass resists the action of acids better than either of them."

"What do you propose?" he asked.

"Gold and silver," I said, "are the bases of the world's currency. If they are abundant, all forms of paper money are abundant. If they are scarce, the paper money must shrink in proportion to the shrinkage of its foundation; if not, there come panics and convulsions, in the effort to make one dollar of gold pay three, six or ten of paper. For one hundred and fifty years *the production of gold and silver has been steadily shrinking, while the pop-ulation and business of the world have been rapidly increasing.*

"Take a child a few years old; let a blacksmith weld around his waist an iron band. At first it causes him little inconvenience. He plays. As he grows older it becomes tighter; it causes him pain; he scarcely knows what ails him. He still grows. All his internal organs are cramped and displaced. He grows still larger; he has the head, shoulders and limbs of a man and the waist of a child. He is a monstrosity. He dies. This is a picture of the world of to-day, bound in the silly superstition of some prehistoric nation. But this is not all. Every decrease in the quantity, actual or relative, of gold and silver increases the purchasing power of the dollars made out of them; and the dollar becomes the equivalent for a larger amount of the labor of man and his productions. This makes the rich man richer and the poor man poorer. The iron band is displacing the organs of life. As the dollar rises in value, man sinks. Hence the decrease in wages; the increase in the power of wealth; the luxury of the few; the misery of the many."

"How would you help it?" he asked.

"I would call the civilized nations together in council, and devise an international paper money, to be issued by the different nations, but to be receivable as legal tender for all debts in all countries. It should hold a fixed ratio to population, never to be exceeded; and it should be secured on all the property of the civilized world, and acceptable in payment of all taxes, national, state and municipal, everywhere. I should declare gold and silver legal tenders only for debts of five dollars or less. An international greenback that was good in New York, London, Berlin, Melbourne, Paris and Amsterdam, would be good anywhere. The world, released from its iron band, would leap forward to marvelous prosperity; there would be no financial panics, for there could be no contraction; there would be no more torpid 'middle ages,' dead for lack of currency, for the money of a nation would expand, *pari passu*, side by side with the growth of its population. There would be no limit to the development of mankind, save the capacities of the planet; and even these, through the skill of man, could be increased a thousand-fold beyond what our ancestors dreamed of. The very seas and lakes, judiciously farmed, would support more people than the earth now maintains. A million fish ova now go to waste where one grows to maturity.

"The time may come when the slow processes of agriculture will be largely discarded, and the food of man be created out of the chemical elements of which it is composed, transfused by electricity and magnetism. We have already done something in that direction in the way of synthetic chemistry. Our mountain ranges may, in after ages, be leveled down and turned into bread for the support of the most enlightened, cultured, and, in its highest sense, religious people that ever dwelt on the globe. All this is possible if civilization is preserved from the destructive power of the ignorant and brutal Plutocracy, who now threaten the safety of mankind. They are like the slave-owners of 1860; they blindly and imperiously insist on their own destruction; they strike at the very hands that would save them."

"But," said Maximilian, "is it not right and necessary that the intellect of the world should rule the world?"

"Certainly," I replied; "but what is intellect? It is breadth of comprehension; and this implies gentleness and love. The man whose scope of thought takes in the created world, and apprehends man's place in nature, cannot be cruel to his fellows. Intellect, if it is selfish, is wisely selfish. It perceives clearly that such a shocking abomination as our present condition cannot endure. It knows that a few men cannot safely batten down the hatches over the starving crew and passengers, and then riot in drunken debauchery on the deck. When the imprisoned wretches in the hold become desperate enough—and it is simply a question of time—they will fire the ship or scuttle it, and the fools and their victims will all perish together. True intellect is broad, fore-sighted, wide-ranging, merciful, just. Some one said of old that 'the gods showed what they thought of riches by the kind of people they gave them to.' It is not the poets, the philosophers, the philanthropists, the historians, the sages, the scholars, the really intellectual of any generation who own the great fortunes. No; but there is a subsection of the brain called *cunning;* it has nothing to do with elevation of mind, or purity of soul, or knowledge, or breadth of view; it is the lowest, basest part of the intellect. It is the trait of foxes, monkeys, crows, rats and other vermin. It delights in holes and subterranean shelters; it will not disdain filth; it is capable of lying, stealing, trickery, knavery. Let me give you an example:

"It is recorded that when the great war broke out in this country against slavery, in 1861, there was a rich merchant in this city, named A. T. Stewart. Hundreds of thousands of men saw in the war only the great questions of the Union and the abolition of human bondage—the freeing of four millions of

human beings, and the preservation of the honor of
the flag; and they rushed forward eager for the fray.
They were ready to die that the Nation and Liberty
might live. But while their souls were thus inflamed
with great and splendid emotions, and they forgot
home, family, wealth, life, everything, Stewart, the
rich merchant, saw simply the fact that the war
would cut off communication between the North and
the cotton-producing States, and that this would result in a rise in the price of cotton goods; and so,
amid the wild agitations of patriotism, the beating
of drums and the blaring of trumpets, he sent out his
agents and bought up all the cotton goods he could
lay his hands on. He made a million dollars, it is
said, by this little piece of cunning. But if all men
had thought and acted as Stewart did, we should
have had no Union, no country, and there would
be left to-day neither honor nor manhood in all the
world. The nation was saved by those poor fellows
who did not consider the price of cotton goods in the
hour of America's crucial agony. Their dust now
billows the earth of a hundred battle-fields; but their
memory will be kept sweet in the hearts of men
forever! On the other hand, the fortune of the great
merchant, as it did no good during his life, so, after
his death, it descended upon an alien to his blood;
while even his wretched carcass was denied, by the
irony of fate, rest under his splendid mausoleum, and
may have found its final sepulchre in the stomachs of
dogs!

"This little incident illustrates the whole matter.
It is not *Intellect* that rules the world of wealth, it is
Cunning. *Muscle* once dominated mankind — the
muscle of the baron's right arm; and *Intellect* had

to fly to the priesthood, the monastery, the friar's gown, for safety. Now *Muscle* is the world's slave, and *Cunning* is the baron—the world's master.

"Let me give you another illustration: Ten thousand men are working at a trade. One of them conceives the scheme of an invention, whereby their productive power is increased tenfold. Each of them, we will say, had been producing, by his toil, property worth four dollars and a half per day, and his wages were, we will say, one dollar and a half per day. Now, he is able with the new invention to produce property worth forty-five dollars per day. Are his wages increased in due proportion, to fifteen dollars per day, or even to five dollars per day? Not at all. *Cunning* has stepped in and examined the poor workman's invention; it has bought it from him for a pittance; it secures a patent—a monopoly under the shelter of unwise laws. The workmen still get their $1.50 per day, and *Cunning* pockets the remainder. But this is not all: If one man can now do the work of ten, then there are nine men thrown out of employment. But the nine men must live; they want the one man's place; they are hungry; they will work for less; and down go wages, until they reach the lowest limit at which the workmen can possibly live. Society has produced one millionaire and thousands of paupers. The millionaire cannot eat any more or wear any more than one prosperous yeoman, and therefore is of no more value to trade and commerce; but the thousands of paupers have to be supported by the tax-payers, and they have no money to spend, and they cannot buy the goods of the merchants, or the manufacturers, and all business languishes. In short, the most utterly useless, destructive and damnable crop a country can grow is—millionaires. If a community were to send to India and import a lot of man-eating tigers, and turn them loose on the streets, to prey on men, women and children, they would not inflict a tithe of the misery that is caused by a like number of millionaires. And there would be this further disadvantage: the inhabitants of the city could turn out and kill the tigers, but the human destroyers are protected by the benevolent laws of the very people they are immolating on the altars of wretchedness and vice."

"But what is your remedy?" asked Max.

"Government," I replied; "government—national, state and municipal—is the key to the future of the human race.

"There was a time when the town simply represented cowering peasants, clustered under the shadow of the baron's castle for protection. It advanced slowly and reluctantly along the road of civic development, scourged forward by the whip of necessity. We have but to expand the powers of government to solve the enigma of the world. Man separated is man savage; man gregarious is man civilized. A higher development in society requires that this instrumentality of co-operation shall be heightened in its powers. There was a time when every man provided, at great cost, for the carriage of his own letters. Now the government, for an infinitely small charge, takes the business off his hands. There was a time when each house had to provide itself with water. Now the municipality furnishes water to all. The same is true of light. At one time each family had to educate its own children; now

9

the state educates them. Once every man went
armed to protect himself. Now the city protects him
by its armed police. These hints must be followed
out. The city of the future must furnish doctors for
all; lawyers for all; entertainments for all; business
guidance for all. It will see to it that no man is
plundered, and no man starved, who is willing to
work."

"But," said Max, "if you do away with interest
on money and thus scatter coagulated capital into
innumerable small enterprises, how are you going to
get along without the keen-brained masters of business, who labor gigantically for gigantic personal
profits; but who, by their toil and their capital, bring
the great body of producers into relation with the
great body of consumers? Are these men not necessary to society? Do they not create occasion and
opportunity for labor? Are not their active and
powerful brains at the back of all progress? There
may be a thousand men idling, and poorly fed and
clothed, in a neighborhood: along comes one of these
shrewd adventurers; he sees an opportunity to utilize
the bark of the trees and the ox-hides of the farmers'
cattle, and he starts a tannery. He may accumulate
more money than the thousand men he sets to work;
but has he not done more? Is not his intellect im-
measurably more valuable than all those unthinking
muscles?"

"There is much force in your argument," I replied,
"and I do not think that society should discourage
such adventurers. But the muscles of the many are
as necessary to the man you describe as his intellect
is to the muscles; and as they are all men together
there should be some equity in the distribution of the

profits. And remember, we have gotten into a way of thinking as if numbers and wealth were everything. It is better for a nation to contain thirty million people, prosperous, happy and patriotic, than one hundred millions, ignorant, wretched and longing for an opportunity to overthrow all government. The over-population of the globe will come soon enough. We have no interest in hurrying it. The silly ancestors of the Americans called it 'national development' when they imported millions of foreigners to take up the public lands, and left nothing for their own children.

"And here is another point: Men work at first for a competence — for enough to lift them above the reach of want in those days which they know to be rapidly approaching, when they can no longer toil. But, having reached that point, they go on laboring for vanity — one of the shallowest of the human passions. The man who is worth $100,000 says to himself, 'There is Jones; he is worth $500,000; he lives with a display and extravagance I cannot equal. I must increase my fortune to half a million.' Jones, on the other hand, is measuring himself against Brown, who has a million. He knows that men cringe lower to Brown than they do to him. He must have a million — half a million is nothing. And Brown feels that he is overshadowed by Smith, with his ten millions; and so the childish emulation continues. Men are valued, not for themselves, but for their bank account. In the meantime these vast concentrations of capital are made at the expense of mankind. If, in a community of a thousand persons, there are one hundred millions of wealth, and it is equally divided between them, all are comfortable and happy. If, now, ten men, by cunning devices, grasp three-fourths of all this wealth, and put it in their pockets, there is but one-fourth left to divide among the nine hundred and ninety, and they are therefore poor and miserable. Within certain limits accumulation in one place represents denudation elsewhere.

"And thus, under the stimulus of shallow vanity," I continued, "a rivalry of barouches and bonnets — an emulation of waste and extravagance — all the powers of the minds of men are turned — not to lift up the world, but to degrade it. A crowd of little creatures — men and women — are displayed upon a high platform, in the face of mankind, parading and strutting about, with their noses in the air, as tickled as a monkey with a string of beads, and covered with a glory which is not their own, but which they have been able to purchase; crying aloud: 'Behold what I *have got!*' not, 'Behold what I *am!*'

"And then the inexpressible servility of those below them! The fools would not recognize Socrates if they fell over him in the street; but they can perceive Crœsus a mile off; they can smell him a block away; and they will dislocate their vertebræ abasing themselves before him. It reminds one of the time of Louis XIV. in France, when millions of people were in the extremest misery — even unto starvation; while great grandees thought it the acme of earthly bliss and honor to help put the king to bed, or take off his dirty socks. And if a common man, by any chance, caught a glimpse of royalty changing its shirt, he felt as if he had looked into heaven and beheld Divinity creating worlds. Oh, it is enough to make a man loathe his species."

"Come, come," said Maximilian, "you grow bitter. Let us go to dinner before you abolish all the evils of the world, or I shall be disposed to quit New York and buy a corner lot in Utopia."

CHAPTER XIII.

THE COUNCIL OF THE OLIGARCHY.

PRECISELY as Rudolph had forecast, things came to pass. I arrived at the palace of the Prince at half past six; at half past seven, my ordinary suit was covered with a braided livery, and I accompanied Rudolph to the council-chamber. We placed the table, chairs, pens, ink, paper, etc., in order. Watching our opportunity, we drew aside a heavy box in which grew a noble specimen of the *cactus grandiflorus* in full bloom, the gorgeous flowers just opening with the sunset, and filling the chamber with their delicious perfume. I crawled through the opening; took off my liveried suit; handed it back to Rudolph; he pushed the box into its place again; I inserted the hooks in their staples, and the barricade was complete. With many whispered injunctions and directions he left me. I heard him go out and lock the door — not the door by which we had entered — and all was silence.

There was room, by doubling up my limbs, Turk-fashion, to sit down in the inclosure. I waited. I thought of Estella. Rudolph had assured me that she had not been disturbed. They were waiting for hunger to compel her to eat the drugged food. Then I wondered whether we would escape in safety. Then my thoughts dwelt on the words she had spoken of me, and I remembered the pleased look upon her face when we met in Rudolph's room, and my visions became very pleasant. Even the dead silence and oppressive solitude of the two great rooms could not still the rapid beatings of my heart. I forgot my mission and thought only of Estella and the future.

I was recalled to earth and its duties by the unlocking of the farther door. I heard Rudolph say, as if in answer to a question:

"Yes, my lord, I have personally examined the rooms and made sure that there are no spies concealed anywhere."

"Let me see," said the Prince; "lift up the tapestry."

I could hear them moving about the council-chamber, apparently going around the walls. Then I heard them advancing into the conservatory. I shrank down still lower; they moved here and there among the flowers, and even paused for a few moments before the mass of flowering *cacti.*

"That *flagelliformis,*" said the Prince, "looks sickly. The soil is perhaps too rich. Tell the gardener to change the earth about it."

"I shall do so, my lord," said Rudolph; and to my great relief they moved off. In a few minutes I heard them in the council-chamber. With great caution I rose slowly. A screen of flowers had been cunningly placed by Rudolph between the *cacti* and that apartment. At last, half-stooping, I found an aperture in the rich mass of blossoms. The Prince was talking to Rudolph. I had a good view of his person. He was dressed in an evening suit. He was a large man, somewhat corpulent; or, as Rudolph had said, bloated. He had a Hebraic cast of countenance; his face seemed to be all angles. The brow was square and prominent, projecting at the corners;

the nose was quite high and aquiline; the hair had
the look of being dyed; a long, thick black mustache
covered his upper lip, but it could not quite conceal
the hard, cynical and sneering expression of his
mouth; great bags of flesh hung beneath the small,
furtive eyes. Altogether the face reminded me of
the portraits of Napoleon the Third, who was
thought by many to have had little of Napoleon in
him except the name.

There was about Prince Cabano that air of confidence and command which usually accompanies
great wealth or success of any kind. Extraordinary
power produces always the same type of countenance. You see it in the high-nosed mummied kings
of ancient Egypt. There is about them an aristo-
cratic *hauteur* which even the shrinking of the dry
skin for four thousand years has not been able to
quite subdue. We feel like taking off our hats even
to their parched hides. You see it in the cross-legged
monuments of the old crusaders, in the venerable
churches of Europe; a splendid breed of ferocious
barbarians they were, who struck ten blows for conquest and plunder where they struck one for Christ.
And you can see the same type of countenance in the
present rulers of the world—the great bankers, the
railroad presidents, the gigantic speculators, the
uncrowned monarchs of commerce, whose golden
chariots drive recklessly over the prostrate bodies of
the people.

And then there is another class who are everywhere the aids and ministers of these oppressors.
You can tell them at a glance—large, coarse, corpulent men; red-faced, brutal; decorated with vulgar
taste; loud-voiced, selfish, self-assertive; cringing

sycophants to all above them, slave-drivers of all
below them. They are determined to live on the best
the world can afford, and they care nothing if the
miserable perish in clusters around their feet. The
howls of starvation will not lessen one *iota* their ap-
petite or their self-satisfaction. These constitute the
great man's *world*. He mistakes their cringings,
posturings and compliments for the approval of
mankind. He does not perceive how shallow and
temporary and worse than useless is the life he leads;
and he cannot see, beyond these well-fed, corpulent
scamps, the great hungry, unhappy millions who are
suffering from his misdeeds or his indifference.

While I was indulging in these reflections the members of the government were arriving. They were
accompanied by servants, black and white, who,
with many bows and flexures, relieved them of their
wraps and withdrew. The door was closed and
locked. Rudolph stood without on guard.

I could now rise to my feet with safety, for the
council-chamber was in a blaze of electric light, while
the conservatory was but partially illuminated.

The men were mostly middle-aged, or advanced in
years. They were generally large men, with finely
developed brows—natural selection had brought the
great heads to the top of affairs. Some were clean-
cut in feature, looking merely like successful business men; others, like the Prince, showed signs of
sensuality and dissipation, in the baggy, haggard
features. They were unquestionably an able assembly. There were no orators among them; they
possessed none of the arts of the rostrum or the
platform. They spoke sitting, in an awkward, hesi-
tating manner; but what they said was shrewd and

always to the point. They had no secretaries or reporters. They could trust no one with their secrets. Their conclusions were conveyed by the president—Prince Cabano—to one man, who at once communicated what was needful to their greater agents, and these in turn to the lesser agents; and so the streams of authority flowed, with lightning-like speed, to the remotest parts of the so-called Republic; and many a man was struck down, ruined, crushed, destroyed, who had little suspicion that the soundless bolt which slew him came from that faraway chamber.

The Prince welcomed each newcomer pleasantly, and assigned him to his place. When all were seated he spoke:

"I have called you together, gentlemen," he said, "because we have very important business to transact. The evidences multiply that we are probably on the eve of another outbreak of the restless _canaille;_ it may be upon a larger scale than any we have yet encountered. The filthy wretches seem to grow more desperate every year; otherwise they would not rush upon certain death, as they seem disposed to do.

"I have two men in this house whom I thought it better that you should see and hear face to face. The first is General Jacob Quincy, commander of the forces which man our ten thousand air-ships, or _Demons_, as they are popularly called. I think it is understood by all of us that, in these men, and the deadly bombs of poisonous gas with which their vessels are equipped, we must find our chief dependence for safety and continued power. We must not forget that we are outnumbered a thousand to one, and the world grows very restive under our domination. If it were not for the *Demons* and the poison-bombs, I should fear the results of the coming contest — with these, victory is certain.

"Quincy, on behalf of his men, demands another increase of pay. We have already several times yielded to similar applications. We are somewhat in the condition of ancient Rome, when the prætorians murdered the emperor Pertinax, and sold the imperial crown to Didius Julianus. These men hold the control of the continent in their hands. Fortunately for us, they are not yet fully aware of their own power, and are content to merely demand an increase of pay. We cannot quarrel with them at this time, with a great insurrection pending. A refusal might drive them over to the enemy. I mention these facts so that, whatever demands General Quincy may make, however extravagant they may be, you will express no dissatisfaction. When he is gone we can talk over our plans for the future, and decide what course we will take as to these troublesome men when the outbreak is over. I shall have something to propose after he leaves us."

There was a general expression of approval around the table.

"There is another party here to-night," continued the Prince. "He is a very shrewd and cunning spy; a member of our secret police service. He goes by the name of Stephen Andrews in his intercourse with me. What his real name may be I know not.

"You are aware we have had great trouble to ascertain anything definitely about this new organization, and have succeeded but indifferently. Their plans seem to be so well taken, and their cunning so great, that all our attempts have come to naught.

Many of our spies have disappeared; the police cannot learn what becomes of them; they are certainly dead, but none of their bodies are ever found. It is supposed that they have been murdered, loaded with weights and sunk in the river. This man Andrews has so far escaped. He works as a mechanic—in fact, he really is such—in one of the shops; and he is apparently the most violent and bitter of our enemies. He will hold intercourse with no one but me, for he suspects all the city police, and he comes here but seldom—not more than once in two or three months—when I pay him liberally and assign him to new work. The last task I gave him was to discover who are the leaders of the miserable creatures in this new conspiracy. He has found it very difficult to obtain any positive information upon this point. The organization is very cunningly contrived. The Brotherhood is made up in groups of ten. No one of the rank and file knows more than nine other members associated with him. The leaders of these groups of ten are selected by a higher power. These leaders are again organized in groups of ten, under a leader again selected by a higher power; but in this second group of ten no man knows his fellow's name or face; they meet always masked. And so the scale rises. The highest body of all is a group of one hundred, selected out of the whole force by an executive committee. Andrews has at length, after years of patient waiting and working, been selected as one of this upper hundred. He is to be initiated to-morrow night. He came to me for more money; for he feels he is placing himself in great danger in going into the den of the chief conspirators. I told him that I thought you would like to question him, and so he has returned again to-night, disguised in the dress of a woman, and he is now in the library awaiting your pleasure. I think we had better see him before we hear what Quincy has to say. Shall I send for him?"

General assent being given, he stepped to the door and told Rudolph to bring up the woman he would find in the library. In a few moments the door opened and a tall personage, dressed like a woman, with a heavy veil over her face, entered. The Prince said:

"Lock the door and come forward."

The figure did so, advanced to the table and removed the bonnet and veil, disclosing the dark, bronzed face of a workman — a keen, shrewd, observant, watchful, strong face.

CHAPTER XIV.

"ANDREWS," said the Prince, "tell these gentlemen what you have found out about the extent of this organization and the personality of its leaders?"

"My lord," replied the man, "I can speak only by hearsay — from whispers which I have heard in a thousand places, and by piecing together scraps of information which I have gathered in a great many ways. I do not yet speak positively. After to-morrow night I hope to be able to tell you everything."

"I understand the difficulties you have to contend with," replied the Prince; "and these gentlemen will not hold you to a strict accountability for the correctness of what you have gathered in that way."

"You can have no idea," said Andrews, "of the difficulty of obtaining information. It is a terrible organization. I do not think that anything like it has ever existed before on the earth. One year ago there were fifteen of us engaged in this work; I am the only one left alive to-night."

His face grew paler as he spoke, and there was a visible start and sensation about the council board.

"This organization," he continued, "is called '*The Brotherhood of Destruction.*' It extends all over Europe and America, and numbers, I am told, *one hundred million members.*"

"Can that be possible?" asked one gentleman, in astonishment.

"I believe it to be true," said Andrews, solemnly. "Nearly every workman of good character and sober habits in New York belongs to it; and so it is in all our great cities; while the blacks of the South are members of it to a man. Their former masters have kept them in a state of savagery, instead of civilizing and elevating them; and the result is they are as barbarous and bloodthirsty as their ancestors were when brought from Africa, and fit subjects for such a terrible organization."

"What has caused such a vast movement?" asked another gentleman.

"The universal misery and wretchedness of the working classes, in the cities, on the farms — everywhere," replied Andrews.

"Are they armed?" asked another of the Council.

"It is claimed," said Andrews, "that every one of the hundred millions possesses a magazine rifle of the most improved pattern, with abundance of fixed ammunition."

"I fear, my good man," said another member of the Council, with a sneer, "that you have been frightened by some old woman's tales. Where could these men buy such weapons? What would they buy them with? Where would they hide them? Our armories and manufacturers are forbidden by law to sell firearms, unless under special permit, signed by one of our trusty officers. The value of those guns would in itself be a vast sum, far beyond the means of those miserable wretches. And our police are constantly scouring the cities and the country for weapons, and they report that the people possess none, except a few old-fashioned, worthless fowling-pieces, that have come down from father to son."

"As I said before," replied Andrews, "I tell you only what I have gleaned among the workmen in those secret whispers which pass from one man's mouth to another man's ear. I may be misinformed; but I am told that these rifles are manufactured by the men themselves (for, of course, all the skilled work of all kinds is done by workingmen) in some remote and desolate parts of Europe or America; they are furnished at a very low price, at actual cost, and paid for in small installments, during many years. They are delivered to the captains of tens and by them buried in rubber bags in the earth."

"Then that accounts," said one man, who had not yet spoken, "for a curious incident which occurred the other day near the town of Zhitomir, in the province of Volhynia, Russia, not very far from the borders of Austria. A peasant made an offer to the police to deliver up, for 200 rubles, and a promise of pardon for himself, nine of his fellow conspirators and their rifles. His terms were accepted and he was paid the money. He led the officers to a place in his barnyard, where, under a manure-heap, they dug up ten splendid rifles of American make, with fixed ammunition, of the most improved kind, the whole inclosed in a rubber bag to keep out the damp. Nine other peasants were arrested; they were all subjected to the knout; but neither they nor their captain could tell anything more than he had at first revealed. The Russian newspapers have been full of speculations as to how the rifles came there, but could arrive at no reasonable explanation."

"What became of the men?" asked Andrews, curiously.

"Nine of them were sent to Siberia for life; the tenth man, who had revealed the hiding-place of the guns, was murdered that night with his wife and all his family, and his house burned up. Even two of his brothers, who lived near him, but had taken no part in the matter, were also slain."

"I expected as much," said Andrews quietly.

This unlooked-for corroboration of the spy's story produced a marked sensation, and there was profound silence for some minutes.

At last the Prince spoke up:

"Andrews," said he, "what did you learn about the leaders of this organization?"

"There are three of them, I am told," replied the spy; "they constitute what is known as 'the Executive Committee.' The commander-in-chief, it is whispered, is called, or was called—for no one can tell what his name is now—Cæsar Lomellini; a man of Italian descent, but a native of South Carolina. He is, it is said, of immense size, considerable ability, and the most undaunted courage. His history is singular. He is now about forty-five years of age. In his youth, so the story goes, he migrated to the then newly settled State of Jefferson, on the upper waters of the Saskatchewan. He had married early, like all his race, and had a family. He settled down on land and went to farming. He was a quiet, peaceable, industrious man. One year, just as he was about to harvest his crops, a discharge of lightning killed his horses; they were the only ones he had. He was without the means to purchase another team, and without horses he could not gather his harvest. He was therefore forced to mortgage his land for enough to buy another pair of

10

horses. The money-lender demanded large interest
on the loan and an exorbitant bonus besides; and as
the 'bankers,' as they called themselves, had an organization, he could not get the money at a lower
rate anywhere in that vicinity. It was the old story.
The crops failed sometimes, and when they did not
fail the combinations and trusts of one sort or
another swept away Cæsar's profits; then he had to
renew the loan, again and again, at higher rates of
interest, and with still greater bonuses; then the
farm came to be regarded as not sufficient security
for the debt; and the horses, cattle, machinery,
everything he had was covered with mortgages.
Cæsar worked like a slave, and his family toiled
along with him. At last the crash came; he was
driven out of his home; the farm and all had been
lost for the price of a pair of horses. Right on the
heels of this calamity, Cæsar learned that his eldest
daughter—a beautiful, dark-eyed girl—had been se-
duced by a lawyer—the agent of the money-lender—
and would in a few months become a mother. Then
all the devil that lay hid in the depths of the man's
nature broke forth. That night the lawyer was attacked in his bed and literally hewed to pieces: the
same fate overtook the money-lender. Before morning Cæsar and his family had fled to the inhospitable
mountain regions north of the settlement. There he
gathered around him a band of men as desperate as
himself, and waged bloody and incessant war on society. He seemed, however, to have a method in his
crimes, for, while he spared the poor, no man who
preyed upon his fellow-men was safe for an hour. At
length the government massed a number of troops
in the vicinity; the place got too hot for him; Cæsar

and his men fled to the Pacific coast; and nothing
more was heard of him for three or four years. Then
the terrible negro insurrection broke out in the lower
Mississippi Valley, which you all remember, and a
white man, of gigantic stature, appeared as their
leader, a man of great daring and enterprise. When
that rebellion had been suppressed, after many
battles, the white man disappeared; and it is now
claimed that he is in this city at the head of this terrible Brotherhood of Destruction; and that he is the
same Cæsar Lomellini who was once a peaceful farmer
in the State of Jefferson."

The spy paused. The Prince said:

" Well, who are the others ? "

"It is reported that the second in command, but
really 'the brains of the organization,' as he is called
by the men, is a Russian Jew. His name I could not
learn; very few have seen him or know anything
about him. He is said to be a cripple, and to have a
crooked neck. It is reported he was driven out of his
synagogue in Russia, years ago, for some crimes he
had committed. He is believed to be the man who
organized the Brotherhood in Europe, and he has
come here to make the two great branches act
together. If what is told of him be true, he must be
a man of great ability, power and cunning."

" Who is the third ? " asked the Prince.

"There seems to be more obscurity about him
than either of the others," replied the spy. "I
heard once that he was an American, a young man
of great wealth and ability, and that he had furnished much of the money needed to carry on the
Brotherhood. But this again is denied by others.
Jenkins, who was one of our party, and who was

killed some months since, told me, in our last interview, that he had penetrated far enough to find out
who the third man was; and he told me this curious
story, which may or may not be true. He said that
several years ago there lived in this city a man of
large fortune, a lawyer by education, but not engaged in the practice of his profession, by the name
of Arthur Phillips. He was a benevolent man, of
scholarly tastes, and something of a dreamer. He
had made a study of the works of all the great
socialist writers, and had become a convert to their
theories, and very much interested in the cause of
the working people. He established a monthly journal for the dissemination of his views. He spoke at
the meetings of the workmen, and was very much
beloved and respected by them. Of course, so
Jenkins said, all this was very distasteful to the ruling class (I am only repeating the story as it was
told to me, your lordships will please remember),
and they began to persecute him. First he was
ostracised from his caste. But this did not trouble
him much. He had no family but his wife and
one son who was away at the university. He
redoubled his exertions to benefit the working
classes. At this time he had a lawsuit about some
property with a wealthy and influential man, a
member of the government. In the course of the
trial Phillips produced a writing, which purported
to be signed by two men, and witnessed by two
others; and Phillips swore he saw all of them sign it.
Whereupon not only the men themselves, but the
two witnesses to the paper, came up and swore, point-
blank, that their alleged signatures were forgeries.
There were four oaths against one. Phillips lost his

case. But this was not the worst of it. The next day he was indicted for forgery and perjury; and, despite his wealth and the efforts of the ablest counsel he could employ, he was convicted and sentenced to twenty years' penal servitude in the state prison. His friends said he was innocent; that he had been sacrificed by the ruling class, who feared him and desired to destroy him; that all the witnesses had been suborned by large sums of money to swear as they did; that the jury was packed, the judge one of their tools, and even his own lawyers corrupted. After several years his son—who bore the same name as himself—Arthur Phillips—returned from the university; and Jenkins told me that he had learned, in some mysterious way, that this was really the man who, out of revenge for the wrongs inflicted on his father, was now the third member of the Executive Committee of the Brotherhood, and had furnished them with large sums of money."

As this story progressed, listened to most attentively by all, I noticed that one large man, flashily dressed, flushed somewhat, and that the rest turned and looked at him. When Andrews stopped, the Prince said, quietly:

"Count, that is your man."

"Yes," replied the man spoken to, very coolly. "There is, however, no truth," he added, "in the latter part of the story; for I have had detectives shadow young Phillips ever since he returned to the city, and they report to me that he is a shallow, dissipated, drunken, worthless fellow, who spends his time about saloons and running after actresses and singers; and that it will not be long until he will have neither health nor fortune left."

I need not say that I was an intent listener to everything, and especially to the latter part of the spy's story. I pieced it out with what Maximilian had told me, and felt certain that Maximilian Petion and Arthur Phillips were one and the same person. I could now understand why it was that a gentleman so intelligent, frank and kindly by nature could have engaged in so desperate and bloody a conspiracy. Nor could I, with that awful narrative ringing in my ears, blame him much. What struck me most forcibly was that there was no attempt, on the part of the Count, to deny the sinister part of Jenkins' story; and the rest of the Council evidently had no doubt of its truth; nor did it seem to lessen him a particle in their esteem. In fact, one man said, and the rest assented to the sentiment:

"Well, it is a lucky thing the villain is locked up, anyhow."

There were some among these men whose faces were not bad. Under favorable circumstances they might have been good and just men. But they were the victims of a pernicious system, as fully as were the poor, shambling, ragged wretches of the streets and slums, who had been ground down by their acts into drunkenness and crime.

"When will the outbreak come?" asked one of the Council.

"That I cannot tell," said Andrews. "They seem to be waiting for something, or there is a hitch in their plans. The men are eager to break forth, and are only held back by the leaders. By their talk they are confident of success when the insurrection does come."

"What are their plans?" asked the Prince.

"They have none," replied Andrews, "except to burn, rob, destroy and murder. They have long lists of the condemned, I am told, including all those here present, and hundreds of thousands besides. They will kill all the men, women and children of the aristocracy, except the young girls, and these will be reserved for a worse fate—at least that is what the men about the beer-houses mutter between their cups."

The members of the government looked uneasy; some even were a trifle pale.

"Can you come here Wednesday night next and tell us what you learn during your visit to their 'Council of One Hundred'?" asked the Prince.

"Yes," replied Andrews—"if I am alive. But it is dangerous for me to come here."

"Wait in the library," said the Prince, "until I am at liberty, and I will give you an order for the thousand dollars I promised you; and also a key that will admit you to this house at any hour of the day or night. Gentlemen," he said, turning to his associates, "have you any further questions to ask this man?"

They had none, and Andrews withdrew.

"I think," said the Prince, "we had better reassemble here on Wednesday night. Matters are growing critical."

This was agreed to. The Prince stepped to the door and whispered a few words to Rudolph.

CHAPTER XV.

THE MASTER OF "THE DEMONS."

THE door, in a few minutes, opened, and closed behind a tall, handsome, military-looking man, in a bright uniform, with the insignia of a brigadier-general of the United States army on his shoulders.

The Prince greeted him respectfully and invited him to a seat.

"General Quincy," said the Prince, "I need not introduce you to these gentlemen; you have met them all before. I have told them that you desired to speak to them about matters relating to your command; and they are ready to hear you."

"Gentlemen," said the General, rising to his feet, "I regret to have to approach you once more in reference to the pay of the officers and men of my command. I fear you will think them importunate, if not unreasonable. I am not here of my own volition, but as the mouthpiece of others. Neither have I incited them to make these demands for increased pay. The officers and men seem to have a high sense of their great importance in the present condition of public affairs. They openly declare that those they maintain in power are enjoying royal affluence, which they could not possess for a single day without their aid; and therefore they claim that they should be well paid."

The General paused, and the Prince said, in his smoothest tones:

"That is not an unreasonable view to take of the matter. What do they ask?"

"I have here," replied the General, drawing a paper from his pocket, "a schedule of their demands, adopted at their last meeting." He handed it to the Prince.

"You will see," he continued, "that it ranges from $5,000 per year, for the common soldiers, up through the different grades, to $25,000 per year for the commanding officer."

Not a man at the Council table winced at this extraordinary demand. The Prince said:

"The salaries asked for are high; but they will come out of the public taxes and not from our pockets; and if you can assure me that your command, in view of this increase of compensation, will work with increased zeal, faithfulness and courage on behalf of law, order and society, I, for one, should be disposed to accede to the demand you make. What say you, gentlemen?"

There was a general expression of assent around the table.

The commander of the Demons thanked them, and assured them that the officers and men would be glad to hear that their request was granted, and that the Council might depend upon their valor and devotion in any extremity of affairs.

"Have you an abundant supply of the death-bombs on hand?" asked the Prince.

"Yes, many tons of them," was the reply.

"Are they well guarded?"

"Yes, with the utmost care. A thousand men of my command watch over them constantly."

"Your air-vessels are in perfect order?"

"Yes; we drill and exercise with them every day."

"You anticipate an outbreak?"

"Yes; we look for it any hour."

"Have you any further questions to ask General Quincy?" inquired the Prince.

"None."

He was bowed out and the door locked behind him. The Prince returned to his seat.

"Gentlemen," he said, "that matter is settled, and we are safe for the present. But you can see the ticklish ground we stand on. These men will not rest satisfied with the immense concessions we have made them; they will demand more and more as the consciousness of their power increases. They know we are afraid of them. In time they will assume the absolute control of the government, and our power will be at an end. If we resist them, they will have but to drop a few of their death-bombs through the roofs of our palaces, and it is all over with us."

"What can we do?" asked two or three.

"We must have recourse to history," he replied, "and profit by the experience of others similarly situated. In the thirteenth century the sultan of Egypt, Malek-ed-Adell the Second, organized a body of soldiery made up of slaves, bought from the Mongols, who had taken them in battle. They were called the *Bahri Mamelukes*. They formed the Sultan's body-guard. They were mounted on the finest horses in the world, and clad in the most magnificent dresses. They were of our own white race—Circassians. But Malek had unwittingly created, out of the slaves, a dangerous power. They, not many years afterward, deposed and murdered his son, and placed their general on the throne. For several generations they ruled Egypt. To circumscribe their power a new army of Mamelukes was formed, called the *Borgis*. But the cure was as bad as the disease. In 1382 the *Borgi Mamelukes* rose up, overthrew their predecessors, and made their leader, Barkok, supreme ruler. This dynasty held power until 1517, when the Ottoman Turks conquered Egypt. The Turks perceived that they must either give up Egypt or destroy the Mamelukes. They massacred them in great numbers; and, at last, Mehemet Ali beguiled four hundred and seventy of their leaders into the citadel of Cairo, and closed the gates, and ordered his mercenaries to fire upon them. But one man escaped. He leaped his horse from the ramparts and escaped unhurt, although the horse was killed by the prodigious fall.

"Now, let us apply this teaching of history. I propose that after this outbreak is over we shall order the construction of ten thousand more of these air-vessels, and this will furnish us an excuse for sending a large force of apprentices to the present command to learn the management of the ships. We will select from the circle of our relatives some young, able, reliable man to command these new troops. We will then seize upon the magazine of bombs and arrest the officers and men. We will charge them with treason. The officers we will execute, and the men we will send to prison for life; for it would not be safe, with their dangerous knowledge, to liberate them. After that we will keep the magazine of bombs and the secret of the poison in the custody of men of our own caste, so that the troops commanding the air-ships will never again feel that sense of power which now possesses them."

These plans met with general approval.

"But what are we to do with the coming out-break?" asked one of the councilors.

"I have thought of that, too," replied the Prince. "It is our interest to make it the occasion of a tre-mendous massacre, such as the world has never before witnessed. There are too many people on the earth, anyhow. In this way we will strike such terror into the hearts of the *canaille* that they will remain submissive to our will, and the domination of our children, for centuries to come."

"But how will you accomplish that?" asked one.

"Easily enough," replied the Prince. "You know that the first step such insurgents usually take is to tear up the streets of the city and erect barricades of stones and earth and everything else they can lay their hands on. Heretofore we have tried to stop them. My advice is that we let them alone—let them build their barricades as high and as strong as they please, and if they leave any outlets unob-structed, let our soldiers close them up in the same way. We have then got them in a rat-trap, sur-rounded by barricades, and every street and alley outside occupied by our troops. If there are a million in the trap, so much the better. Then let our flock of Demons sail up over them and begin to drop their fatal bombs. The whole streets within the barricades will soon be a sea of invisible poison. If the insurgents try to fly they will find in their own barricades the walls of their prison-house; and if they attempt to scale them they will be met, face to face, with our massed troops, who will be instructed to take no prisoners. If they break into the adja-cent houses to escape, our men will follow from the back streets and gardens and bayonet them at their leisure, or fling them back into the poison. If ten millions are slain all over the world, so much the better. There will be more room for what are left, and the world will sleep in peace for centuries.

"These plans will be sent out, with your approval, to all our cities, and to Europe. When the rebellion is crushed in the cities, it will not take long to subdue it among the wretched peasants of the country, and our children will rule this world for ages to come."

CHAPTER XVI.

GABRIEL'S FOLLY.

WHILE the applause that followed this diabolical scheme rang loud and long around the council-chamber, I stood there paralyzed. My eyes dilated and my heart beat furiously. I was overwhelmed with the dreadful, the awful prospect, so coolly presented by that impassive, terrible man. My imagination was always vivid, and I saw the whole horrid reality unrolled before me like a panorama. The swarming streets filled with the oppressed people; the dark shadows of the Demons floating over them; the first bomb; the terror; the confusion; the gasping of the dying; the shrieks, the groans— another and another bomb falling here, there, everywhere; the surging masses rushing from death to death; the wild flight; the barricades a line of fire and bayonets; the awful and continuous rattle of the guns, sounding like the grinding of some dreadful machinery that crunches the bones of the living; the recoil from the bullets to the poison; the wounded stumbling over the dead, now covering the streets in strata several feet thick; and still the bombs crash and the poison spreads. Death! death! nothing but death! *Ten million dead!* Oh, my God!

I clasped my head—it felt as if it would burst. I must save the world from such a calamity. These men are human. They cannot be insensible to an appeal for mercy— for justice!

Carried away by these thoughts, I stooped down and unclasped the hooks; I pushed aside the box; I crawled out; the next moment I stood before them in the full glare of the electric lamps.

"For God's sake," I cried, "save the world from such an awful calamity! Have pity on mankind; even as you hope that the Mind and Heart of the Universe will have pity on you. I have heard all. Do not plunge the earth into horrors that will shock the very stars in their courses. The world can be saved! It can be saved! You have power. Be pitiful. Let me speak for you. Let me go to the leaders of this insurrection and bring you together."

"He is mad," said one.

"No, no," I replied, "I am not mad. It is you that are mad. It is the wretched people who are mad—mad with suffering and misery, as you with pride and hardness of heart. You are all *men*. Hear their demands. Yield a little of your surperfluous blessings; and touch their hearts with kindness, and love will spring up like flowers in the track of the harrow. For the sake of Christ Jesus, who died on the cross for *all* men, I appeal to you. Be just, be generous, be merciful. Are they not your brethren? Have they not souls like yourselves? Speak, speak, and I will toil as long as I can breathe. I will wear the flesh from off my bones, if I can reconcile the castes of this wretched society, and save civilization."

The Prince had recoiled with terror at my first entrance. He had now rallied his faculties.

"How did you come here?" he asked.

Fortunately the repulsive coldness with which the Council had met my earnest appeals, which I had fairly shrieked at them, had restored to some extent the balance of my reason. The thought flashed over me that I must not betray Rudolph.

"Through yonder open window," I replied.

"How did you reach it?" asked the Prince.

"I climbed up the ivy vine to it."

"What did you come here for?" he asked.

"To appeal to you, in the name of God, to prevent the coming of this dreadful outbreak."

"The man is a religious fanatic," said one of the Council to another; "probably one of the street preachers."

The Prince drew two or three of the leaders together, and they whispered for a few minutes. Then he went to the door and spoke to Rudolph. I caught a few words: "Not leave—alive—send for Macarius—midnight—garden."

Rudolph advanced and took me by the arm. The revulsion had come. I was dazed—overwhelmed. There swept over me, like the rush of a flood, the dreadful thought: "What will become of Estella?" I went with him like a child. I was armed, but an infant might have slain me.

When we were in the hall, Rudolph said to me, in a hoarse whisper:

"I heard everything. You meant nobly; but you were foolish—wild. You might have ruined us all. But there is a chance of escape yet. It will be an hour before the assassin will arrive. I can secure that much delay. In the meantime, be prudent and silent, and follow my directions implicitly."

I promised, very humbly, to do so.

CHAPTER XVII.

THE FLIGHT AND PURSUIT.

HE opened the door of a room and pushed me into it. "Wait," he whispered, "for my orders." I looked around me. It was Rudolph's room—the one I had been in before. I was not alone. There was a young gentleman standing at a window, looking out into the garden. He turned around and advanced toward me, with his hand extended and a smile on his face. It was Estella! looking more charming than ever in her masculine dress. I took her hand. Then my heart smote me; and I fell upon my knees before her.

"O Estella," I cried, "pardon me. I would have sacrificed you for mankind—you that are dearer to me than the whole human race. Like a fool I broke from my hiding-place, and appealed to those hearts of stone—those wild beasts—those incarnate fiends —to spare the world the most dreadful calamity it has ever known. They proposed to murder *ten million human beings!* I forgot my task—my duty— you—my own safety—everything, to save the world."

Her eyes dilated as I spoke, and then, without a trace of mock modesty, without a blush, she laid her hand upon my head and said simply:

"If you had done less, I should have loved you less. What am I in the presence of such a catastrophe? But if you are to die we can at least perish

11

together. In that we have the mastery of our enemies. Our liberty is beyond their power."

"But you shall not die," I said, wildly, springing to
my feet. "The assassin comes! Give me the poisoned
knife. When he opens the door I shall slay him.
I shall bear you with me. Who will dare to arrest
our departure with that dreadful weapon—that instantaneous death—shining in my hand. Besides, I
carry a hundred lives at my girdle. Once in the
streets, we can escape."

She took from the pocket of her coat the sheathed
dagger and handed it to me.

"We must, however, be guided by the counsels of
Rudolph," she quietly said; "he is a faithful friend."

"True," I replied.

We sat near each other. I presumed nothing upon
the great admission she had so gravely made. This
was a woman to be worshiped rather than wooed.
I told her all the story of my life. I described my
home in that strange, wild, ancient, lofty land; my
mother, my brothers; the wide, old, roomy house;
the trees, the flowers, the clustering, bleating sheep.

A half hour passed. The door opened. A burst of
laughter and the clinking of glasses resounded
through it. Rudolph entered.

"The Prince and his friends," he said, "make
merry over their assured victory. If you will tell
Maximilian all you have heard to-night, the result
may be different from what they anticipate. Come
with me."

He led the way through a suite of two or three
rooms which communicated with his apartment.

"We must throw the hounds off the scent of the
fox," he said; and, to our astonishment, he proceeded

to tear down the heavy curtains from two windows, having first locked the door and closed the outer shutters. He then tore the curtains into long strips, knotting them together; we pulled upon them to test their strength. He then opened one of the windows and dropped the end of the long rope thus formed out of it, fastening the other end to a heavy piece of furniture, within the room.

"That will account for your escape," he said. "I have already thrown the rope ladder from the window of the room Estella occupied. These precautions are necessary for my own safety."

Then, locking the communicating doors, we returned to his room.

"Put this cloak over your shoulders," he said; "it will help disguise you. Walk boldly down these stairs," opening another door—not the one we had entered by; "turn to the right—to the right, remember—and on your left hand you will soon find a door—the first you will come to. Open it. Say to the man on guard: 'Show me to the carriage of Lord Southworth.' There is no such person; but that is the signal agreed upon. He will lead you to the carriage. Maximilian is the footman. Farewell, and may God bless you."

We shook hands. I followed his directions; we met no one; I opened the door; the guard, as soon as I uttered the pass-word, led me, through a mass of carriages, to where one stood somewhat back under some overhanging trees. The footman hurried to open the door. I gave my hand to Estella; she sprang in; I followed her. But this little movement of instinctive courtesy on my part toward a woman had been noticed by one of the many spies hanging around. He thought it strange that one man should offer his hand to assist another into a carriage. He whispered his suspicions to a comrade. We had hardly gone two blocks from the palace when Maximilian leaned down and said: "I fear we are followed."

Our carriage turned into another street, and then into another. I looked out and could see—for the streets were very bright with the magnetic light—that, some distance behind us, came two carriages close together, while at a greater distance, behind them, I caught sight of a third vehicle. Maximilian leaned down again and said:

"We are certainly pursued by two carriages. The third one I recognize as our own—the man with the bombs. We will drive to the first of the houses we have secured. Be ready to spring out the moment we stop, and follow me quickly into the house, for all depends on the rapidity of our movements."

In a little while the carriage suddenly stopped. I took Estella's hand. She needed no help. Maximilian was ascending the steps of a house, key in hand. We followed. I looked back. One of our pursuers was a block away; the other a little behind him. The carriage with the bombs I could not see—it might be obscured by the trees, or it might have lost us in the fierce speed with which we had traveled.

"Quick," said Maximilian, pulling us in and locking the door.

We followed him, running through a long, lighted hall, out into a garden; a gate flew open; we rushed across the street and sprang into another carriage; Maximilian leaped to his place; crack went the whip, and away we flew; but on the instant the quick eyes of my friend saw, rapidly whirling around the next corner, one of the carriages that had been pursuing us.

"They suspected our trick," said he. "Where, in heaven's name, is the man with the bombs?" he added, anxiously.

Our horses were swift, but still that shadow clung to us; the streets were still and deserted, for it was after midnight; but they were as bright as if the full moon shone in an unclouded sky.

"Ah! there he comes, at last," said Maximilian, with a sigh of relief. "I feared we might meet another carriage of the police, and this fellow behind us would call it to his help, and our case would be desperate, as they would know our trick. We should have to fight for it. Now observe what takes place."

Estella, kneeling on the cushions, looked out through the glass window in the back of the carriage; I leaned far out at the side.

"See, Estella," I cried, "how that hindmost team flies! They move like race-horses on the course."

Nearer and nearer they come to our pursuers; they are close behind them; the driver of the front carriage seems to know that there is danger; he lashes his horses furiously; it is in vain. Now they are side by side—side by side for a time; but now our friends forge slowly ahead. The driver of the beaten team suddenly pulls his horses back on their haunches. It is too late. A man stands up on the seat of the front carriage—it is an open barouche. I could see his arm describe an arc through the air; the next instant the whole street was ablaze with a flash of brilliant red light, and the report of a tre-

mendous explosion rang in my ears. Through the
smoke and dust I could dimly see the horses of our
pursuers piled in a heap upon the street, kicking,
plunging, dying.

"It is all right now," said Maximilian quietly;
and then he spoke to the driver: "Turn the next
corner to the left."

After having made several changes of direction
—with intent to throw any other possible pursuers
off the track—and it being evident that we were not
followed, except by the carriage of our friends, we
drove slowly to Maximilian's house and alighted.

The sweet-faced old lady took the handsome,
seeming boy, Estella, in her arms, and with hearty
cordiality welcomed her to her new home. We left
them together, mingling tears of joy.

Max and I adjourned to the library, and there, at
his request, I told him all that had happened in the
council-chamber. He smoked his cigar and listened
attentively. His face darkened as I repeated the
spy's story, but he neither admitted nor denied the
truth of that part which I thought related to himself.
When I told him about the commander of the air-
ships, his interest was so great that his cigar went
out; and when I narrated the conversation which
occurred after General Quincy had left the room his
face lighted up with a glow of joy. He listened
intently to the account of the Prince's plan of battle,
and smiled grimly. But when I told how I came from
my hiding-place and appealed to the Oligarchy to
spare mankind, he rose from his chair and walked
the room, profoundly agitated; and when I had finished, by narrating how Rudolph led me to his room,
to the presence of Estella, he threw his arms around

my neck, and said, "You dear old fool! It was just like you;" but I could see that his eyes were wet with emotion.

Then he sat for some time in deep thought. At last he said:

"Gabriel, would you be willing to do something more to serve me?"

"Certainly," I replied; "anything."

"Would you go with me to-morrow night and tell this tale to the council of our Brotherhood? My own life and the lives of my friends, and *the liberty of one dear to me*, may depend upon your doing so."

"I shall go with you most willingly," I said. "To tell you the truth," I added, "while I cannot approve of your terrible Brotherhood, nevertheless what I have seen and heard to-night satisfies me that the Plutocrats should no longer cumber the earth with their presence. Men who can coolly plot, amid laughter, the death of ten million human beings, for the purpose of preserving their ill-gotten wealth and their ill-used power, should be exterminated from the face of the planet as enemies of mankind — as poisonous snakes — vermin."

He grasped my hand and thanked me.

It was pleasant to think, that night, that Estella loved me; that I had saved her; that we were under the same roof; and I wove visions in my brain brighter than the dreams of fairyland; and Estella moved everywhere amid them, a radiant angel,

CHAPTER XVIII.

THE EXECUTION.

"Now, GABRIEL," said Max, "I will have to blind-fold you—not that I mistrust you, but that I have to satisfy the laws of our society and the scruples of others."

This was said just before we opened the door. He folded a silk handkerchief over my face, and led me down the steps and seated me in a carriage. He gave some whispered directions to the driver, and away we rolled. It was a long drive. At last I observed that peculiar salty and limy smell in the air, which told me we were approaching the river. The place was very still and solitary. There were no sounds of vehicles or foot-passengers. The carriage slowed up, and we stopped.

"This way," said Max, opening the door of the carriage, and leading me by the hand. We walked a few steps; we paused; there were low whisperings. Then we descended a long flight of steps; the air had a heavy and subterranean smell; we hurried forward through a large chamber; I imagined it to be the cellar of some abandoned warehouse; the light came faintly through the bandage over my face, and I inferred that a guide was carrying a lantern before us. Again we stopped. There was more whispering and the rattle of paper, as if the guards were examining some document. The whispering was renewed; then we entered and descended again a flight of steps, and again went forward for a short distance. The air was very damp and the smell earthy. Again I heard the whispering and the rattling of paper. There was delay. Some one within was sent for and came out. Then the door was flung open, and we entered a room in which the air appeared to be drier than in those we had passed through, and it seemed to be lighted up. There were little movements and stirrings of the atmosphere which indicated that there were a number of persons in the room. I stood still.

Then a stern, loud voice said:

"Gabriel Weltstein, hold up your right hand."

I did so. The voice continued:

"You do solemnly swear, in the presence of Almighty God, that the statements you are about to make are just and true; that you are incited to make them neither by corruption, nor hate, nor any other unworthy motive; and that you will tell the truth and all the truth; and to this you call all the terrors of the unknown world to witness; and you willingly accept death if you utter anything that is false."

I bowed my head.

"What brother vouches for this stranger?" asked the same stern voice.

Then I heard Maximilian. He spoke as if he was standing near my side. He said:

"I do. If I had not been willing to vouch for him with my life, I should not have asked to bring him—not a member of our Brotherhood—into this presence. He saved my life; he is a noble, just and honorable man—one who loves his kind, and would bless and help them if he could. He has a story to tell which concerns us all."

"Enough," said the voice. "Were you present in the council-chamber of the Prince of Cabano last night? If so, tell us what you saw and heard?"

Just then there was a slight noise, as if some one was moving quietly toward the door behind me, by which I had just entered. Then came another voice, which I had not before heard—a thin, shrill, strident, imperious voice—a voice that it seemed to me I shoud recognize again among a million. It cried out:

"Back to your seat! Richard, tell the guards to permit no one to leave this chamber until the end of our meeting."

There was a shuffling of feet, and whispering, and then again profound silence.

"Proceed," said the stern voice that had first spoken.

Concealing all reference to Estella, and omitting to name Rudolph, whom I referred to simply as one of their Brotherhood known to Maximilian, I told, in the midst of a grave-like silence, how I had been hidden in the room next to the council-chamber; and then I went on to give a concise history of what I had witnessed and heard.

"Uncover his eyes!" exclaimed the stern voice.

Maximilian untied the handkerchief. For a moment or two I was blinded by the sudden glare of light. Then, as my eyes recovered their function, I could see that I stood, as I had supposed, in the middle of a large vault or cellar. Around the room, on rude benches, sat perhaps one hundred men. At the end, on a sort of dais, or raised platform, was a man of gigantic stature, masked and shrouded. Below him, upon a smaller elevation, sat another, whose head, I noticed even then, was crooked to one side,

Still below him, on a level with the floor, at a table, were two men who seemed to be secretaries. Every man present wore a black mask and a long cloak of dark material. Near me stood one similarly shrouded, who, I thought, from the size and figure, must be Maximilian.

It was a solemn, silent, gloomy assemblage, and the sight of it thrilled through my very flesh and bones. I was not frightened, but appalled, as I saw all those eyes, out of those expressionless dark faces, fixed upon me. I felt as if they were phantoms, or dead men, in whom only the eyes lived.

The large man stood up. He was indeed a giant. He seemed to uncoil himself from his throne as he rose.

"Unmask," he said.

There was a rustle, and the next moment the masks were gone and the cloaks had fallen down.

It was an extraordinary assemblage that greeted my eyes; a long array of stern faces, dark and toil-hardened, with great, broad brows and solemn or sinister eyes.

Last night I had beheld the council of the Plutocracy. Here was the council of the Proletariat. The large heads at one end of the line were matched by the large heads at the other. A great injustice, or series of wrongs, working through many generations, had wrought out results that in some sense duplicated each other. Brutality above had produced brutality below; cunning there was answered by cunning here; cruelty in the aristocrat was mirrored by cruelty in the workman. High and low were alike victims—unconscious victims—of a system. The crime was not theirs: it lay at the door of the shallow, indifferent, silly generations of the past.

My eyes sought the officers. I noticed that Maximilian was disguised—out of an excess of caution, as I supposed—with eye-glasses and a large dark mustache. His face, I knew, was really beardless.

I turned to the president. Such a man I had never seen before. He was, I should think, not less than six feet six inches high, and broad in proportion. His great arms hung down until the monstrous hands almost touched the knees. His skin was quite dark, almost negroid; and a thick, close mat of curly black hair covered his huge head like a thatch. His face was muscular, ligamentous; with great bars, ridges and whelks of flesh, especially about the jaws and on the forehead. But the eyes fascinated me. They were the eyes of a wild beast, deep-set, sullen and glaring; they seemed to shine like those of the cat-tribe, with a luminosity of their own. This, then —I said to myself—must be Cæsar, the commander of the dreaded Brotherhood.

A movement attracted me to the man who sat below him; he had spoken to the president.

He was in singular contrast with his superior. He was old and withered. One hand seemed to be shrunken, and his head was permanently crooked to one side. The face was mean and sinister; two fangs alone remained in his mouth; his nose was hooked; the eyes were small, sharp, penetrating and restless; but the expanse of brow above them was grand and noble. It was one of those heads that look as if they had been packed full, and not an inch of space wasted. His person was unclean, however, and the hands and the long finger-nails were black with dirt. I should have picked him out anywhere as a very able and a very dangerous man. He was evidently the vice-president of whom the spy had spoken—the nameless Russian Jew who was accounted "the brains of the Brotherhood."

"Gabriel Weltstein," said the giant, in the same stern, loud voice, "each person in this room will now pass before you,—the officers last; and,—under the solemn oath you have taken,—I call upon you to say whether the spy you saw last night in the council-chamber of the Prince of Cabano is among them. But first, let me ask, did you see him clearly, and do you think you will be able to identify him?"

"Yes," I replied; "he faced me for nearly thirty minutes, and I should certainly know him if I saw him again."

"Brothers," said the president, "you will now——"

But here there was a rush behind me. I turned toward the door. Two men were scuffling with a third, who seemed to be trying to break out. There were the sounds of a struggle; then muttered curses; then the quick, sharp report of a pistol. There was an exclamation of pain and more oaths; knives flashed in the air; others rushed pell-mell into the melee; and then the force of numbers seemed to triumph, and the crowd came, dragging a man forward to where I stood. His face was pale as death; the blood streamed from a flesh wound on his forehead; an expression of dreadful terror glared out of his eyes; he gasped and looked from right to left. The giant had descended from his dais. He strode forward. The wretch was laid at my feet.

"Speak," said Cæsar, "is that the man?"

"It is," I replied.

The giant took another step, and he towered over the prostrate wretch.

"Brothers," he asked, "what is your judgment upon the spy?"

"Death!" rang the cry from a hundred throats.

The giant put his hand in his bosom; there was a light in his terrible face as if he had long waited for such an hour.

"Lift him up," he said.

Two strong men held the spy by his arms; they lifted him to his feet; he writhed and struggled and shrieked, but the hands that held him were of iron.

"Stop!" said the thin, strident voice I had heard before, and the cripple advanced into the circle. He addressed the prisoner:

"Were you followed to this place?"

"Yes, yes," eagerly cried the spy. "Spare me, spare me, and I will tell you everything. Three members of the police force were appointed to follow, in a carriage, the vehicle that brought me here. They were to wait about until the meeting broke up and then shadow the tallest man and a crook-necked man to their lodgings and identify them. They are now waiting in the dark shadows of the warehouse."

"Did you have any signal agreed upon with them?" asked the cripple.

"Yes," the wretch replied, conscious that he was giving up his associates to certain death, but willing to sacrifice the whole world if he might save his own life. "Spare me, spare me, and I will tell you all."

"Proceed," said the cripple.

"I would not trust myself to be known by them. I agreed with Prince Cabano upon a signal between us. I am to come to them, if I need their help, and say: 'Good evening, what time is it?' The reply is, 'It is thieves' time.' Then I am to say, 'The more the better;' and they are to follow me."

"Richard," said the cripple, "did you hear that?"

"Yes."

"Take six men with you; leave them in the brew-house cellar; lead the police thither; throw the bodies in the river."

The man called Richard withdrew, with his men, to his work of murder.

The prisoner rolled his eyes appealingly around that dreadful circle.

"Spare me!" he cried. "I know the secrets of the banks. I can lead you into the Prince of Cabano's house. Do not kill me."

"Is that all?" asked the giant.

"Yes," replied the cripple.

In an instant the huge man, like some beast that had been long held back from its prey, gave a leap forward, his face revealing terrible ferocity; it was a tiger that glares, plunges and devours. I saw something shining, brilliant and instantaneous as an electric flash; then there was the sound of a heavy blow. The spy sprang clean out of the hands that were holding him, high up in the air; and fell, close to me, stone dead. He had been dead, indeed, when he made that fearful leap. His heart was split in twain. His spring was not the act of the man; it was the protest of the body against the rush of the departing spirit; it was the clay striving to hold on to the soul.

The giant stooped and wiped his bloody knife upon the clothes of the dead man. The cripple

laughed a crackling, hideous laugh. I hope God
will never permit me to hear such a laugh again.
Others took it up—it echoed all around the room.
I could think of nothing but the cachinnations of
the fiends as the black gates burst open and new
hordes of souls are flung, startled and shrieking, into
hell.

"Thus die all the enemies of the Brotherhood!"
cried the thin voice of the cripple.

And long and loud they shouted.

"Remove the body through the back door," said
the giant, "and throw it into the river."

"Search his clothes first," said the cripple.

They did so, and found the money which the
Prince had ordered to be given him—it was the price
of his life—and also a bundle of papers. The former
was handed over to the treasurer of the Brotherhood; the latter were taken possession of by the vice-
president.

Then, resuming his seat, the giant said:

"Gabriel Weltstein, the Brotherhood thank you
for the great service you have rendered them. We
regret that your scruples will not permit you to
become one of us; but we regard you as a friend and
we honor you as a man; and if at any time the
Brotherhood can serve you, be assured its full powers
shall be put forth in your behalf."

I was too much shocked by the awful scene I had
just witnessed to do more than bow my head.

"There is one thing more," he continued, "we shall
ask of you; and that is that you will repeat your
story once again to another man, who will soon be
brought here. We knew from Maximilian what you
were about to tell, and we made our arrangements

accordingly. Do not start," he said, "or look alarmed—there will be no more executions."

Turning to the men, he said: "Resume your masks." He covered his own face, and all the rest did likewise.

CHAPTER XIX.

THE MAMELUKES OF THE AIR.

THE vice-president of the Brotherhood leaned forward and whispered to one of the secretaries, who, taking two men with him, left the room. A seat was given me. There was a pause of perhaps ten minutes. Not a whisper broke the silence. Then there came a rap at the door. The other secretary went to it. There was whispering and consultation; then the door opened and the secretary and his two companions entered, leading a large man, blindfolded. He wore a military uniform. They stopped in the middle of the room.

"General Jacob Quincy," said the stern voice of the president, "before we remove the bandage from your eyes I ask you to repeat, in this presence, the pledge you made to the representative of the Brotherhood, who called upon you to-day."

The man said:

"I was informed by your messenger that you had a communication to make to me which involved the welfare, and perhaps the lives, of the officers and men commanding and manning the air-vessels, or war-ships, called by the people 'The Demons.' You invited me here under a pledge of safe conduct; you left your messenger with my men, as hostage for my return; and I promised never to reveal to mortal ear anything that I might see or hear, except so far as it might be necessary, with your consent, to do so to warn my command of those dangers which you assure me threaten them. This promise I here renew, and swear by the Almighty God to keep it forever inviolate."

"Remove his bandage," said the president.

They did so, and there stood before me the handsome and intelligent officer whom I had seen last night in the Prince of Cabano's council-chamber.

The president nodded to the cripple, as if by some pre-arrangement, and said, "Proceed."

"General Jacob Quincy," said the thin, penetrating voice of the vice-president of the Order, "you visited a certain house last night, on a matter of business, connected with your command. How many men knew of your visit?"

"Three," said the general, with a surprised look. "I am to communicate the results to a meeting of my command to-morrow night; but I thought it better to keep the matter pretty much to myself until that time."

"May I ask who were the men to whom you spoke of the matter?"

"I might object to your question," he said, "but that I suppose something important lies behind it. The men were my brother, Col. Quincy; my adjutant-general, Captain Underwood, and my friend Major Hartwright."

"Do you think any of these men would tell your story to any one else?"

"Certainly not. I would venture my life upon their prudence and secrecy, inasmuch as I asked them to keep the matter to themselves. But why do you ask such questions?"

"Because," said the wily cripple, "I have a wit-

ness here who is about to reveal to you everything
you said and did in that council-chamber last night,
even to the minutest detail. If you had told your
story to many, or to untrustworthy persons, there
might be a possibility that this witness had gleaned
the facts from others; and that he had not been
present, as he claims; and therefore that you could
not depend upon what he says as to other matters
of importance. Do you recognize the justice of my
reasoning?"

"Certainly," said the general. "If you produce
here a man who can tell me just where I was last
night, what I said, and what was said to me, I shall
believe that he was certainly present; for I well
know he did not get it from me or my friends;
and I know, equally well, that none of those
with whom I had communication would tell what
took place to you or to any friend of yours."

"Be kind enough to stand up," said the cripple to
me. I did so.

"Did you ever see that man before?" he asked
the general.

The general looked at me intently.

"Never," he replied.

"Have you ever seen this man before?" he asked
me.

"Yes," I replied.

"When and where?"

"Last night; at the palace of Prince Cabano—in
his council-chamber."

"Proceed, and tell the whole story."

I did so. The general listened closely, never re-
laxing his scrutiny of my face. When I had finished
my account of the interview, the cripple asked the

general whether it was a faithful narration of what had taken place. He said it was — wonderfully accurate in every particular.

"You believe him, then, to be a truthful witness," asked the cripple, "and that he was present at your interview, with the Council of the Plutocracy?"

"I do," said General Quincy.

"Now proceed," he said to me, "to tell what took place after this gentleman left the room."

I did so. The face of the general darkened into a scowl as I proceeded, and he flushed with rage when I had concluded my story.

"Do you desire to ask the witness any questions?" said the cripple.

"None at all," he replied.

He stood for several minutes lost in deep thought. I felt that the destiny of the world hung tremblingly in the balance. At last he spoke, in a low voice.

"Who represents your organization?" he asked.

"The Executive Committee," replied the president.

"Who are they?" he inquired.

"Myself, — the vice-president" — pointing to the cripple — "and yonder gentleman" — designating the cowled and masked figure of Maximilian, who stood near me.

"Could I have a private conference with you?" he asked.

"Yes," replied the president, somewhat eagerly; "come this way."

All four moved to a side door, which seemed to lead into another subterranean chamber; — the cripple carried a torch.

"Wait here for me," said Maximilian, as he passed me.

I sat down. The cowled figures remained seated around the walls. Not a sound broke the profound silence. I could see that all eyes were fixed upon the door by which the Executive Committee had. left us, and my own were riveted there also.

We all felt the gravity of the occasion. Five minutes — ten minutes — fifteen minutes — twenty minutes passed. The door opened. We thought the conference was over. No; it was only the cripple; his face was uncovered and flushed with excitement. He walked quickly to the secretary's table; took up pen, ink and paper, and returned to the other cellar, closing the door after him. There was a movement among the cowled figures — whispers — excitement; they augured that things were going well — the agreement was to be reduced to writing! Five minutes more passed — then ten — then fifteen. The door opened, and they came out:— the gigantic Cæsar ahead. All the faces were uncovered, and I thought there was a look of suppressed triumph upon the countenances of the Executive Committee. The commander of the Demons looked sedate and thoughtful, like a man who had taken a very grave and serious step.

The president resumed the chair. He spoke to the secretary.

"You will cover the eyes of General Quincy," he said. "Take two men with you; accompany him to his carriage, then go with him to his residence, and bring back our hostage.—General," he said, "good night," and then added meaningly, *"Au revoir!"*

"Au revoir," said the general, as the handkerchief was adjusted over his face.

The commander of the Demons and his escort

withdrew. The president sat consulting his watch, and when he was sure that they were beyond hearing, he sprang to his feet, his eyes glowing and his whole frame dilated with excitement.

"Brothers," he cried out, "we have got the world in our hands at last. The day is near we have so long toiled and waited for! The Demons are with us!"

The wildest demonstrations of joy followed — cheer after cheer broke forth; the men embraced each other.

"The world's slavery is at an end," cried one.

"Death to the tyrants!" shouted another.

"Down with the Oligarchy!" roared a third.

"Come," said Maximilian, taking me by the arm, "it is time to go."

He replaced the bandage over my eyes and led me out. For some time after I left the room, and while in the next cellar, I could hear the hoarse shouts of the triumphant conspirators. Victory was now assured. My heart sank within me. That monstrous chorus was chanting the requiem of a world.

In the carriage Maximilian was trembling with excitement. One thought seemed to be uppermost in his mind. "He will be free! He will be free!" he continually cried. When at last he grew more calm, he embraced me, and called me the preserver of himself; and all his family; and all his friends; and all his work, — the savior of his father! Then he became incoherent again. He cursed the baseness of mankind. "It was noble," he said, "to crush a rotten world for revenge, or for justice' sake; but to sell out a trust, for fifty millions of the first plunder, was execrable — it was damnable. It was a shame to have to use such instruments. But the whole world was corrupt to the very core; there was not enough consistency in it to make it hang together. Yet there was one consolation—the end was coming! Glory be to God! The end was coming!"

And he clapped his hands and shouted, like a madman.

When he grew quieter I asked him what day the blow was to be struck. Not for some time, he said. In the morning the vice-president would take an airship to Europe, with a cipher letter from General Quincy to the commandant of the Demons in England—to be delivered in case it was thought safe to do so. The cripple was subtle and cunning beyond all men. He was to arrange for the purchase of the officers commanding the Demons all over Europe; and he was to hold a council of the leaders of the Brotherhood, and arrange for a simultaneous outbreak on both sides of the Atlantic, so that one continent should not come to the help of the other. If, however, this could not be effected, he was to return home, and the Brotherhood would precipitate the revolution all over America at the same hour, and take the chances of holding their own against the banker-government of Europe.

That night I lay awake a long time, cogitating; and the subject of my thoughts was—Estella.

It had been my intention to return to Africa before the great outbreak took place. I could not remain and witness the ruin of mankind. But neither could I leave Estella behind me. Maximilian might be killed. I knew his bold and desperate nature; he seemed to me to have been driven almost, if not quite, to insanity, by the wrongs of his father. Revenge had become a mania with him. If he perished in the battle what would become of Estella, in a world torn to pieces? She had neither father, nor mother, nor home. But she loved me and I must protect her!

On the other hand, she was powerless and dependent on the kindness of strangers. Her speech in that moment of terror might have expressed more than she felt. Should I presume upon it? Should I take advantage of her distress to impose my love upon her? But, if the Brotherhood failed, might not the Prince recover her, and bear her back to his hateful palace and his loathsome embraces? Dangers environed her in every direction. I loved her; and if she would not accompany me to my home as my wife, she must go as my sister. She could not stay where she was. I must again save her.

I fell asleep and dreamed that Estella and I were flying into space on the back of a dragon, that looked very much like Prince Cabano.

CHAPTER XX.

I HAVE told you, my dear Heinrich, that I have
latterly attended, and even spoken at, a number of
meetings of the workingmen of this city. I have just
returned from one of the largest I have seen. It was
held in a great underground chamber, or series of
cellars, connected with each other, under an ancient
warehouse. Before I retire to my couch I will give
you some description of the meeting, not only
because it will enable you to form some idea of the
state of feeling among the mechanics and workmen,
but because this one, unfortunately, had a tragical
ending.

There were guards stationed at the door to give
warning of the coming of the police. There were
several thousand persons present. It was Saturday
night. When we arrived the hall was black with people—a gloomy, silent assemblage. There were no
women present; nó bright colors—all dark and sad-
hued. The men were nearly all workingmen, many
of them marked by the grime of their toil. Maximilian whispered to me that the attendance was larger
than usual, and he thought it indicated that, by a
kind of instinct, the men knew the great day of deliverance was near at hand.

The president of a labor organization had taken
the chair before we came in. As I walked up the hall
I was greeted with cheers, and invited to the platform. Maximilian accompanied me.

A man in a blouse was speaking. He was discussing the doctrines of Karl Marx and the German socialists of the last century. He was attentively listened to, but his remarks aroused no enthusiasm; they all seemed familiar with the subjects of his discourse.

He was followed by another workman, who spoke upon the advantages of co-operation between the employers and the employed. His remarks were moderate and sensible. He was, however, answered by another workman, who read statistics to show that, after a hundred years of trial, the co-operative system had not extended beyond a narrow circle. "There were too many greedy employers and too many helpless workmen. Competition narrowed the margin of profit and hardened the heart of the master, while it increased the number of the wretchedly poor, who must work at any price that would maintain life." [Applause.] "The cure must be more radical than that." [Great applause.]

He was followed by a school teacher, who thought that the true remedy for the evils of society was universal education. If all men were educated they could better defend their rights. Education meant intelligence, and intelligence meant prosperity. It was the ignorant hordes from Europe who were crowding out the American workingmen and reducing them to pauperism." [Applause.]

Here a rough-looking man, who, I inferred, was an English miner, said he begged leave to differ from the gentleman who had last spoken. (I noticed that these workingmen, unless very angry, used in their discussions the courteous forms of speech common in all parliamentary bodies.)

"A man who knew how to read and write," he continued, "did not command any better wages for the work of his hands than the man who could not." [Applause.] "His increased knowledge tended to make him more miserable." [Applause.] "Education was so universal that the educated man, without a trade, had to take the most inadequate pittance of compensation, and was not so well off, many times, as the mechanic." [Applause.] "The prisons and alms-houses were full of educated men; and three-fourths of the criminal class could read and write. Neither was the gentleman right when he spoke of the European immigrants as 'ignorant hordes.' The truth was, the proportion of the illiterate was much less in some European despotisms than it was in the American Republic." [Applause from the foreigners present.] "Neither did it follow that because a man was educated he was intelligent. There was a vast population of the middle class, who had received good educations, but who did not have any opinion upon any subject, except as they derived it from their daily newspapers." [Applause.] "The rich men owned the newspapers and the newspapers owned their readers; so that, practically, the rich men cast all those hundreds of thousands of votes. If these men had not been able to read and write they would have talked with one another upon public affairs, and have formed some correct ideas; their education simply facilitated their mental subjugation; they were chained to the chariots of the Oligarchy; and they would never know the truth until they woke up some bright morning and found it was the Day of Judgment." [Sensation and great applause.]

Here I interposed:

"Universal education is right; it is necessary," I said; "but it is not all-sufficient. Education will not stop corruption or misgovernment. No man is fit to be free unless he possesses a reasonable share of education; but every man who possesses that reasonable share .of education is not fit to be free. A man may be able to read and write and yet be a fool or a knave." [Laughter and applause.] "What is needed is a society which shall bring to Labor the aid of the same keenness, penetration, foresight, and even cunning, by which wealth has won its triumphs. Intellect should have its rewards, but it should not have everything. But this defense of labor could only spring from *the inspiration of God,* for the natural instinct of man, in these latter days, seems to be to prey on his fellow. We are sharks that devour the wounded of our own kind."

I paused, and in the midst of the hall a thin gentleman, dressed in black, with his coat buttoned to his throat, and all the appearance of a clergyman, arose and asked whether a stranger would be permitted to say a few words. He was received in sullen silence, for the clergy are not popular with the proletariat. His manner, however, was quiet and unassuming, and he appeared like an honest man.

The chairman said he had no doubt the audience would be glad to hear his views, and invited him to the platform.

He said, in a weak, thin voice:

"I have listened, brethren, with a great deal of interest and pleasure to the remarks that have been made by the different speakers. There is no doubt the world has fallen into evil conditions; and it is very right that you should thus assemble and consider the causes and the remedy. And, with your kind permission, I will give you my views on the subject.

"Brethren, your calamities are due, in my opinion, to the loss of religion in the world and the lack of virtue among individuals. What is needed for the reformation of mankind is a new interest in the church — a revival of faith. If every man will purify his own heart, all hearts will then be pure; and when the hearts of all are pure, and filled with the divine sentiment of justice and brotherhood, no man will be disposed to treat his neighbor unjustly. But, while this is true, you must remember that, after all, this world is only a place of temporary trial, to prepare us for another and a better world. This existence consists of a few troubled and painful years, at best, but there you will enjoy eternal happiness in the company of the angels of God. We have the assurance of the Holy Scriptures that riches and prosperity here are impediments to happiness hereafter. The beggar Lazarus is shown to us in the midst of everlasting bliss, while the rich man Dives, who had supported him for years, by the crumbs from his table, and was clothed in purple and fine linen, is burning in an eternal hell. Remember that it is 'less difficult for a camel to pass through the eye of a needle than for a rich man to enter the kingdom of heaven;' and so, my friends, you may justly rejoice in your poverty and your afflictions, for 'those whom the Lord loveth he chasteneth;' and the more wretched your careers may be, here on earth, the more assured you are of the delights of an everlasting heaven. And do not listen, my brethren, to the men who tell you that you must hate government and law. 'The powers that be are ordained of God,' saith the Scripture; and by patient resignation to the evils of this world you will lay up treasures for yourselves in heaven, where the moth and rust cannot consume, and where thieves do not break in and steal. They tell you that you should improve your condition. But suppose you possessed all the pleasures which this transitory world could give you, of what avail would it be if your earthly happiness made you lose the eternal joys of heaven? 'What will it profit a man if he gain the whole world and lose his own soul?' Nothing, my brethren, nothing. Be patient, therefore——"

As the reverend gentleman had proceeded the murmurs and objections of the audience kept increasing, until at last it broke forth in a storm of howls and execrations which completely drowned his voice. The whole audience—I could see their faces from where I sat on the platform—were infuriated. Arms were waving in the air, and the scene was like Bedlam. I requested the clergyman to sit down, and, as soon as he did so, the storm began to subside. A man rose in the midst of the audience and mounted a bench. Loud cries and applause greeted him. I could distinguish the name on a hundred lips, "Kelker! Kelker!" As I ascertained afterwards, he was a professor, of German descent, a man of wide learning, who had lost his position in the university, and in society as well, by his defense of the rights of the people. He now earned a meager living at shoemaking. He was a tall, spare man, with gold eyeglasses (sole relic of his past station), poorly clad; and he had the wild look of a man who had been hunted all his life. He spoke with great vehemence, and in a penetrating voice, that could be heard all over that vast assemblage, which, as soon as he opened his mouth, became as still as death.

"Friends and brothers," he said; "friends by the ties of common wrongs, brothers in misery, I regret that you did not permit the reverend gentleman to proceed. Ours is a liberality that hears all sides; and, for one, I should have been glad to hear what this advocate of the ancient creeds had to say for them. But since he has taken his seat I shall reply to him.

"He tells us that his religion is the one only thing which will save us; and that it is better for us to be miserable here that we may be happy here-after. If that is so, heaven must be crowded now-a-days, for the misery of the earth is unlimited and unspeakable; and it is rapidly increasing." [Laughter and applause.] "But religion has had control of the world for nearly two thousand years, and this is what it has brought us to. It has been, in all ages, the moral police-force of tyrants." [Great applause.] "It has chloroformed poverty with promises of heaven, while the robbers have plundered the world." [Continued applause.] "It has kept the people in submission, and has sent uncountable millions through wretched lives to shameful graves." [Great applause.] "With a lot of myths and super-stitions, derived from a dark and barbarous past, it has prevented civilization from protecting mankind; and, Nero-like, has fiddled away upon its ridiculous dogmas while the world was burning." [Great cheers.]

"When have your churches helped man to improve his condition? They are gorgeous palaces,

where once a week the women assemble to display
their millinery and the men to maintain their
business prestige." [Laughter and applause.] "What
great reform have they not opposed? What new
discoveries in science have they not resisted?" [Ap-
plause.] "Man has only become great when he has
escaped out of their clutches." [Cheers.] "They have
preached heaven and helped to turn earth into a hell."
[Great cheers.] "They stood by, without a murmur,
and beheld mankind brought down to this awful
condition; and now, in the midst of our unbearable
calamities, they tell us it is well for us to starve;
that starvation is the especial gate of heaven; and
that Dives deserved hell because he had plenty to eat
while on earth." [Great cheering.] "And why do
they do this? Because, if they can get possession of
our consciences and persuade us to starve to death
patiently, and not resist, they will make it so much
the easier for the oppressors to govern us; and the
rich, in return, will maintain the churches." [Sensa-
tion.] "They are throttling us in the name of God!"
[Tremendous applause.] "Our sons march in endless
procession to the prison and the scaffold; our
daughters take their places in the long line of the
bedizened cortege of the brothel; and every fiber of
our poor frames and brains shrieks out its protest
against insufficient nourishment; and this man
comes to us and talks about his Old-World, worn-out
creeds, which began in the brains of half-naked barbarians, and are a jumble of the myths of a hundred —— "

Here the speaker grew wild and hoarse with
passion, and the audience, who had been growing
more and more excited and turbulent as he pro-
13

ceeded, burst into a tremendous uproar that
drowned every other sound. A crowd of the more
desperate—dark-faced, savage-looking workingmen
—made a rush for the platform to seize the clergyman; and they would soon have had possession of
him. But in this extremity I sprang to the front of
the platform, between him and the oncoming mob,
and by my mere presence, and the respect they have
for me as their friend, I stilled the tempest and
restored order.

"My dear friends!" I said, "be patient! Are you
the men who boast of your toleration? You meet
to discuss your sufferings and their remedy; and
when one tells you how he would cure you, you rise
up to slay him. Be just. This poor man may be
mistaken—the body of which he is a member may be
mistaken—as to the best way to serve and save
mankind; but that his purpose is good, and that he
loves you, who can doubt? Look at him! Observe
his poor garments; his emaciated figure. What
joys of life does he possess? He has given up everything to help you. Into your darkest alleys—into
your underground dens—where pestilence and
starvation contend for their victims, he goes at high
noon and in the depths of the blackest night, and he
brings to the parting soul consolation and hope.
And why not? Who can doubt that there is another
life? Who that knows the immortality of matter,
its absolute indestructibility, can believe that mind,
intelligence, soul,—which must be, at the lowest esti-
mate—if they are not something higher—a form
of matter,—are to perish into nothingness? If it be
true, as we know it is, that the substance of the poor
flesh that robes your spirits—nay, of the very gar-

ments you wear—shall exist, undiminished by the friction of eternity, æons after our planet is blotted out of space and our sun forgotten, can you believe that this intelligence, whereby I command your souls into thought, and communicate with the unsounded depths of your natures, can be clipped off into annihilation? Nay, out of the very bounty and largess of God I speak unto you; and that in me which speaks, and that in you which listens, are alike part and parcel of the eternal Maker of all things, without whom is nothing made." [Applause.]

"And so, my friends, every good man who loves you, and would improve your condition, in time or in eternity, is your friend, and to be venerated by you." [Applause.] "And while we may regret the errors of religion, in the past, or in the present, let us not forget its virtues. Human in its mechanism, it has been human in its infirmities. In the doctrine of the brotherhood of man and the fatherhood of God, which are the essential principles of Christianity, lies the redemption of mankind. But some of the churchmen have misconceived Christ, or perverted him to their own base purposes. He who drove the money-changers out of the temple, and denounced the aristocrats of his country as whited sepulchres, and preached a communism of goods, would not view to-day with patience or equanimity the dreadful sufferings of mankind. We have inherited Christianity without Christ; we have the painted shell of a religion, and that which rattles around within it is not the burning soul of the Great Iconoclast, but a cold and shriveled and meaningless tradition. Oh! for the quick-pulsing, warm-beating, mighty human heart of the man of Galilee! Oh! for his uplifted hand, armed with a whip of scorpions, to depopulate the temples of the world, and lash his recreant preachers into devotion to the cause of his poor afflicted children!" [Great applause.]

"There is no power in the world too great or too sacred to be used by Goodness for the suppression of Evil. Religion—true religion—not forms or ceremonies, but *inspired purpose*—should take possession of the *governments* of the world and enforce *justice!* The purified individual soul we may not underestimate. These are the swept and garnished habitations in which the angels dwell, and look with unpolluted eyes upon the world. But this is not all. To make a few virtuous where the many are vicious is to place goodness at a disadvantage. To teach the people patience and innocence in the midst of craft and cruelty, is to furnish the red-mouthed wolves with woolly, bleating lambs. Hence the grip of the churches on humanity has been steadily lessening during the past two hundred years. Men permanently love only those things that are beneficial to them. The churches must come to the rescue of the people or retire from the field. A babe in the claws of a tiger is not more helpless than a small virtuous minority in the midst of a cruel and bloody world. Virtue we want, but virtue growing out of the bosom of universal justice. While you labor to save one soul, poverty crushes a million into sin. You are plucking brands from a constantly increasing conflagration. The flames continue to advance and devour what you have saved. The religion of the world must be built on universal prosperity, and this is only possible on a foundation of universal justice. If the web of the cloth is knotted in one place it is because the threads have, in an unmeaning tangle, been withdrawn from another part. Human misery is the correlative and equivalent of injustice somewhere else in society.

"What the world needs is a new organization—a great world-wide Brotherhood of Justice. It should be composed of all men who desire to lift up the oppressed and save civilization and society. It should work through governmental instrumentalities. Its altars should be the schools and the ballot-boxes. It should combine the good, who are not yet, I hope, in a minority, against the wicked. It should take one wrong after another, concentrate the battle of the world upon them, and wipe them out of existence. It should be sworn to a perpetual crusade against every evil. It is not enough to heal the wounds caused by the talons of the wild beasts of injustice: it should pursue them to their bone-huddled dens and slay them." [Great applause.] "It should labor not alone to relieve starvation, but to make starvation impossible;—*to kill it in its causes.*

"With the widest toleration toward those who address themselves to the future life, even to the neglect of this, the sole dogma of our society should be Justice. If there is an elysium in the next world, and not a continuation of the troubled existence through which we are now passing, we will be all the better fitted to enjoy it if we have helped to make this world a heaven. And he who has labored to make earth a hell should enjoy his workmanship in another and more dreadful world, forever and forever.

"And oh, ye churches! Will ye not come up to

the help of the people against the mighty? Will ye
not help us break the jaws of the spoiler and drag
the prey from between his teeth? Think what you
could do if all your congregations were massed together to crush the horrid wrongs that abound in
society! To save the world *you must fight corruption and take possession of government.* Turn
your thoughts away from Moses and his ragged
cohorts, and all the petty beliefs and blunders of the
ancient world. Here is a world greater than Moses
ever dreamed of. Here is a population infinitely
vaster in numbers, more enlightened, more capable
of exquisite enjoyment, and exquisite suffering, than
all the children of Israel and all the subjects of imperial Rome combined. Come out of the past into
the present. God is as much God to-day as he was
in the time of the Pharaohs. If God loved man
then he loves him now. Surely the cultured denizen
of this enlightened century, in the midst of all the
splendors of his transcendent civilization, is as
worthy of the tender regard of his Creator as the
half-fed and ignorant savage of the Arabian desert
five thousand years ago. God lives yet, and he lives
for *us.*"

Here I paused. Although the vast audience had
listened patiently to my address, and had, occasionally, even applauded some of its utterances, yet it
was evident that what I said did not touch their
hearts. In fact, a stout man, with a dark, stubbly
beard, dressed like a workingman, rose on one of the
side benches and said :

"Fellow-toilers, we have listened with great respect to what our friend Gabriel Weltstein has said
to us, for we know he would help us if he could —

that his heart is with us. And much that he has said is true. But the time has gone by to start such a society as he speaks of. Why, if we formed it, the distresses of the people are so great that our very members would sell us out on election day." [Applause.] "The community is rotten to the core; and so rotten that it is not conscious that it is rotten." [Applause.] "There is no sound place to build on. There is no remedy but the utter destruction of the existing order of things." [Great applause.] "It cannot be worse for us than it is; it may be better." [Cheers.]

"But," I cried out, "do you want to destroy civilization?"

"Civilization," he replied solemnly; "what interest have we in the preservation of civilization? Look around and behold its fruits! Here are probably ten thousand industrious, sober, intelligent workingmen; I doubt if there is one in all this multitude that can honestly say he has had, during the past week, enough to eat." [Cries of "That's so."] "I doubt if there is one here who believes that the present condition of things can give him, or his children, anything better for the future." [Applause.] "Our masters have educated us to understand that we have no interest in civilization or society. We are its victims, not its members. They depend on repression, on force alone; on cruelty, starvation, to hold us down until we work our lives away. *Our lives are all we have;*—it may be all we will ever have! They are as dear to us as existence is to the millionaire.

"What is civilization worth which means happiness for a few thousand men and inexpressible misery for hundreds of millions? No, down with it!" [Immense cheering. Men rising and waving their hats.] "If they have set love and justice adrift and depend only on force, why should we not have recourse to force also?" [Cheers and applause, mingled with cries of "Take care!" "Look out!" "Spies!" etc.] "Yes," continued the speaker, "I mean, of course, the force of argument and reason." [Great laughter and applause.] "Of course none of us would advocate a violation of the law—that blessed law which it has cost our masters so much hard-earned money to purchase;" [renewed laughter and applause,] "and which restrains us and not them; for under it no injustice is forbidden to them, and no justice is permitted to us. Our labor creates everything; we possess nothing. Yes, we have the scant supply of food necessary to enable us to create more." [Applause.] "We have ceased to be men— we are machines. Did God die for a machine? Certainly not.

"We are crushed under the world which we maintain, and our groans are drowned in the sounds of music and laughter." [Great applause.] "We have a hell that is more desperate and devilish than any dreamed of by the parsons—for we have to suffer to maintain the pleasures of heaven, while we have no share in what we ourselves create." [Laughter and applause.] "Do you suppose that if heaven were blown to pieces hell would be any worse off? At least, the work would stop." [Great applause, long-continued, with cries of "That's so!"]

Here a great uproar broke out near the end of the hall. A man had been caught secretly taking notes of the speaker's remarks. He was evidently a detective. On the instant a hundred men sprang upon him, and he was beaten and trampled under foot, until not only life, but all semblance of humanity, had been crushed out of him; and the wretched remains were dragged out and thrown upon the pavement. It is impossible to describe the uproar and confusion which ensued. In the midst of it a large platoon of police, several hundred strong, with their belts strung with magazine pistols, and great clubs in their hands, broke into the room, and began to deal blows and make arrests right and left, while the crowd fled through all the doors. Maximilian seized me and the poor clergyman, who had been sitting in a dazed and distraught state for some time, and dragged us both up a back stairway and through a rear exit into the street. There we took a carriage, and, after we had left the bewildered clergyman at his residence, Maximilian said to me as we rode home:

"You see, my dear Gabriel, I was right and you were wrong. That workman told the truth. You have arrived on the scene too late. A hundred years ago you might have formed your Brotherhood of Justice and saved society. Now there is but one cure —the Brotherhood of *Destruction*."

"Oh, my dear friend," I replied, "do not say so. *Destruction!* What is it? The wiping out of the slow accumulations made by man's intelligence during thousands of years. A world cataclysm. A day of judgment. A day of fire and ashes. A world burned and swept bare of life. All the flowers of art; the beautiful, gossamer-like works of glorious literature; the sweet and lovely creations of the souls of men long since perished, and now the inestimable heritage of humanity; all, all crushed, torn, leveled in the dust. And all that is savage, brutal, cruel, demoniac in man's nature let loose to ravage the face of the world. Oh! horrible — most horrible! The mere thought works in me like a convulsion; what must the inexpressible reality be? To these poor, suffering, hopeless, degraded toilers; these children of oppression and the dust; these chained slaves, anything that would break open the gates of their prison-house would be welcome, even though it were an earthquake that destroyed the planet. But you and I, my dear friend, are educated to higher thoughts. We know the value of the precious boon of civilization. We know how bare and barren, and wretched and torpid, and utterly debased is soulless barbarism. I see enough to convince me that the ramifications of your society are like a net-work of wires, all over the earth, penetrating everywhere, and at every point touching the most deadly explosives of human passions and hates; and that it needs but the pressure of your finger upon the pedal to blow up the world. The folly of centuries has culminated in the most terrible organization that ever grew out of the wretchedness of mankind. But oh, my friend — you have a broad mind and a benevolent soul — tell me, is there no remedy? Cannot the day of wrath be averted?"

The tears flowed down my face as I spoke, and Maximilian placed his hand gently upon my arm, and said in the kindliest manner:

"My dear Gabriel, I have thought such thoughts as these many times; not with the fervor and vehemence of your more imaginative nature, but because I shrank, at first, from what you call 'a world-cataclysm.' But facts are stronger than the opin-

ions of man. There is in every conflagration a time
when a few pails of water would extinguish it; then
there comes a time when the whole fire-department,
with tons of water, can alone save what is left of the
property; but sometimes a point is reached where
even the boldest firemen are forced to recoil and give
up the building to the devouring element. Two hundred years ago a little wise statesmanship might
have averted the evils from which the world now
suffers. One hundred years ago a gigantic effort, of
all the good men of the world, might have saved
society. Now the fire pours through every door, and
window and crevice; the roof crackles; the walls tot-
ter; the heat of hell rages within the edifice; it is
doomed; there is no power on earth that can save it;
it must go down into ashes. What can you or I do?
What will it avail the world if we rush into the
flames and perish? No; we witness the working-out of
great causes which we did not create. When man permits the establishment of self-generating evil he must
submit to the effect. Our ancestors were blind, indifferent, heartless. We live in the culmination of their
misdeeds. They have crawled into their graves and
drawn the earth over them, and the flowers bloom on
their last resting-places, and we are the inheritors of
the hurricane which they invoked. Moreover," he
continued, "how can reformation come? You have
seen that audience to-night. Do you think they are
capable of the delicate task of readjusting the disarranged conditions of the world? That workman was
right. In the aggregate they are honest—most
honest and honorable; but is there one of them
whose cramped mind and starved stomach could
resist the temptation of a ten-dollar bill? Think

what a ten-dollar bill is to them! It represents all they crave: food, clothes, comfort, joy. It opens the gate of heaven to them; it is paradise, for a few hours at least. Why, they would mortgage their souls, they would trade their Maker, for a hundred dollars! The crime is not theirs, but the shallow creatures who once ruled the world, and permitted them to be brought to this state. And where else can you turn? Is it to the newspapers? They are a thousand times more dishonest than the working-men. Is it to the halls of legislation? There corruption riots and rots until the stench fills the earth. The only ones who could reform the world are the rich and powerful: but they see nothing to reform. Life is all sunshine for them; civilization is a success for them; they need no better heaven than they enjoy. They have so long held mankind in subjection that they laugh at the idea of the great, dark, writhing masses, rising up to overthrow them. Government is, to them, an exquisitely adjusted piece of mechanism whose object is to keep the few happy and the many miserable."

"But," said I, "if an appeal were made to them; if they were assured of the dangers that really threatened them; if their better and kindlier natures were appealed to, do you not think they might undertake the task of remedying the evils endured by the multitude? They cannot all be as abandoned and utterly vicious as Prince Cabano and his Council."

"No," he replied; "have you not already made the test? The best of them would probably hang you for your pains. Do you think they would be willing to relinquish one-tenth of their pleasures, or their possessions, to relieve the distresses of their fellows?

If you do, you have but a slight conception of the callousness of their hearts. You were right in what you said was the vital principle of Christianity— brotherly love, not alone of the rich for the rich, but of the poor and rich for each other. But that spirit has passed away from the breasts of the upper classes. Science has increased their knowledge one hundred per cent. and their vanity one thousand per cent. The more they know of the material world the less they can perceive the spiritual world around and within it. The acquisition of a few facts about nature has closed their eyes to the existence of a God."

"Ah," said I, "that is a dreadful thought! It seems to me that the man who possesses his eyesight must behold a thousand evidences of a Creator denied to a blind man; and in the same way the man who knows most of the material world should see the most conclusive evidences of design and a Designer. The humblest blade of grass preaches an incontrovertible sermon. What force is it that brings it up, green and beautiful, out of the black, dead earth? Who made it succulent and filled it full of the substances that will make flesh and blood and bone for millions of gentle, grazing animals? What a gap would it have been in nature if there had been no such growth, or if, being such, it had been poisonous or inedible? Whose persistent purpose is it—whose everlasting will—that year after year, and age after age, stirs the tender roots to life and growth, for the sustenance of uncounted generations of creatures? Every blade of grass, therefore, points with its tiny finger straight upward to heaven, and proclaims an eternal, a benevolent God. It is to me a dreadful thing that men can penetrate farther and farther into nature with their senses, and leave their reasoning faculties behind them. Instead of mind recognizing mind, dust simply perceives dust. This is the suicide of the soul."

"Well, to this extremity," said Maximilian, "the governing classes of the world have progressed. We will go to-morrow—it will be Sunday—and visit one of their churches; and you shall see for yourself to what the blind adoration of wealth and the heartless contempt of humanity have brought the world."

CHAPTER XXI.

A SERMON OF THE TWENTIETH CENTURY.

MAX and I entered the church together. It is a magnificent structure—palatial, cathedral-like, in its proportions—a gorgeous temple of fashion, built with exquisite taste, of different-colored marbles, and surrounded by graceful columns. Ushers, who looked like guards in uniform, stood at the doors, to keep out the poorly-dressed people, if any such presented themselves; for it was evident that this so-called church was exclusively a club-house of the rich.

As we entered we passed several marble statues. It is a curious illustration of the evolution of religion, in these latter days, that these statues are not representations of any persons who have ever lived, or were supposed to have lived on earth, or anywhere else; and there was not in or about them any hint whatever of myth or antique belief. In the pre-Christian days the work of the poet and sculptor taught a kind of history in the statues of the pagan divinities. Bacchus told of some ancient race that had introduced the vine into Europe and Africa. Ceres, with her wheat-plant, recited a similar story as to agriculture. And Zeus, Hercules, Saturn and all the rest were, in all probability—as Socrates declared—deified men. And, of course, Christian art was full of beautiful allusions to the life of the Savior, or to his great and holy saints and martyrs. But here we

had simply splendid representations of naked human figures, male and female, wondrously beautiful,
but holding no associations whatever with what you
and I, my dear Heinrich, call religion.

Passing these works of art, we entered a magnificent hall. At the farther end was a raised platform,
almost embowered in flowers of many hues, all in
full bloom. The light entered through stained windows, on the sides of the hall, so colored as to cast a
weird and luxurious effulgence over the great chamber. On the walls were a number of pictures; some
of a very sensuous character; all of great beauty
and perfect workmanship; but none of them of a religious nature, unless we might except one of the nude
Venus rising from the sea.

The body of the hall was arranged like a great
lecture-room; there were no facilities for or suggestions of devotion, but the seats were abundantly
cushioned, and with every arrangement for the comfort of the occupants. The hall was not more than
half full, the greater part of those present being
women. Most of these were fair and beautiful; and
even those who had long passed middle age retained,
by the virtue of many cunning arts, well known to
these people, much of the appearance and freshness
of youth. I might here note that the prolongation of
life in the upper classes, and its abbreviation in the
lower classes, are marked and divergent characteristics of this modern civilization.

I observed in the women, as I had in those of
the Darwin Hotel, associated with great facial perfection, a hard and soulless look out of the eyes; and
here, even more than there, I could not but notice a
sensuality in the full, red lips, and the quick-glancing

eyes, which indicated that they were splendid animals, and nothing more.

An usher led us up one of the thickly carpeted aisles to a front pew; there was a young lady already seated in it. I entered first, and Max followed me. The young lady was possessed of imperial beauty. She looked at us both quite boldly, without shrinking, and smiled a little. We sat down. They were singing a song—I could not call it a hymn; it was all about the "Beautiful and the Good"—or something of that sort. The words and tune were fine, but there were no allusions to religion, or God, or heaven, or anything else of a sacred character. The young lady moved toward me and offered to share her song-book with me. She sang quite sweetly, but there was no more soul in her voice than there was in the song.

After a little time the preacher appeared on the platform. Max told me his name was Professor Odyard, and that he was one of the most eminent philosophers and orators of the day, but that his moral character was not of the best. He was a large, thick-set, florid, full-bearded man, with large lips, black hair and eyes, and swarthy skin. His voice was sweet and flute-like, and he had evidently perfected himself in the graces of elocution. He spoke with a great deal of animation and action; in fact, he was a very vivacious actor.

He commenced by telling the congregation of some new scientific discoveries, recently made in Germany, by Professor Von der Slahe, to the effect that the whole body of man, and of all other animals and even inanimate things, was a mass of living microbes—not in the sense of disease or parasites, but

14

that the intrinsic matter of all forms was life-forms; the infinite molecules were creatures; and that there was no substance that was not animated; and that life was therefore infinitely more abundant in the world than matter; that life was matter.

And then he went on to speak of the recent great discoveries made by Professor Thomas O'Connor, of the Oregon University, which promise to end the reign of disease on earth, and give men patriarchal leases of life. More than a century ago it had been observed, where the bacteria of contagious disorders were bred in culture-infusions, for purposes of study, that after a time they became surrounded by masses of substance which destroyed them. It occurred to Professor O'Connor, that it was a rule of Nature that life preyed on life, and that every form of being was accompanied by enemies which held its over-growth in check: the deer were eaten by the wolves; the doves by the hawks; the gnats by the dragon-flies.

> " Big fleas had little fleas to bite 'em,
>   And these had lesser still, *ad infinitum.*"

Professor O'Connor found that, in like manner, bacteria, of all kinds, were devoured by minuter forms of life. Recovery from sickness meant that the microbes were destroyed by their natural enemies before they had time to take possession of the entire system; death resulted where the vital powers could not hold out until the balance of nature was thus re-established. He found, therefore, that the remedy for disease was to take some of the culture-infusion in which malignant *bacteria* had just perished, and inject it into the veins of the sick man. This was like stocking a rat-infested barn with weasles. The invisible, but greedy swarms of *bacilli* penetrated every part of the body in search of their prey, and the man recovered his health. Where an epidemic threatened, the whole community was to be thus inoculated, and then, when a wandering microbe found lodgment in a human system, it would be pounced upon and devoured before it could reproduce its kind. He even argued that old age was largely due to bacteria; and that perpetual youth would be possible if a germicide could be found that would reach every fiber of the body, and destroy the swarming life-forms which especially attacked the vital forces of the aged.

And then he referred to a new invention by a California scientist, named Henry Myers, whereby telephonic communication had been curiously instituted with intelligences all around us—not spirits or ghosts, but forms of life like our own, but which our senses had hitherto not been able to perceive. They were new forms of matter, but of an extreme tenuity of substance; and with intellects much like our own, though scarcely of so high or powerful an order. It was suggested by the preacher that these shadowy earth-beings had probably given rise to many of the Old-World beliefs as to ghosts, spirits, fairies, goblins, angels and demons. The field in this direction, he said, had been just opened, and it was difficult to tell how far the diversity and multiplicity of creation extended. He said it was remarkable that our ancestors had not foreseen these revelations, for they knew that there were sound-waves both above and below the register of our hearing; and light-waves of which our eyes were able to take no cognizance; and therefore it followed, *a priori*, that nature might possess an infinite number of forms of life which our

senses were not fitted to perceive. For instance, he
added, there might be right here, in this very hall,
the houses and work-shops and markets of a multitude of beings, who swarmed about us, but of such
tenuity that they passed through our substance, and
we through theirs, without the slightest disturbance
of their continuity. All that·we knew of Nature
taught us that she was tireless in the prodigality of
her creative force, and boundless in the diversity of
her workmanship; and we now knew that what the
ancients called *spirit* was simply an attenuated condition of matter.

The audience were evidently keenly intellectual
and highly educated, and they listened with great
attention to this discourse. In fact, I began to perceive that the office of preacher has only survived,
in this material age, on condition that the priest
shall gather up, during the week, from the literary
and scientific publications of the whole world, the
gems of current thought and information, digest
them carefully, and pour them forth, in attractive
form, for their delectation on Sunday. As a sort of
oratorical and poetical reviewer, essayist and rhap-
sodist, the parson and his church had survived the
decadence of religion.

"Nature," he continued, "is as merciless as she is
prolific. Let us consider the humblest little creature
that lives—we will say the field-mouse. Think what
an exquisite compendium it is of bones, muscles,
nerves, veins, arteries—all sheathed in such a delicate, flexible and glossy covering of skin. Observe
the innumerable and beautiful adjustments in the little animal: the bright, pumping, bounding blood; the
brilliant eyes, with their marvelous powers; the ap-

prehending brain, with its sentiments and emotions, its loves, its fears, its hopes; and note, too, that wonderful net-work, that telegraphic apparatus of nerves which connects the brain with the eyes and ears and quick, vivacious little feet. One who took but a half view of things would say, 'How benevolent is Nature, that has so kindly equipped the tiny field-mouse with the means of protection—its quick, listening ears; its keen, watchful eyes; its rapid, glancing feet!' But look a little farther, my brethren, and what do you behold? This same benevolent Nature has formed another, larger creature, to watch for and spring upon this 'timorous little beastie,' even in its moments of unsuspecting happiness, and rend, tear, crush and mangle it to pieces. And to this especial work Nature has given the larger animal a set of adjustments as exquisitely perfect as those it has conferred on the smaller one; to-wit: eyes to behold in the darkness; teeth to tear; claws to rend; muscles to spring; patience to wait; and a stomach that clamors for the blood of its innocent fellow-creature.

"And what lesson does this learned and cultured age draw from these facts? Simply this: that the plan of Nature necessarily involves cruelty, suffering, injustice, destruction, death.

"We are told by a school of philanthropists more numerous in the old time, fortunately, than they are at present, that men should not be happy while their fellow-men are miserable; that we must decrease our own pleasures to make others comfortable; and much more of the same sort. But, my brethren, does Nature preach that gospel to the cat when it destroys the field-mouse? No; she equips it with special aptitudes for the work of slaughter.

"If Nature, with her interminable fecundity, pours forth millions of human beings for whom there is no place on earth, and no means of subsistence, what affair is that of ours, my brethren? We did not make them; we did not ask Nature to make them. And it is Nature's business to feed them, not yours or mine. Are we better than Nature? Are we wiser? Shall we rebuke the Great Mother by caring for those whom she has abandoned? If she intended that all men should be happy, why did she not make them so? She is omnipotent. She permits evil to exist, when with a breath of her mouth she could sweep it away forever. But it is part of her scheme of life. She is indifferent to the cries of distress which rise up to her, in one undying wail, from the face of the universe. With stony eyes the thousand-handed goddess sits, serene and merciless, in the midst of her worshipers, like a Hindoo idol. Her skirts are wet with blood; her creation is based on destruction; her lives live only by murder. The cruel images of the pagan are truer delineations of Nature than the figures which typify the impotent charity of Christendom — an exotic in the midst of an alien world.

"Let the abyss groan. Why should we trouble ourselves. Let us close our ears to the cries of distress we are not able to relieve. It was said of old time, 'Many are called, but few chosen.' Our ancestors placed a mythical interpretation on this text; but we know that it means:— many are called to the sorrows of life, but few are chosen to inherit the delights of wealth and happiness. Buddha told us, 'Poverty is the curse of Brahma;' Mahomet declared that 'God smote the wicked with misery;' and Christ said, 'The poor ye have always with you.' Why, then, should we concern ourselves about the poor? They are part of the everlasting economy of human society. Let us leave them in the hands of Nature. She who made them can care for them.

"Let us rejoice that out of the misery of the universe *we* are reserved for happiness. For us are music, painting, sculpture, the interweaving glories of the dance, the splendors of poetry and oratory, the perfume of flowers, all delicate and dainty viands and sparkling wines and nectars; and above all Love! Love! Entrancing, enrapturing Love! With its glowing cheeks—its burning eyes—its hot lips— its wreathing arms—its showering kisses—its palpitating bosoms—its intertwining symmetry of beauty and of loveliness."

Here the young lady with the song book drew up closer to me, and looked up into my eyes with a gaze which no son of Adam could misunderstand. I thought of Estella, like a true knight, and turned my face to the preacher. While his doctrines were, to me, utterly heartless and abominable, there was about him such an ecstasy of voluptuousness, associated with considerable intellectual force and passionate oratory, that I was quite interested in him as a psychological study. I could not help but think by what slow stages, through many generations, a people calling themselves Christians could have been brought to this curious commingling of intellectuality and bestiality; and all upon the basis of indifference to the sorrows and sufferings of their fellow-creatures.

"On with the dance!" shouted the preacher, "though we dance above graves. Let the very calamities of the world accentuate our pleasures, even as the warm and sheltered fireside seems more delightful when we hear without the roar of the tempest. The ancient Egyptians brought into their banquets the mummied bodies of the dead, to remind them of mortality. It was a foolish custom. Men are made to feast and made to die; and the one is as natural as the other. Let us, on the other hand, when we rejoice together, throw open our windows, that we may behold the swarming, starving multitudes who stream past our doors. Their pinched and ashy faces and hungry eyes, properly considered, will add a flavor to our viands. We will rejoice to think that if, in this ill-governed universe, all cannot be blest, we at least rise above the universal wretchedness and are reserved for happiness.

"Rejoice, therefore, my children, in your wealth, in your health, in your strength, in your bodies, and in your loves. Ye are the flower and perfection of mankind. Let no plea shorten, by one instant, your pleasures. Death is the end of all things — of consciousness; of sensation; of happiness. Immortality is the dream of dotards. When ye can no longer enjoy, make ready for the grave; for the end of Love is death.

"And what is Love? Love is the drawing together of two beings, in that nature-enforced affinity and commingling, when out of the very impact and identity of two spirits, life, triumphant life, springs into the universe.

"What a powerful impulse is this Love? It is nature-wide. The rushing together of the chemical elements; the attraction of suns and planets — all are Love. See how even the plant casts its pollen abroad on the winds, that it may somewhere reach and rest upon the loving bosom of a sister-flower; and there, amid perfume and sweetness and the breath of zephyrs, the great mystery of life is re-enacted. The plant is without intellect, but it is sensible to Love.

"And who shall doubt, when he contemplates the complicated mechanism by which, everywhere, this God-Nature—blind as to pain and sin and death, but tender and solicitous as to birth and life—makes Love possible, imperative, soulful, overwhelming, that the purposed end and aim of life is Love. And how pitiful and barren seem to us the lives of the superstitious and ascetic hermits of the ancient world, who fled to desert places, to escape from Love, and believed that they were overcoming the foul fiend by prayers and fastings and scourgings. But outraged Nature, mighty amid the ruins of their blasted hearts, reasserted herself, and visited them even in dreams; and the white arms and loving lips of woman overwhelmed them with hot and passionate caresses, in visions against which they strove in vain.

"Oh, my brethren, every nerve, fiber, muscle, and 'petty artery of the body,' participates in Love. Love is the conqueror of death, because Love alone perpetuates life. Love is life! Love is religion! Love is the universe! Love is God!"

And with this climax he sat down amid great applause, as in a theater.

I need scarcely say to you, my dear Heinrich, that I was absolutely shocked by this sermon. Knowing, as you do, the kind and pure and gentle doctrines taught in the little church in our mountain home, where love means charity for man and worship of God, you may imagine how my blood boiled at this

cruel, carnal and heartless harangue. The glowing
and picturesque words which he poured out were simply a carpet of flowers spread over crawling serpents.

The audience of course were familiar with these
doctrines. The preacher owed his success, indeed, to
the fact that he had courageously avowed the sentiments which had dwelt in the breasts of the people
and had been enacted in their lives for generations.
The congregation had listened with rapt attention
to this eloquent echo of their own hearts; this justifi-
cation of their Nature-worship; this re-birth of
Paganism. The women nestled closer to the men at
the tender passages; and I noticed many a flashing
interchange of glances, between bold, bright eyes,
which told too well that the great preacher's adjura-
tions were not thrown away upon unwilling listeners.

Another song was sung; and then there was a
rustle of silks and satins. The audience were about
to withdraw. The preacher sat upon his sofa, on
the platform, mopping his broad forehead with his
handkerchief, for he had spoken with great energy.
I could restrain myself no longer. I rose and said in
a loud voice, which at once arrested the movement
of the congregation:

"Reverend sir, would you permit a stranger to
make a few comments on your sermon?"

"Certainly," he replied, very courteously; "we
welcome discussion. Will you step to the platform?"

"No," I replied; "with your permission I shall
speak from where I stand.

"I can only say to you that I am inexpressibly
shocked and grieved by your discourse.

"Are you blind? Can you not see that Christianity was intended by God to be something better and nobler, superimposed, as an after-birth of time, on the brutality of the elder world? Does not the great doctrine of Evolution, in which you believe, preach this gospel? If man rose from a brute form, then advanced to human and savage life, yet a robber and a murderer; then reached civility and culture, and philanthropy; can you not see that the finger-board of God points forward, unerringly, along the whole track of the race; and that it is still pointing forward to stages, in the future, when man shall approximate the angels? But this is not your doctrine. Your creed does not lead forward; it leads backward, to the troglodyte in his cavern, splitting the leg-bones of his victim to extract the marrow for his cannibalistic feast. *He* would have enjoyed your sermon!" [Great excitement in the congregation.]

"And your gospel of Love. What is it but beastliness? Like the old Greeks and Romans, and all undeveloped antiquity, you deify the basest traits of the fleshly organism; you exalt an animal incident of life into the end of life. You drive out of the lofty temples of the soul the noble and pure aspirations, the great charities, the divine thoughts, which should float there forever on the pinions of angels; and you cover the floor of the temple with crawling creatures, toads, lizards, vipers—groveling instincts, base appetites, leprous sensualities, that befoul the walls of the house with their snail-like markings, and climb, and climb, until they look out of the very windows of the soul, with such repellent and brutish eyes, that real love withers and shrinks at the sight, and dies like a blasted flower.

"O shallow teacher of the blind, do you not see that Christianity was a new force, Heaven-sent, to overcome that very cruelty and heartlessness of Nature which you so much commend? Nature's offspring was indeed the savage, merciless as the creed you preach. Then came God, who breathed a *soul* into the nostrils of the savage. Then came One after Him who said the essence of all religion was man's love for his fellow man, and for the God that is over all; that the highest worship of the Father was to heal the sick, and feed the hungry, and comfort the despised and rejected, and lift up the fallen. And love!—that was true love, made up in equal parts of adoration and of pity! Not the thing you call love, which makes these faces flush with passion and these eyes burn with lust!"

I had gotten thus far, and was proceeding swimmingly, very much to my own satisfaction, when an old woman who stood near me, and who was dressed like a girl of twenty, with false rubber shoulders and neck and cheeks, to hide the ravages of time, hurled a huge hymn-book, the size of a Bible, at me. Age had not impaired the venerable woman's accuracy of aim, nor withered the strength of her good right arm; and the volume of diluted piety encountered me, with great force, just below my right ear, and sent me reeling over against Max. As I rose, nothing disconcerted, to renew my discourse, I found the air full of hymn-books, cushions, umbrellas, overshoes, and every other missile they could lay their hands on; and then I perceived that the whole congregation, men, women, children, preacher, clerks and ushers, were all advancing upon me with evil intent. I would fain have staid to have argued the matter out with them, for I was full of a great many fine points, which I had not yet had time to present, but Max, who never had any interest in theological discussions, and abhorred a battle with Amazons, seized me by the arm and literally dragged me out of the church. I continued, however, to shout back my anathemas of the preacher, and that worthy answered me with floods of abuse; and the women screamed, and the men howled and swore; and altogether it was a very pretty assemblage that poured forth upon the sidewalk.

"Come along," said Max; "you will be arrested, and that will spoil everything."

He hurried me into a carriage and we drove off. Although still full of the debate, I could not help but laugh when I looked back at the multitude in front of the church. Every one was wildly ejaculating, except some of the sisters, who were kissing the hands and face of the preacher — dear, good man — to console him for the hateful insults I had heaped upon him! They reminded me of a swarm of hornets whose paper domicile had been rudely kicked by the foot of some wandering country boy.

"Well, well," said Max, "you are a strange character! Your impulses will some time cost you your life. If I did not think so much of you as I do, I should tell you you were a great fool. Why couldn't you keep quiet? You surely didn't hope to convert that congregation, any more than you could have converted the Council of the Plutocracy."

"But, my dear fellow," I replied, "it was a great comfort to me to be able to tell that old rascal just what I thought of him. And you can't tell — it may do some good."

"No, no," said Max; "the only preacher that will
ever convert that congregation is Cæsar Lomellini.
Cæsar is a bigger brute than they are—which is saying a good deal. The difference is, they are brutes
who are in possession of the good things of this
world; and Cæsar is a brute who wants to get into
possession of them. And there is another difference: they are polished and cultured brutes, and
Cæsar is the brute natural,—'the unaccommodated
man' that Lear spoke of."

CHAPTER XXII.

ESTELLA AND I.

I NEED not say to you, my dear Heinrich, how greatly I love Estella. It is not alone for her beauty, although that is as perfect and as graceful as the dream of some Greek artist hewn in immortal marble. That alone would have elicited merely my admiration. But there is that in her which wins my profoundest respect and love—I had almost said my veneration. Her frame is but the crystal-clear covering of a bright and pure soul, without stain or shadow or blemish. It does not seem possible for her to be otherwise than good. And yet, within this goodness, there is an hereditary character intrenched, capable, under necessity, of all heroism—a fearless and a potent soul. And, besides all this, she is a woman, womanly; a being not harsh and angular in character, but soft and lovable—

> "A countenance in which do meet
> Sweet records, promises as sweet;
> A creature not too bright or good
> For human nature's daily food;
> For transient sorrows, simple wiles,
> Praise, blame, love, kisses, tears and smiles."

You may judge, my dear brother, having gone through a similar experience, how profoundly I was drawn to her; how absolute a necessity she seemed to my life. Neither was I a despairing lover; for had she not, at a time when death seemed imminent, avowed her love for me? Yes, *"love"*—that was the word she used; and the look which accompanied it gave the word a double emphasis. But there was a giant difficulty in my path. If she had compromised her maiden reserve in that particular, how could I take advantage of it? And how could I still further take advantage of her lonely and friendless condition to press my suit? And yet I could not leave her alone to encounter all the dangers of the dreadful time which I know too well is approaching. If she had stood, happy and contented, in the midst of her family, under the shelter of father and mother, surrounded by brothers and sisters, with a bright and peaceful future before her, I could have found courage enough to press my suit, to throw myself at her feet, and woo her boldly, as man woos woman. But this poor, unhappy, friendless, lovely girl! What could I do? Day and night I pondered the problem, and at last an expedient occurred to me.

I called upon her. She had fled from the palace without a wardrobe. A woman may be a heroine, but she is still a woman. Joan of Arc must have given considerable thought to her cap and ribbons. Estella was busy, with a dressmaker, contriving several dresses. I asked her if I could speak with her. She started, blushed a little, and led the way into another room. I closed the door.

"My dear Estella," I said, "I have been amusing my leisure by composing a fairy story."

"Indeed," she said, smiling, "a strange occupation for a philanthropist and philosopher, to say nothing of a poet."

"It is, perhaps," I replied, in the same playful vein, "the poetical portion of my nature that has set me at this work. But I cannot satisfy myself as to the *denouement* of my story, and I desire your aid and counsel."

"I am all attention," she replied; "proceed with your story;—but first, wait a moment. I will get some of my work; and then I can listen to you without feeling that I am wasting precious time."

"Otherwise you would feel," I said, "that your time was wasted listening to me?"

"No," she said, laughing, "but in listening to a fairy tale."

She returned in a few moments, and we took seats, I covering my real feeling by an assumed gayety, and Estella listening attentively, with her eyes on her work.

"You must know," I commenced, "that my tale is entitled:

THE STORY OF PRINCESS CHARMING AND THE KNIGHT WEAKHART.

"'Once upon a time'—you know all fairy stories are dated from that eventful period of the world's history—there was a beautiful princess, who lived in a grand palace, and her name was Princess Charming; and she was every way worthy of her name; for she was as good as she was handsome. But a dreadful dwarf, who had slain many people in that country, slew her father and mother, and robbed the poor Princess of her fine house, and carried her off and delivered her to an old fairy, called Cathel, a wicked and bad old sorceress and witch, who sat all day surrounded by black cats, weaving incantations and making charms, which she sold to all who would buy of her. Now, among the customers of Cathel was a

15

monstrous and bloody giant, whose castle was not far away. He was called The Ogre Redgore. He was a cannibal, and bought charms from Cathel, with which to entice young men, women and children into his dreadful den, which was surrounded with heaps of bones of those he had killed and devoured. Now it chanced that when he came one day to buy his charms from Cathel, the old witch asked him if he did not desire to purchase a beautiful young girl. He said he wanted one of that very kind for a banquet he was about to give to some of his fellow giants. And thereupon the wicked old woman showed him the fair and lovely Princess Charming, sitting weeping, among the ashes, on the kitchen hearth. He felt her flesh, to see if she was young and tender enough for the feast, and, being satisfied upon this important point, he and the old witch were not long in coming to terms as to the price to be paid for her.

"And so he started home, soon after, with poor Princess Charming under his arm; she, the while, filling the air with her piteous lamentations and appeals for help.

"And now it so chanced that a wandering knight, called Weakhart, from a far country, came riding along the road that very day, clad in steel armor, and with his lance in rest. And when he heard the pitiful cries of Princess Charming, and beheld her beauty, he drove the spurs into his steed and dashed forward, and would have driven the lance clear through the giant's body; but that worthy saw him coming, and, dropping the Princess and springing aside with great agility, he caught the lance and broke it in many pieces. Then they drew their

swords and a terrible battle ensued; and Princess
Charming knelt down, the while, by the roadside, and
prayed long and earnestly for the success of the
good Knight Weakhart. But if he was weak of
heart he was strong of arm, and at last, with a tremendous blow, he cut the ugly ogre's head off; and
the latter fell dead on the road, as an ogre naturally
will when his head is taken off. And then the Knight
Weakhart was more afraid of being alone with the
Princess than he had been of the giant. But she rose
up, and dried her tears, and thanked him. And then
the Princess and the Knight were in a grave quan-
dary; for, of course, she could not go back to the
den of that wicked witch, Cathel, and she had
nowhere else to go. And so Weakhart, with many
tremblings, asked her to go with him to a cavern
in the woods, where he had taken shelter.''

Here I glanced at Estella, and her face was pale
and quiet, and the smile was all gone from it. I continued:

"There was nothing else for it; and so the poor
Princess mounted in front of the Knight on his
horse, and they rode off together to the cavern.
And there Weakhart fitted up a little room for the
Princess, and made her a bed of the fragrant boughs
of trees, and placed a door to the room and showed
her how she could fasten it, and brought her flowers.
And every day he hunted the deer and the bear, and
made a fire and cooked for her; and he treated
her with as much courtesy and respect as if she had
been a queen sitting upon her throne.

"'And, oh! how that poor Knight Weakhart loved
the Princess! He loved the very ground she walked
on; and he loved all nature because it surrounded

her; and he loved the very sun, moon and stars because they shone down upon her. Nay, not only did
he love her; he worshiped her, as the devotee
worships his god. She was all the constellations of
the sky to him. Universal nature had nothing that
could displace her for a moment from his heart.
Night and day she filled his soul with her ineffable
image; and the birds and the breeze and the whispering trees seemed to be all forever speaking her beloved name in his ears.

"But what could he do? The Princess was poor,
helpless, dependent upon him. Would it not be un-
manly of him to take advantage of her misfortunes
and frighten or coax her into becoming his wife?
Might she not mistake gratitude for love? Could
she make a free choice unless she was herself free?

"And so the poor Knight Weakhart stilled the
beating of the fluttering bird in his bosom, and
hushed down his emotions, and continued to hunt
and cook and wait upon his beloved Princess.

"At last, one day, the Knight Weakhart heard
dreadful news. A people called Vandals, rude and
cruel barbarians, bloodthirsty and warlike, conquer-
ors of nations, had arrived in immense numbers
near the borders of that country, and in a few days
they would pour over and ravage the land, killing
the men and making slaves of the women. He must
fly. One man could do nothing against such numbers. He could not leave the Princess Charming
behind him: she would fall into the hands of the
savages. He knew that she had trust enough in him
to go to the ends of the earth with him. He had a
sort of dim belief that she loved him. What should
he do? Should he overcome his scruples and ask

the lady of his love to wed him; or should he invite her to accompany him as his friend and sister? Would it not be mean and contemptible to take advantage of her distresses, her solitude and the very danger that threatened the land, and thus coerce her into a marriage which might be distasteful to her?

"Now, my dear Estella," I said, with a beating heart, "thus far have I progressed with my fairy tale; but I know not how to conclude it. Can you give me any advice?"

She looked up at me, blushing, but an arch smile played about her lips.

"Let us play out the play," she said. "I will represent the Princess Charming—a very poor representative, I fear;—and you will take the part of the good Knight Weakhart—a part which I imagine you are especially well fitted to play. Now," she said, "you know the old rhyme:

> "'He either fears his fate too much,
>   Or his desert is small,
> Who fears to put it to the touch,
>   And win or lose it all.'

"Therefore, I would advise that you—acting the Knight Weakhart, of course—take the bolder course and propose to Princess Charming to marry you."

I began to see through her device, and fell on my knees, and grasped the Princess's hand, and poured forth my love in rapturous words, that I shall not pretend to repeat, even to you, my dear brother. When I had paused, for want of breath, Estella said:

"Now I must, I suppose, act the part of Princess Charming, and give the foolish Knight his answer."

And here she put her arms around my neck—I

still kneeling—and kissed me on the forehead, and said, laughing, but her eyes glistening with emotion:

"You silly Knight Weakhart, you are well named; and really I prefer the ogre whose head you were cruel enough to cut off, or even one of those hideous Vandals you are trying to frighten me with. What kind of a weak heart or weak head have you, not to know that a woman never shrinks from dependence upon the man she loves, any more than the ivy regrets that it is clinging to the oak and cannot stand alone? A true woman must weave the tendrils of her being around some loved object; she cannot stand alone any more than the ivy. And so—speaking, of course, for the Princess Charming!—I accept the heart and hand of the poor, weak-headed Knight Weakhart."

I folded her in my arms and began to give her all the kisses I had been hoarding up for her since the first day we met. But she put up her hand playfully, and pushed me back, and cried out:

"Stop! stop! the play is over!"

"No! no!" I replied, "it is only beginning; and it will last as long as we two live."

Her face grew serious in an instant, and she whispered:

"Yes, until death doth us part."

CHAPTER XXIII.

MAX'S STORY — THE SONGSTRESS.

WHEN Max came home the next evening I observed that his face wore a very joyous expression — it was indeed radiant. He smiled without cause; he moved as if on air. At the supper table his mother noticed these significant appearances also, and remarked upon them, smiling. Max laughed and said:

"Yes, I am very happy; I will tell you something surprising after supper."

When the evening meal was finished we adjourned to the library. Max closed the doors carefully, and we all sat down in a group together, Max holding the withered hand of the gentle old lady in his own, and Estella and I being near together.

"Now," said Max, "I am about to tell you a long story. It may not be as interesting to you as it is to me; but you are not to interrupt me. And, dear mother," he said, turning to her with a loving look, "you must not feel hurt that I did not make you my confidante, long ere this, of the events I am about to detail; I did not really know myself how they were going to end — I never knew until to-day.

"You must understand," he continued, "that, while I have been living under my own name elsewhere, but in disguise, as I have told you; and conscious that my actions were the subject of daily espionage, it was my habit to frequent all the resorts where men congregate in great numbers, from the

highest even to the lowest. I did this upon principle:
not only to throw my enemies off the track as to my
real character, but also because it was necessary to
me, in the great work I had undertaken, that I
should sound the whole register of humanity, down
to its bass notes.

"There is, in one of the poorer portions of the city,
a great music hall, or 'variety theater,' as they
call it, frequented by multitudes of the middle and
lower orders. It is arranged, indeed, like a huge
theater, but the audience are furnished with beer and
pipes, and little tables, all for an insignificant
charge; and there they sit, amid clouds of smoke,
and enjoy the singing, dancing and acting upon the
stage. There are many of these places in the city,
and I am familiar with them all. They are the poor
man's club and opera. Of course, the performers are
not of a high order of talent, and generally not of a
high order of morals; but occasionally singers. or
actors of real merit and good character begin on
these humble boards, and afterwards rise to great
heights in their professions.

"One night I wandered into the place I speak of,
took a seat and called for my clay pipe and pot of
beer. I was paying little attention to the performance on the stage, for it was worn threadbare with
me; but was studying the faces of the crowd around
me, when suddenly I was attracted by the sound of
the sweetest voice I ever heard. I turned to the
stage, and there stood a young girl, but little more
than a child, holding her piece of music in her hand,
and singing, to the thrumming accompaniment of a
wheezy piano, a sweet old ballad. The girl was slight
of frame and small, not more than about five feet

high. She was timid, for that was her first appearance, as the play-bills stated; and the hand trembled
that held the music. I did not infer that she had had
much training as a musician; but the voice was the
perfection of nature's workmanship; and the singing
was like the airy warbling of children in the happy
unconsciousness of the household, or the gushing
music of birds welcoming the red light of the dawning day while yet the dew and the silence lie over all
nature. A dead quiet had crept over the astonished
house; but at the close of the first stanza a thunderous burst of applause broke forth that shook the
whole building. It was pleasant to see how the
singer brightened into confidence, as a child might,
at the sound; the look of anxiety left the sweet face;
the eyes danced; the yellow curls shook with half-
suppressed merriment; and when the applause had
subsided, and the thrumming of the old piano began
again, there was an abandon in the rush of lovely
melody which she poured forth, with delicate instinctive touches, fine cadences and joyous, bird-like warb-
lings, never dreamed of by the composer of the old
tune. The vast audience was completely carried
away. The voice entered into their slumbering hearts
like a revelation, and walked about in them like a
singing spirit in halls of light. They rose to their
feet; hats were flung in the air; a shower of silver
pieces, and even some of gold—a veritable Danaë
shower—fell all around the singer, while the shouting
and clapping of hands were deafening. The *debu-
tante* was a success. The singer had passed the ordeal. She had entered into the promised land of fame
and wealth. I looked at the programme, as did hundreds of others; it read simply: '*A Solo by Miss Chris-*

tina Carlson—first appearance.' The name was
Scandinavian, and the appearance of the girl confirmed that supposition. She evidently belonged to
the great race of Nilsson and Lind. Her hair, a mass
of rebellious, short curls, was of the peculiar shade of
light yellow common among that people; it looked as
if the xanthous locks of the old Gauls, as described
by Cæsar, had been faded out, in the long nights and
the ice and snow of the Northland, to this paler hue.
But what struck me most, in the midst of those con-
taminated surroundings, was the air of innocence
and purity and light-heartedness which shone over
every part of her person, down to her little feet, and
out to her very finger tips. There was not the slightest suggestion of art, or craft, or double-dealing, or
thought within a thought, or even vanity. She was
delighted to think she had passed the dreadful am-
buscade of a first appearance successfully, and that
employment — and *bread* — were assured for the
future. That seemed to be the only triumph that
danced in her bright eyes.

" 'Who is she?' 'Where did she come from?' were
the questions I heard, in whispers, all around me;
for many of the audience were Germans, Frenchmen
and Jews, all passionate lovers of music, and to them
the ushering in of a new star in the artistic firma-
ment is equal to a new world born before the eyes of
an astronomer.

"When she left the stage there was a rush of the
privileged artists for the green-room. I followed
them. There I found the little singer standing by
the side of a middle-aged, care-worn woman, evidently her mother, for she was carefully adjusting a
poor, thin cloak over the girl's shoulders, while a

swarm of devotees, including many debauched old gallants, crowded around, pouring forth streams of compliments, which Christina heard with pleased face and downcast eyes.

"I kept in the background, watching the scene. There was something about this child that moved me strangely. True, I tried to pooh-pooh away the sentiment, and said to myself: 'Why bother your head about her? She is one of the "refuse;" she will go down into the dark ditch with the rest, baseness to baseness linked.' But when I looked at the modest, happy face, the whole poise of the body— for every fiber of the frame of man or woman partakes of the characteristics of the soul—I could not hold these thoughts steadily in my mind. And I said to myself: 'If she is as pure as she looks I will watch over her. She will need a friend in these scenes. Here success is more dangerous than misery.'

"And so, when Christina and her mother left the theater, I followed them, but at a respectful distance. They called no carriage, and there were no cars going their way; but they trudged along, and I followed them; a weary distance it was—through narrow and dirty streets and back alleys—until at last they stopped at the door of a miserable tenement-house. They entered, and like a shadow I crept noiselessly behind them. Up, up they went; floor after floor, until the topmost garret was reached. Christina gave a glad shout; a door flew open; she entered a room that seemed to be bursting with children; and I could hear the broader voice of a man, mingled with ejaculations of childish delight, as Christina threw down her gifts of gold and silver on the table, and told in tones of girlish ecstasy of her great triumph, calling ever and anon upon her mother to vouch for the truth of her wonderful story. And then I had but time to shrink back into a corner, when a stout, broad-shouldered man, dressed like a workingman, rushed headlong down the stairs, with a large basket in his hand, to the nearest eating-house; and he soon returned bearing cooked meats and bread and butter, and bottles of beer, and pastry, the whole heaped up and running over the sides of the basket. And oh, what a tumult of joy there was in that room! I stood close to the closed door and listened. There was the hurry-scurry of many feet, little and big, as they set the table; the quick commands; the clatter of plates and knives and forks; the constant chatter; the sounds of helping each other and of eating; and then Christina, her mouth, it seemed to me, partly filled with bread and butter, began to give her father some specimens of the cadenzas that had brought down the house; and the little folks clapped their hands with delight, and the mother thanked God fervently that their poverty and their sufferings were at an end.

"I felt like a guilty thing, standing there, sharing in the happiness to which I had not been invited; and at last I stole down the stairs, and into the street. I need not say that all this had vastly increased my interest in the pretty singer. This picture of poverty associated with genius, and abundant love shining over all, was very touching.

"The next day I set a detective agency to work to find out all they could about the girl and her family. One of their men called upon me that evening, with a report. He had visited the place and made inquiries of the neighbors, of the shop-keepers, the police, etc., and this is what he had found out:

"There was no person in the building of the name of 'Carlson,' but in the garret I had described a man resided named 'Carl Jansen,' a Swede by birth, a blacksmith by trade, and a very honest, worthy man and good workman, but excessively poor. He had lived for some years in New York; he had a large family of children; his wife took in washing, and thus helped to fill the many greedy little mouths; the oldest girl was named Christina; she was seventeen years of age; she had attended the public schools, and of late years had worked at embroidery, her earnings going into the common stock. She was a good, amiable girl, and highly spoken of by every one who knew her. She had attended Sunday school, and there it had been discovered that she possessed a remarkably fine voice, and she had been placed in the choir; and, after a time, at the suggestion of some of the teachers, her mother had taken her to the manager of the variety hall, who was so pleased with her singing that he gave her a chance to appear on the boards of his theater. She had made her *début* last night, and the whole tenement-house, and, in fact, the whole alley and neighboring streets, were talking that morning of her great success; and, strange to say, they all rejoiced in the brightening fortunes of the poor family.

"'Then,' I said to myself, 'Carlson was merely a stage name, probably suggested by the manager of the variety show.'

"I determined to find out more about the pretty Christina."

CHAPTER XXIV.

"You may be sure that that night the public took the variety theater by storm; every seat was filled; the very aisles were crowded with men standing; the beer flowed in streams and the tobacco-smoke rose in clouds; the establishment was doing a splendid business. Christina was down on the bills for three solos. Each one was a triumph—encore followed encore—and when the performance closed the little singer was called before the curtain and another Danaë shower of silver and gold, and some bouquets, fell around her. When I went behind the scenes I found the happy girl surrounded by even a larger circle of admirers than the night before, each one sounding her praises. I called the manager aside. He knew me well as a rich young spendthrift. I said to him:

"'How much a week do you pay Christina?'

"'I promised her,' said he, 'five dollars a week; but,' and here he looked at me suspiciously, 'I have determined to double it. I shall pay her ten.'

"'That is not enough,' I said; 'you will find in her a gold mine. You must pay her fifty.'

"'My dear sir,' he said, 'I cannot afford it. I really cannot.'

"'Well,' said I, 'I will speak to Jobson [a rival in business]; he will pay her a hundred. I saw him here to-night. He has already heard of her.'

"'But,' said he, 'she has contracted with me to sing for three months, at five dollars per week; and I have permitted her to take home all the money that was thrown on the stage last night and to-night. Now I shall pay her ten. Is not that liberal?'

"'Liberal!' I said; 'it is hoggish. This girl has made you two hundred dollars extra profit to-night. She is under age. She cannot make a binding contract. And the money that was thrown to her belongs to her and not to you. Come, what do you say—shall I speak to Jobson?'

"'What interest have you in this girl?' he asked, sullenly.

"'That is no matter of yours,' I replied; 'if you will not pay her what I demand, to-morrow night she will sing for Jobson, and your place will be empty.'

"'Well,' said he, 'I will pay it; but I don't see what right you have to interfere in my business.'

"'That is not all,' I said; 'go to her now and tell her you have made a good deal of money to-night, by her help, and ask her to accept fifty dollars from you as a present; and tell her, *in my hearing*, that she is to receive fifty dollars a week hereafter. The family are very poor, and need immediate help. And besides, if she does not know that she is to receive a liberal salary, when the agents of the other houses come for her, she may leave you. Fair play is the wisest thing.'

"He thought a moment; he was very angry with me; but finally he swallowed his wrath, and pushed his way through the crowd to where Christina stood, and said to her with many a bow and smile:

"'Miss Christina, your charming voice has greatly

increased my business to-night; and I think it only fair to give you a part of my profits—here are fifty dollars.'

"Christina was delighted—she took the money—she had never seen so large an amount before—she handed it to her mother; and both were profuse in their thanks, while the crowd vigorously applauded the good and generous manager.

"'But this is not all,' he continued; 'instead of five dollars per week, the sum we had agreed upon, for your singing, I shall pay you hereafter fifty dollars a week!'

"There was still greater applause; Christina's eyes swam with happiness; her mother began to cry; Christina seized the manager's hand, and the old scamp posed, as he received the thanks of those present, as if all this were the outcome of his own generosity, and as if he were indeed the best and noblest of men. I have no doubt that if I had not interfered he would have kept her on the five dollars a week, and the silly little soul would have been satisfied.

"I followed them home. I again listened to their happiness. And then I heard the mother tell the father that they must both go out to-morrow and find a better place to lodge in, for they were rich now. A bright thought flashed across my mind, and I hastened away.

"The next morning, at daybreak, I hurried to the same detective I had employed the day before; he was a shrewd, but not unkindly fellow. I explained to him my plans, and we went out together. We took a carriage and drove rapidly from place to place; he really seemed pleased to find himself engaged, for once in his life, in a good action. What I did will be revealed as I go on with this story.

"At half past eight o'clock that morning the Jansen family had finished their breakfast and talked over and over again, for the twentieth time, their wonderful turn of fortune, and all its incidents, including repeated counting of their marvelous hoard of money. Then Christina was left in charge of the children, and the father and mother sallied forth to look for a new residence. The neighbors crowded around to congratulate them; and they explained,—for, kindly-hearted souls, they did not wish their old companions in poverty to think that they had willingly fled from them, at the first approach of good fortune,—they explained that they must get a new home nearer to the theater, for Christina's sake; and that they proposed that she should have teachers in music and singing and acting; for she was now the bread-winner of the family, and they hoped that some day she would shine in opera with the great artists.

"Did the neighbors know of any place, suitable for them, which they could rent?

"No, they did not; they rarely passed out of their own poor neighborhood.

"But here a plainly dressed man, who looked like a workman, and who had been listening to the conversation, spoke up and said that he had observed, only that morning, a bill of 'To Rent' upon a very neat little house, only a few blocks from the theater; and, as he was going that way, he would be glad to show them the place. They thanked him; and, explaining to him that the business of renting houses was something new to them, for heretofore they had lived in one or two rooms—they might have added, very near the roof—they walked off with the stranger. He led them into a pleasant, quiet, respectable neighborhood, and at last stopped before a small, neat three-story house, with a little garden in front and another larger one in the rear.

"'What a pretty place!' said the mother; 'but I fear the rent will be too high for us.'

"'Well, there is no harm in inquiring,' said the workman, and he rang the bell.

"A young man, dressed like a mechanic, answered the summons. He invited them in; the house was comfortably, but not richly furnished. They went through it and into the garden; they were delighted with everything. And then came the question they feared to ask: What was the rent?

"'Well,' said the young man, pleasantly, 'I must explain my position. I am a printer by trade. My name is Francis Montgomery. I own this house. It was left to me by my parents. It is all I have. I am not married. I cannot live in it alone; it is too big for that; and, besides, I think I should get some income out of it, for there are the taxes to be paid. But I do not want to leave the house. I was born and raised here. I thought that if I could get some pleasant family to take it, who would let me retain one of the upper rooms, and would board me, I would rent the house for'—here he mentioned a ridiculously low price. 'I do not want,' he added, 'any expensive fare. I am content to take "pot-luck" with the family. I like your looks; and if you want the house, at the terms I have named, I think we can get along pleasantly together. I may not be here all the time.'

"The offer was accepted; the workman was dismissed with thanks. That afternoon the whole family moved in. The delight of Christina was unbounded. There was one room which I had foreseen would be assigned to her, and that I had adorned with some flowers. She was introduced to me; we shook hands; and I was soon a member of the family. What a curious flock of little white-heads, of all ages, they were—sturdy, rosy, chubby, healthy, merry, and loving toward one another. They brought very little of their poor furniture with them; it was too shabby for the new surroundings; they gave it away to their former neighbors. But I noticed that the father carefully carried into the kitchen an old chair, time-worn and venerable; the back was gone, and it was nothing but a stool. The next day I observed a pudgy little boy, not quite three years old (the father's favorite, as I discovered), driving wrought nails into it with a little iron hammer.

"'Stop! stop! my man!' I exclaimed; 'you must not drive nails in the furniture.'

"I looked at the chair: the seat of it was a mass of nail-holes. And then Christina, noticing my looks of perplexity, said:

" 'Last Christmas we were very, very poor. Papa was out of work. We could scarcely get enough to eat. Papa saw the preparations in the store windows for Christmas—the great heaps of presents; and he saw the busy parents hurrying about buying gifts for their children, and he felt very sad that he could not give us any presents, not even to little Ole, whom he loves so much. So he went into the blacksmith shop of a friend, and, taking up a piece of iron that had been thrown on the floor, he made that

little hammer Ole has in his hand, and a number of
wrought nails; and he brought them home and
showed Ole how to use the hammer and drive the
nails into that chair; and when he had driven them
all into the wood, papa would pry them out for him,
and the work would commence all over again, and
Ole was happy all day long.'

"I found my eyes growing damp; for I was thinking of the riotous profusion of the rich, and of the
costly toys they heap upon their children; and the
contrast of this poor man, unable to buy a single
cheap toy for his family, and giving his chubby boy
a rude iron hammer and nails, to pound into that
poor stool, as a substitute for doll or rocking-horse,
was very touching. And then I looked with some
wonder at the straightforward honesty of the little
maid, who, in the midst of the new, fine house, was
not ashamed to talk so frankly of the dismal wretchedness and want which a few days before had been
the lot of the family. She saw nothing to be ashamed
of in poverty; while by meaner and more sordid
souls it is regarded as the very abasement of shame
and crime.

"Ole was pounding away at his nails.

" 'Does he not hurt himself sometimes?' I asked.

" 'Oh, yes,' she said, laughing; 'at first he would
hit his little fingers many a hard rap; and he would
start to cry, but papa would tell him that "*men*
never cry;" and then it was funny to see how he
would purse up his little red mouth, while the tears
of pain ran down from his big round eyes, but not a
sound more would escape him.'

"And I said to myself: 'This is the stuff of which
was formed the masterful race that overran the

world under the names of a dozen different peoples. Ice and snow made the tough fiber, mental and physical, which the hot sun of southern climes afterward melted into the viciousness of more luxurious nations. Man is scourged into greatness by adversity, and leveled into mediocrity by prosperity. This little fellow, whose groans die between his set teeth, has in him the blood of the Vikings.'

"There was one thing I did out of policy, which yet went very much against my inclinations, in dealing with such good and honest people. I knew that in all probability I had been traced by the spies of the Oligarchy to this house; they would regard it of course as a crazy adventure, and would naturally assign it to base purposes. But it would not do for me to appear altogether different, even in this family, from the character I had given myself out to be, of a reckless and dissipated man; for the agents of my enemies might talk to the servant, or to members of the household. And so the second night I came home to supper apparently drunk. It was curious to see the looks of wonder, sorrow and sympathy exchanged between the members of the family as I talked ramblingly and incoherently at the table. But this feint served one purpose; it broke down the barrier between landlord and tenants. Indeed, paradoxical as it may seem, I think they thought more of me because of my supposed infirmity.; for 'pity is akin to love;' and it is hard for the tenderer feelings of the heart to twine about one who is so strong and flawless that he demands no sympathy or forbearance at our hands. I ceased to be the rich owner of a house—I was simply one of themselves; a foolish journeyman printer; given to drink, but withal a kindly and pleasant man. Two days afterwards, Christina, who had looked at me several times with a troubled brow, took me aside and tried to persuade me to join a temperance society of which her father was a member. It was very pretty and touching to see the motherly way in which the little woman took my hand, and coaxed me to give up my vice, and told me, with eloquent earnestness, all the terrible consequences which would flow from it. I was not foolish enough to think that any tender sentiment influenced her. It was simply her natural goodness, and her pity for a poor fellow, almost now one of their own family, who was going to destruction. And indeed, if I had been a veritable drunkard, she would have turned me from my evil courses. But I assured her that I would try to reform; that I would drink less than previously, and that, on the next New Year's day, I might be able to summon up courage enough to go with her father to his society, and pledge myself to total abstinence. She received these promises with many expressions of pleasure; and, although I had to keep up my false character, I never afterwards wounded her feelings by appearing anything more than simply elevated in spirit by drink.

"They were a very kind, gentle, good people; quite unchanged by prosperity and unaffected in their manners. Even in their poverty the children had all looked clean and neat; now they were prettily, but not expensively, dressed. Their religious devotion was great; and I endeared myself to them by sometimes joining in their household prayers. And I said to myself: If there is no God—as the miserable philosophers tell us—there surely ought to be one, if for nothing else than to listen to the supplications of these loving and grateful hearts. And I could not believe that such tender devotions could ascend and be lost forever in empty and unresponsive space. The impulse of prayer, it seems to me, presupposes a God."

CHAPTER XXV.

MAX'S STORY CONTINUED—THE DARK SHADOW.

"But a cloud was moving up to cover the fair face of this pleasant prospect; and yet the sun was shining and the birds singing.

"Christina was very busy during the day with her teachers. She loved music and was anxious to excel. She had her lessons on the piano; she improved her mind by a judicious course of reading, in which I helped her somewhat; she went twice a week to a grand Italian *maestro*, who perfected her in her singing. And she took long walks to the poor neighborhood where she had formerly lived, to visit the sick and wretched among her old acquaintances, and she never left them empty-handed.

"At the theater she grew more and more popular. Even the rudest of the audience recognized instinctively in her the goodness which they themselves lacked. Every song was an ovation. Her praises began to resound in the newspapers; and she had already received advances from the manager of one of the grand opera-houses. A bright future opened before her—a vista of light and music and wealth and delight.

"She did not escape, however, the unpleasant incidents natural to such a career. Her mother accompanied her to every performance, and was, in so far, a shield to her; but she was beset with visitors at the house; she was annoyed by men who stopped and claimed acquaintance with her on the streets; she received many gifts, flowers, fruit, jewelry, and all the other tempting sweet nothings which it is thought bewitch the heart of frail woman. But they had no effect upon her. Only goodness seemed to cling to her, and evil fell far off from her. You may set two plants side by side in the same soil — one will draw only bitterness and poison from the earth; while the other will gather, from the same nurture, nothing but sweetness and perfume.

> "'For virtue, as it never will be moved,
>   Though lewdness court it in a shape of heaven;
>   So lust, though to a radiant angel linked,
>   Will sate itself in a celestial bed,
>   And prey on garbage.'

"Among the men who pestered Christina with their attentions was a young fellow named Nathan Brederhagan, the son of a rich widow. He was one of those weak and shallow brains to whom wealth becomes only a vehicle in which to ride to destruction. He was in reality all that I pretended to be — a reckless, drunken, useless spendthrift, with no higher aim in life than wine and woman. He spent his days in vanity and his nights in debauchery. Across the clouded portal of this fool's brain came, like a vision, the beautiful, gentle, gifted Christina. She was a new toy, the most charming he had ever seen, and, like a child, he must possess it. And so he began a series of persecutions. He followed her everywhere; he fastened himself upon her at the theater; he showered all sorts of gifts on her; and, when he found she returned his presents, and that she refused or resisted all his advances, he grew so desperate that he at last offered to marry her, although with a con-

sciousness that he was making a most heroic and
extraordinary sacrifice of himself in doing so. But
even this condescension—to his unbounded astonishment—she declined with thanks. And then the
silly little fool grew more desperate than ever, and
battered up his poor brains with strong drink, and
wept in maudlin fashion to his acquaintances. At
last one of these—a fellow of the same kidney, but
with more enterprise than himself—said to him:
'Why don't you carry her off?' Nathan opened
his eyes very wide, stopped his sniffling and blubber-
ing, and made up his mind to follow this sage advice.
To obtain the necessary nerve for such a prodigious
undertaking he fired up with still more whisky;
and when the night came he was crazy with drink.
Obtaining a carriage and another drunken fool to
help him, he stationed himself beside the pavement,
in the quiet street where Christina lived, and but a
few doors distant from her house; and then, as she
came along with her mother, he seized upon her,
while his companion grasped Mrs. Jansen. He began to drag Christina toward the carriage; but the
young girl was stronger than he was, and not only
resisted him, but began to shriek, ably seconded by
her mother, until the street rang. The door of their
house flew open, and Mr. Jansen, who had recognized the voices of his wife and daughter, was hurrying to their rescue; whereupon the little villain cried
in a tone of high tragedy, 'Then die!' and stabbed
her in the throat with a little dagger he carried. He
turned and sprang into the carriage; while the poor
girl, who had become suddenly silent, staggered and
fell into the arms of her father.

"It chanced that I was absent from the house

that night, on some business of the Brotherhood, and the next morning I breakfasted in another part of the city, at a restaurant. I had scarcely begun my meal when a phonograph, which, in a loud voice, was proclaiming the news of the day before for the entertainment of the guests, cried out:

Probable Murder—A Young Girl Stabbed.

Last night, at about half-past eleven, on Seward Street, near Fifty-first Avenue, a young girl was assaulted and brutally stabbed in the throat by one of two men. The girl is a singer employed in Peter Bingham's variety theater, a few blocks distant from the place of the attack. She was accompanied by her mother, and they were returning on foot from the theater, where she had been singing. The man had a carriage ready, and while one of them held her mother, the other tried to force the young girl into the carriage; it was plainly the purpose of the men to abduct her. She resisted, however; whereupon the ruffian who had hold of her, hearing the footsteps of persons approaching, and seeing that he could not carry her off, drew a knife and stabbed her in the throat, and escaped with his companion in the carriage. The girl was carried into her father's house, No. 1252 Seward Street, and the distinguished surgeon, Dr. Hemnip, was sent for. He pronounced the wound probably fatal. The young girl is named Christina Jansen; she sings under the stage-name of Christina Carlson, and is the daughter of Carl Jansen, living at the place named. Inquiry at the theater showed her to be a girl of good character, very much esteemed by her acquaintances, and greatly admired as a very brilliant singer.

Later.—A young man named Nathan Brederhagan, belonging to a wealthy and respectable family, and residing with his mother at No. 637 Sherman Street, was arrested this morning at one o'clock, in his bed, by police officer No. 18,333, on information furnished by the family of the unfortunate girl. A bloody dagger was found in his pocket. As the girl is likely to die he was committed to jail and bail refused. He is represented to be a dissipated, reckless young fellow, and it seems was in love with the girl, and sought her hand in marriage; and she refused him; whereupon, in his rage, he attempted to take her life. His terrible deed has plunged a large circle of relatives and friends into great shame and sorrow.

"I had started to my feet as soon as I heard the words, 'The girl is a singer in Peter Bingham's Variety Theater,' but, when her name was mentioned and her probable death, the pangs that shot through me no words of mine can describe.

"It is customary with us‑all to think that our intellect is our self, and that we are only what we think; but there are in the depths of our nature feelings, emotions, qualities of the soul, with which the mere intelligence has nothing to do; and which, when they rise up, like an enraged elephant from the jungle, scatter all the conventionalities of our training, and all the smooth and automaton-like operations of our minds to the winds. As I stood there, listening to the dead-level, unimpassioned, mechanical voice of the phonograph, pouring forth those deadly sentences, I realized for the first time what the sunny-haired little songstress was to me.

"'Wounded! Dead!'

"I seized my hat, and, to the astonishment of the waiters, I rushed out. I called a hack. I had to alter my appearance. I grudged the time necessary for this very necessary precaution, but, paying the driver double fare, I went, as fast as his horses' legs could carry me, to the place, in a saloon kept by one of the Brotherhood, where I was in the habit of changing my disguises. I dismissed the hack, hurried to my room, and in a few minutes I was again flying along, in another hack, to 1252 Seward Street. I rushed up the steps. Her mother met me in the hall. She was crying.

"'Is she alive?' I asked.

"'Yes, yes,' she replied.

"'What does the doctor say?' I inquired.

"'He says she will not die—*but her voice is gone forever*,' she replied.

"Her tears burst forth afresh. I was shocked—inexpressibly shocked. True, it was joy to know she would live; but to think of that noble instrument of grace and joy and melody silenced forever! It was like the funeral of an angel! God, in the infinite diversity of his creation, makes so few such voices—so few such marvelous adjustments of those vibrating chords to the capabilities of the air and the human sense and the infinite human soul that dwells behind the sense—and all to be the spoil of a ruffian's knife. Oh! if I could have laid my hands on the little villain! I should have butchered him with his own dagger—sanctified, as it was, with her precious blood. The infamous little scoundrel! To think that such a vicious, shallow, drunken brute could have power to 'break into the bloody house of life' and bring to naught such a precious and unparalleled gift of God. I had to clutch the railing of the stairs to keep from falling. Fortunately for me, poor Mrs. Jansen was too much absorbed in her own sorrows to notice mine. She grieved deeply and sincerely for her daughter's sufferings and the loss of her voice; but, worse than all, there rose before her—the *future!* She looked with dilated eyes into that dreadful vista. She saw again the hard, grinding, sordid poverty from which they had but a little time before escaped—she saw again her husband bent down with care, and she heard her children crying once more for bread. I read the poor woman's thoughts. It was not selfishness—it was love for

those dear to her; and I took her hand, and—
scarcely knowing what I said—I told her she must
not worry, that she and her family should never
suffer want again. She looked at me in surprise,
and thanked me, and said I was always good and
kind.

"In a little while she took me to Christina's room.
The poor girl was under the influence of morphine
and sleeping a troubled sleep. Her face was very
pale from loss of blood; and her head and neck were
all bound up in white bandages, here and there
stained with the ghastly fluid that flowed from her
wounds. It was a pitiable sight: her short, crisp
yellow curls broke here and there, rebelliously,
through the folds of the linen bandages; and I
thought how she used to shake them, responsive to
the quiverings of the cadenzas and trills that poured
from her bird-like throat. 'Alas!' I said to myself,
'poor throat! you will never sing again! Poor little curls, you will never tremble again in sympathy
with the dancing delight of that happy voice.' A
dead voice! Oh! it is one of the saddest things in
the world! I went to the window to hide the un-
manly tears which streamed down my face.

"When she woke she seemed pleased to see me
near her, and extended her hand to me with a little
smile. The doctor had told her she must not attempt to speak. I held her hand for awhile, and
told how grieved I was over her misfortune. And
then I told her I would bring her a tablet and pencil,
so that she might communicate her wants to us;
and then I said to her that I was out of a job at my
trade (I know that the angels in heaven do not
record such lies), and that I had nothing to do, and

could stay and wait upon her; for the other children were too small, and her mother too busy to be with her all the time, and her father and I could divide the time between us. She smiled again and thanked me with her eyes.

"And I was very busy and almost happy—moving around that room on tiptoe in my slippers while she slept, or talking to her in a bright and chatty way, about everything that I thought would interest her, or bringing her flowers, or feeding her the liquid food which alone she could swallow.

"The doctor came every day. I questioned him closely. He was an intelligent man, and had, I could see, taken quite a liking to his little patient. He told me that the knife had just missed, by a hair's breadth, the carotid artery, but unfortunately it had struck the cervical plexus, that important nerve-plexus, situated in the side of the neck; and had cut the recurrent laryngeal nerve, which arises from the cervical plexus and supplies the muscles of the larynx; and it had thereby caused instant paralysis of those muscles, and aphonia, or loss of voice. I asked him if she would ever be able to sing again. He said it was not certain. If the severed ends of the nerve reunited fully her voice might return with all its former power. He hoped for the best.

"One morning I was called down stairs by Mrs. Jansen; it was three or four days after the assault had been made on Christina. There I found the chief of police of that department. He said it had become necessary, in the course of the legal proceedings, that Brederhagan should be identified by Christina as her assailant. The doctor had reported that there was now no danger of her death; and the family of the little rascal desired to get him out on bail. I told him I would confer with the physician, when he called, as to whether Christina could stand the excitement of such an interview, and I would notify him. He thanked me and took his leave. That day I spoke upon the subject to Dr. Hemnip, and he thought that Christina had so far recovered her strength that she might see the prisoner the day after the next. At the same time he cautioned her not to become nervous or excited, and not to attempt to speak. She was simply to write 'Yes' on her tablet, in answer to the question asked her by the police. The interview was to be as brief as possible. I communicated with the chief of police, as I had promised, giving him these details, and fixed an hour for him to call."

CHAPTER XXVI.

"THE next day, about ten in the morning, I went out to procure some medicine for Christina. I was gone but a few minutes, and on my return, as I mounted the stairs, I was surprised to hear a strange voice in the sick-room. I entered and was introduced by Mrs. Jansen to 'Mrs. Brederhagan,' the rich widow, the mother of the little wretch who had assaulted Christina. She was a large, florid woman, extravagantly dressed, with one of those shallow, unsympathetic voices which betoken a small and flippant soul. Her lawyers had told her that Nathan would probably be sent to prison for a term of years; and so she had come to see if she could not beg his victim to spare him. She played her part well. She got down on her knees by the bedside in all her silks and furbelows, and seized Christina's hand and wept; and told of her own desolate state as a widow — drawing, incidentally, a picture of the virtues of her deceased husband, which he himself — good man — would not have recognized in this world or any other. And then she descanted on the kind heart of her poor boy, and how he had been led off by bad company, etc., etc. Christina listened with an intent look to all this story; but she flushed when the widow proceeded to say how deeply her son loved her, Christina, and that it was his love for her that had caused him to commit his desperate act; and she

17   257

actually said that, although Christina was but a poor singer, with no blood worth speaking of, in comparison with her own illustrious long line of nobodies, yet she brought Christina an offer from her son—sanctioned by her own approval—that he would—if she would spare him from imprisonment and his family from disgrace—marry her outright and off-hand; and that she would, as a magnanimous and generous, upper-crust woman, welcome her, despite all her disadvantages and drawbacks, to her bosom as a daughter! All this she told with a great many tears and ejaculations, all the time clinging to Christina's hand.

"When she had finished and risen, and readjusted her disarranged flounces, Christina took her tablet and wrote:

"'I could not marry your son. As to the rest, I will think it over. Please do not come again.'

"The widow would have gotten down on her knees and gone at it again; but I took her aside and said to her:

"'Do you not see that this poor girl is very weak, and your appeals distress her? Go home and I will communicate with you.'

"And I took her by the arm, and firmly but respectfully led her out of the room, furbelows, gold chains and all. She did not feel at all satisfied with the success of her mission; but I saw her into her carriage and told the driver to take her home. I was indignant. I felt that the whole thing was an attempt to play upon the sympathies of my poor little patient, and that the woman was a hollow, heartless old fraud.

"The next day, at the appointed hour, the chief of

police came, accompanied by the prisoner. The latter had had no liquor for several days and was collapsed enough. All his courage and vanity had oozed out of him. He was a dilapidated wreck. He knew that the penitentiary yawned for him, and he felt his condition as deeply as such a shallow nature could feel anything. I scowled at the wretch in a way which alarmed him for his personal safety, and he trembled and hurried behind the policeman.

"Christina had been given a strengthening drink. The doctor was there with his finger on her pulse; she was raised up on some pillows. Her father and mother were present. When we entered she looked for an instant at the miserable, dejected little creature, and I saw a shudder run through her frame, and then she closed her eyes.

"'Miss Jansen,' said the chief of police, 'be kind enough to say whether or not this is the man who tried to kill you.'

"I handed her the tablet and pencil. She wrote a few words. I handed it to the chief.

"'What does this mean?' he said, in evident astonishment.

"I took the tablet out of his hand, and was thunderstruck to find on it these unexpected words:

"'*This is not the man.*'

"'Then,' said the chief of police, 'there is nothing more to do than to discharge the prisoner.'

"Her father and mother stepped forward; but she waved them back with her hand; and the chief led the culprit out, too much stunned to yet realize that he was free.

"'What does this mean, Christina?' I asked, in a tone that expressed indignation, if not anger.

"She took her tablet and wrote:

"'What good would it do to send that poor, foolish boy to prison for many years? He was drunk or he would not have hurt me. It will do no good to bring disgrace on a respectable family. This great lesson may reform him and make him a good man.'

"At that moment I made up my mind to make Christina my wife, if she would have me. Such a soul was worth a mountain of rubies. There are only a few of them in each generation, and fortunate beyond expression is the man who can call one of them his own!

"But I was not going to see my poor love, or her family, imposed on by that scheming old widow. I hurried out of the house; I called a hack, and drove to Mrs. Brederhagan's house. I found her and her son in the first paroxysm of joy—locked in each other's arms.

"'Mrs. Brederhagan,' I said, 'your vicious little devil of a son here has escaped punishment so far for his cruel and cowardly assault upon a poor girl. He has escaped through her unexampled magnanimity and generosity. But do you know what he has done to her? He has silenced her exquisite voice forever. He has ruthlessly destroyed that which a million like him could not create. That poor girl will never sing again. She was the sole support of her family. This imp here has taken the bread out of their mouths—they will starve. You owe it to her to make a deed of gift whereby you will endow her with the amount she was earning when your son's dagger pierced her poor throat and silenced her voice; that is—fifty dollars a week.'

"The widow ruffled up her feathers, and said she

did not see why she should give Christina fifty dollars a week. She had declared that her son was not the one who had assaulted her, and he was a free man, and that was the end of their connection with the matter.

"'Ha! ha!' said I, 'and so, that is your position? Now you will send at once for a notary and do as I tell you, or in one hour your son shall be arrested again. *Christina's mother knows him perfectly well, and will identify him;* and Christina herself will not swear in court to the generous falsehood she told to screen you and yours from disgrace. You are a worthy mother of such a son, when you cannot appreciate one of the noblest acts ever performed in this world.'

"The widow grew pale at these threats; and after she and her hopeful son—who was in a great fright— had whispered together, she reluctantly agreed to my terms. A notary was sent for, and the deed drawn and executed, and a check given, at my demand, for the first month's payment.

"'Now,' said I, turning to Master Nathan, 'permit me to say one word to you, young man. If you ever again approach, or speak to, or molest in any way, Miss Christina Carlson, I will,'—and here I drew close to him and put my finger on his breast,—'I will kill you like a dog.'

"With this parting shot I left the happy pair."

CHAPTER XXVII.

"I NEED not describe the joy there was in the Jansen family when I brought home Mrs. Brederhagan's deed of gift and the money. Christina did not yet know that her voice was destroyed, and hence was disposed to refuse what she called 'the good lady's great generosity.' But we reminded her that the widow was rich, and that her son had inflicted great and painful wounds upon her, which had caused her weeks of weary sickness, to say nothing of the doctor's bills and the other expenses they had been subjected to; and so, at last, she consented, and agreed that, for the present at least, she would receive the widow's money, but only until she could resume her place on the boards of the theater. But the deed of gift drove the brooding shadows out of the heart and eyes of poor Mrs. Jansen.

"I need not tell you all the details of Christina's recovery. Day by day she grew stronger. She began to speak in whispers, and gradually she recovered her power of speech, although the voice at first sounded husky. She was soon able to move about the house, for youth and youthful spirits are great medicines. One day she placed her hand on mine and thanked me for all my great kindness to her; and said, in her arch way, that I was a good, kindhearted friend, and it was a pity I had any weaknesses; and that I must not forget my promise to her about the next New Year's day. But she feared that I had neglected my business to look after her.

"At length she learned from the doctor that she could never sing again; that her throat was paralyzed. It was a bitter grief to her, and she wept quietly for some hours. And then she comforted herself with the reflection that the provision made for her by Mrs. Brederhagan had placed herself and her family beyond the reach of poverty. But for this I think she would have broken her heart.

"I had been cogitating for some days upon a new idea. It seemed to me that these plain, good people would be much happier in the country than in the city; and, besides, their income would go farther. They had country blood in their veins, and it takes several generations to get the scent of the flowers out of the instincts of a family; they have subtle promptings in them to walk in the grass and behold the grazing kine. And a city, after all, is only fit for temporary purposes—to see the play and the shops and the mob—and wear one's life out in nothingnesses. As one of the poets says:

> "'Thus is it in the world-hive; most where men
> Lie deep in cities as in drifts—death drifts—
> Nosing each other like a flock of sheep;
> Not knowing and not caring whence nor whither
> They come or go, so that they fool together.'

"And then I thought, too, that Mr. Jansen was unhappy in idleness. He was a great, strong man, and accustomed all his life to hard work, and his muscles cried out for exercise.

"So I started out and made little excursions in all directions. At last I found the very place I had been looking for. It was about twelve miles beyond the built-up portions of the suburbs, in a high and airy neighborhood, and contained about ten acres of land. There was a little grove, a field, a garden, and an old-fashioned, roomy house. The house needed some repairs, it is true; but beyond the grove two roads crossed each other, and at the angle would be an admirable place for a blacksmith shop. I purchased the whole thing very cheaply. Then I set carpenters to work to repair the house and build a blacksmith shop. The former I equipped with furniture, and the latter with anvil, bellows and other tools, and a supply of coal and iron.

"When everything was ready I told Christina another of my white lies. I said to her that Mrs. Brederhagan, learning that her voice was ruined forever by her son's dagger, had felt impelled, by her conscience and sense of right, to make her a present of a little place in the country, and had deputed me to look after the matter for her, and that I had bought the very place that I thought would suit them.

"And so we all started out to view the premises. It would be hard to say who was most delighted, Christina or her mother or her father; but I am inclined to think the latter took more pure happiness in his well-equipped little shop, with the big sign, 'CARL JANSEN, BLACKSMITH,' and the picture of a man shoeing a horse, than Christina did in the flower-bed, or her mother in the comfortable household arrangements.

"Soon after the whole family moved out. I was right. A race that has lived for several generations in the country is an exotic in a city."

CHAPTER XXVIII.

MAX'S STORY CONCLUDED — THE UNEXPECTED HAPPENS.

"I USED to run out every other day, and I was as welcome as if I had been really a member of the family. The day before yesterday I found the whole household in a state of joyous excitement. Christina had been enjoined to put the baby to sleep; and while rocking it in its cradle she had, all unconsciously, begun to sing a little nursery song. Suddenly she sprang to her feet, and, running to her mother, cried out:

"'Oh, mother! I can sing! Listen.'

"She found, however, that the voice was still quite weak, and that if she tried to touch any of the higher notes there was a pain in her throat.

"I advised her to forbear singing for some time, and permit the organs of the voice to resume their natural condition. It might be that the doctor was wrong in his prognosis of her case; or it might be that the injured nerve, as he had said was possible, had resumed its function, through the curative power of nature. But it was a great delight to us all, and especially to the poor girl herself, to think that her grand voice might yet be restored to her.

"To-day I went out again.

"I thought that Mr. Jansen met me with a constrained manner; and when Mrs. Jansen saw me, instead of welcoming me with a cordial smile, as was usual with her, she retreated into the house. And

when I went into the parlor, Christina's manner was
still more embarrassing. She blushed as she extended her hand to me, and seemed very much confused; and yet her manner was not unkind or un-
friendly. I could not understand it.

"'What is the matter, Christina?' I asked.

"The little woman was incapable of double-dealing, and so she said:

"'You know it came into my head lately, very
often, that Mrs. Brederhagan had been exceedingly,
I might say extraordinarily, kind to me. It is true
her son had done me a great injury, and might have
killed me; and I refused to testify against him. But
she had not only given me that deed of gift you
brought me, but she had also presented papa with
this charming home. And so I said to myself that
she must think me very rude and ungrateful, since I
had never called upon her to thank her in person.
And so, knowing that Nathan had been sent to Europe, I made up my mind, yesterday, that I would
go into town, and call upon Mrs. Brederhagan, and
thank her for all her kindness.

"'I took a hack to her house from the station,
and sent up my card. She received me quite kindly.
After a few inquiries and commonplaces I thanked
her as I had intended doing. She smiled and made
light of it; then I spoke of the house, and the garden, and the blacksmith shop, and how grateful we
all were to her.

"'"Why," said she, "what on earth are you talking about? I never gave you a house, or a garden,
or a blacksmith shop."

"'You may imagine my surprise.

"'"Why," said I, "did you not give Mr. Frank

Montgomery the money to purchase it, and tell him
to have the deed made out to my father?"

"""My dear," said she, "you bewilder me; I never
in all my life heard of such a person as Mr. Frank
Montgomery; and I certainly never gave him any
money to buy a house for anybody."

"""Why," said I, "do you pretend you do not
know Mr. Frank Montgomery, who brought me your
deed of gift?"

"""That," she said, "was not Mr. Frank Montgomery, but Mr. Arthur Phillips."

"""No, no," I said, "you are mistaken; it was
Frank Montgomery, a printer by trade, who owns
the house we used to live in, at 1252 Seward Street.
I am well acquainted with him."

"""Well," said she, "this is certainly astonishing!
Mr. Arthur Phillips, whom I have known for years, a
young gentleman of large fortune, a lawyer by profession, comes to me and tells me, the very day you
said my son was not the man who assaulted you,
that unless I settled fifty dollars a week on you for
life, by a deed of gift, he would have Nathan rear-
rested for an attempt to murder you, and would
prove his guilt by your mother; and now you come
and try to make me believe that Arthur Phillips, the
lawyer, is Frank Montgomery, the printer; that he
lives in a little house on Seward Street, and that I
have been giving him money to buy you houses and
gardens and blacksmith shops in the country! I
hope, my dear, that the shock you received, on that
dreadful night, has not affected your mind. But I
would advise you to go home to your parents."

"'And therewithal she politely bowed me out.'

"'I was very much astonished and bewildered. I

stood for some time on the doorstep, not knowing what to do next. Then it occurred to me that I would go to your house and ask you what it all meant; for I had no doubt Mrs. Brederhagan was wrong, and that you were, indeed, Frank Montgomery, the printer. I found the house locked up and empty. A bill on the door showed that it was to rent, and referred inquirers to the corner grocery. They remembered me very well there. I asked them where you were. They did not know. Then I asked whether they were not agents for you to rent the house. Oh, no; you did not own the house. But had you not lived in it for years? No; you rented it the very morning of the same day we moved in. I was astounded, and more perplexed than ever. What did it all mean? If you did not own the house and had not been born in it, or lived there all your life, as you said, then the rest of your story was probably false also, and the name you bore was assumed. And for what purpose? And why did you move into that house the same day we rented it from you? It looked like a scheme to entrap us; and yet you had always been so kind and good that I could not think evil of you. Then it occurred to me that I would go and see Peter Bingham, the proprietor of the theater. I desired, anyhow, to tell him that I thought I would recover my voice, and that I might want another engagement with him after awhile. When I met him I fancied there was a shade of insolence in his manner. When I spoke of singing again he laughed, and said he guessed I would never want to go on the boards again. Why? I asked. Then he laughed again, and said "Mr. Phillips would not let me;" and then he began to abuse you, and said you

"had forced him to give me fifty dollars a week for
my singing when it wasn't worth ten dollars; but he
understood then what it all meant, and that now
every one understood it;—that you had lived in the
same house with me for months, and now you had
purchased a cage for your bird in the country." At
first I could not understand what he meant; and when
at last I comprehended his meaning and burst into
tears, he began to apologize; but I would not listen
to him, and hurried home and told everything to
papa and mamma.

"'Now,' she continued, looking me steadily in the
face with her frank, clear eyes, 'we have talked it all
over for hours, and we have come to several conclusions. First, you are not Francis Montgomery, but
Arthur Phillips; second, you are not a poor printer,
but a rich young gentleman; third, you have done
me a great many kindnesses and attributed them to
others. You secured me a large salary from Bingham; you made Mrs. Brederhagan settle an income
upon me; you nursed me through all my sickness,
with the tenderness of a brother, and you have
bought this beautiful place and presented it to papa.
You have done us all nothing but good; and you
claimed no credit for it; and we shall all be grateful to you and honor you and pray for you to the
end of our lives. But,' and here she took my hand
as a sister might, 'but we cannot keep this place.
You will yourself see that we cannot. You a poor
printer, we met on terms of equality. From a rich
young gentleman this noble gift would be universally
considered as the price of my honor and self-respect.
It is so considered already. The deed of gift from
Mrs. Brederhagan I shall avail myself of until I am

able to resume my place on the stage; but here is a deed, signed by my father and mother, for this place, and to-morrow we must leave it. We may not meet again'—and here the large eyes began to swim in tears—'but—but—I shall never forget your goodness to me.'

"'Christina,' I said, 'suppose I had really been Frank Montgomery, the printer, would you have driven me away from you thus?'

"'Oh! no! no!' she cried; 'you are our dearest and best friend. And I do not drive you away. I must leave *you*. The world can have only one interpretation of the relation of two people so differently situated—a very wealthy young gentleman and a poor little singer, the daughter of a poor, foreign-born workman.'

"'Well, then,' said I, taking her in my arms, 'let the blabbing, babbling old world know that that poor little singer sits higher in my heart, yes, in my brain and judgment, than all the queens and princesses of the world. I have found in her the one inestimable jewel of the earth—a truly good and noble woman. If I deceived you it was because I loved you; loved you with my whole heart and soul and all the depths of my being. I wanted to dwell in the same house with you; to study you; to see you always near me. I was happier when I was nursing you through your sickness than I have ever been before or since. I was sorry, to tell the truth, when you got well, and were no longer dependent on me. And now, Christina, if you will say yes, we will fix the day for the wedding.'

"I knew as soon as I began to speak that I had won my case. There was no struggle to escape from my arms; and, as I went on, she relaxed even her rigidity, and reposed on my breast with trusting confidence.

"'Frank,' she said, not looking up, and speaking in a low tone—'I shall always call you Frank—I loved the poor printer from the very first; and if the rich man can be content with the affection I gave the poor one, my heart and life are yours. But stop,' she added, looking up with an arch smile, 'you must not forget the promise you made me about New Year's day!'

"'Ah, my dear,' I replied, 'that was part of poor Frank's character, and I suppose that is what you loved him for; but if you *will* marry a rich man you must be content to forego all those attractions of the poor, foolish printer. I shall not stand up next New Year's day and make a vow to drink no more; but I make a vow now to kiss the sweetest woman in the world every day in the year.'

"And, lest I should forget so sacred an obligation, I began to put my vow into execution right then and there.

"Afterward the old folks were called in, and I told them my whole story. And I said to them, moreover, that there was storm and danger ahead; that the great convulsion might come any day; and so it is agreed that we are to be married, at Christina's home, the day after to-morrow. And to-morrow I want my dear mother, and you, my dear friends, to go with me to visit the truest and noblest little woman that ever promised to make a man happy."

When Max had finished his long story, his mother kissed and cried over him; and Estella and I shook hands with him; and we were a very happy party; and no one would have thought, from our jests and laughter, that the bloodhounds of the aristocracy were hunting for three of us, and that we were sitting under the dark presaging shadow of a storm that was ready to vomit fire and blood at any moment.

Before we retired that night Estella and I had a private conference, and I fear that at the end of it I made the same astonishing vow which Max had made to Christina. And I came to another surprising conclusion—that is, that no woman is worth worshiping unless she is worth wooing. But what I said to Estella, and what she said to me, will never be revealed to any one in this world;—the results, however, will appear hereafter, in this veracious chronicle.

CHAPTER XXIX

ELYSIUM.

IT was a bright and sunny autumn day. We were a very happy party. Estella was disguised with gold spectacles, a black wig and a veil, and she looked like some middle-aged school-teacher out for a holiday. We took the electric motor to a station one mile and a half from Mr. Jansen's, and walked the rest of the way. The air was pure and sweet and light; it seemed to be breathed right out of heaven. The breezes touched us and dallied with us and delighted us, like ministering angels. The whole panoply of nature was magnificent; the soft-hued, grassy fields; the embowered trees; the feeding cattle; the children playing around the houses;—

> "Clowns cracking jokes, and lasses with sly eyes,
> And the smile settling on their sun-flecked cheeks
> Like noon upon the mellow apricot."

My soul rose upon wings and swam in the ether like a swallow; and I thanked God that he had given us this majestic, this beautiful, this surpassing world, and had placed within us the delicate sensibility and capability to enjoy it. In the presence of such things death—annihilation—seemed to me impossible, and I exclaimed aloud:

> "Hast thou not heard
> That thine existence, here on earth, is but
> The dark and narrow section of a life
> Which was with God, long ere the sun was lit,
> And shall be yet, when all the bold, bright stars
> Are dark as death-dust?"

18   273

And oh, what a contrast was all this to the clouded world we had left behind us, in yonder close-packed city, with its poverty, its misery, its sin, its injustice, its scramble for gold, its dark hates and terrible plots. But, I said to myself, while God permits man to wreck himself, he denies him the power to destroy the world. The grass covers the graves; the flowers grow in the furrows of the cannon balls; the graceful foliage festoons with blossoms the ruins of the prison and the torture-chamber; and the corn springs alike under the foot of the helot or the yeoman. And I said to myself that, even though civilization should commit suicide, the earth would still remain—and with it some remnant of mankind; and out of the uniformity of universal misery a race might again arise worthy of the splendid heritage God has bestowed upon us.

Mr. Jansen had closed up his forge in honor of our visit, and had donned a new broadcloth suit, in which he seemed as comfortable as a whale in an overcoat. Christina ran out to meet us, bright and handsome, all in white, with roses in her curly hair. The sweet-faced old lady took her to her arms, and called her "my daughter," and kissed her, and expressed her pleasure that her son was about to marry so good and noble a girl. Mrs. Jansen held back modestly at first, a little afraid of "the great folks," but she was brought forward by Christina, and introduced to us all. And then we had to make the acquaintance of the whole flock of blue-eyed, curly-haired, rosy-cheeked little ones, gay in white dresses and bright ribbons. Even Master Ole forgot, for a time, his enrapturing hammer and nails, and stood, with eyes like saucers, contemplating the irruption of outside barbarians. We went into the house, and there, with many a laugh and jest, the spectacled school-teacher was transformed into my own bright and happy Estella. The two girls flowed into one another, by natural affinity, like a couple of drops of quicksilver; each recognized the transparent soul in the other, and in a moment they were friends for life.

We were a jolly party. Care flew far away from us, and many a laugh and jest resounded.

"There is one thing, Christina," said Max, "that I cannot comprehend, and of which I demand an explanation. Your name is 'Christina Jansen,' and yet you appeared in public by the name of 'Christina Carlson.' Now I refuse to marry you until this thing is explained; for I may be arrested and charged with bigamy for marrying two women at once! I am willing to wed 'Christina Jansen'—but what am I to do with 'Christina Carlson'? I could be 'happy with either were t'other dear charmer away.'"

Christina laughed and blushed and said:

"If you do not behave yourself you shall not have either of the Christinas. But I will tell you, my dear friend, how that happened. You must know that in our Sweden, especially in the northern part of it, where father and mother came from, we are a very primitive people—far 'behind the age,' you will say. And there we have no family names, like Brown or Jones or Smith; but each man is simply the son of his father, and he takes his father's first name. Thus if 'Peter' has a son and he is christened 'Ole,' then he is 'Ole Peterson,' or Ole the son of Peter; and if his son is called 'John,' then he is 'John Oleson.' I think, from what I have read in the books you gave me, Frank, that the same practice prevailed, centuries ago, in England, and that is how all those English names, such as Johnson, Jackson, Williamson, etc., came about. But the females of the family, in Sweden, are called 'daughters' or 'dotters;' and hence, by the custom of my race, I am 'Christina Carl's Dotter.' And when Mr. Bingham asked me my name to print on his play bills, that is what I answered him; but he said 'Christina Carl's Dotter' was no name at all. It would never do; and so he called me 'Christina Carlson.' There you have the explanation of the whole matter."

"I declare," said Frank, "this thing grows worse and worse! Why, there are three of you. I shall have to wed not only 'Christina Jansen,' and 'Christina Carlson,' but 'Christina Carl's Dotter.' Why, that would be not only bigamy, but *trigamy!*"

And then Estella came to the rescue, and said that she felt sure that Max would be glad to have her even if there were a dozen of her.

And Frank, who had become riotous, said to me:

"You see, old fellow, you are about to marry a girl with a pedigree, and I another without one."

"No," said Christina, "I deny that charge; with us the very name we bear declares the pedigree. I am 'Christina Carl's Dotter,' and 'Carl' was the son of 'John,' who was the son of 'Frederick,' who was the son of 'Christian;' and so on for a hundred generations. I have a long pedigree; and I am very proud of it; and, what is more, they were all good, honest, virtuous people." And she heightened up a bit. And then Frank kissed her before us all, and she boxed his ears, and then dinner was announced.

And what a pleasant dinner it was: the vegetables, crisp and fresh, were from their own garden; and the butter and milk and cream and schmearkase from their own dairy; and the fruit from their own trees; and the mother told us that the pudding was of Christina's own making; and thereupon Frank ate more of it than was good for him; and everything was so neat and bright, and everybody so happy; and Frank vowed that there never was before such luscious, golden butter; and Mrs. Jansen told us that that was the way they made it in Sweden, and she proceeded to explain the whole process. The only unhappy person at the table, it seemed to me, was poor Carl, and he had a wretched premonition that he was certainly going to drop some of the food on that brand-new broadcloth suit of his. I feel confident that when we took our departure he hurried to take off that overwhelming grandeur, with very much the feeling with which the dying saint shuffles off the mortal coil, and soars to heaven.

But then, in the midst of it all, there came across me the dreadful thought of what was to burst upon the world in a few days; and I could have groaned aloud in anguish of spirit. I felt we were like silly sheep gamboling on the edge of the volcano. But why not? We had not brought the world to this pass. Why should we not enjoy the sunshine, and that glorious light, brighter than all sunshine—the love of woman? For God alone, who made woman—the true woman—knows the infinite capacities for good which he has inclosed within her soul. And I don't believe one bit of that orthodox story. I think Eve ate the apple to obtain knowledge, and Adam devoured the core because he was hungry.

And these thoughts, of course, were suggested by my looking at Estella. She and Christina were in a profound conference; the two shades of golden hair mingling curiously as they whispered to each other, and blushed and laughed. And then Estella came over to me, and smiled and blushed again, and whispered: "Christina is delighted with the plan."

And then I said to Max, in a dignified, solemn way:

"My dear Max, or Frank, or Arthur, or whatever thy name may be—and 'if thou hast no other name to call thee by I will call thee devil'—I have observed, with great regret, that thou art very much afraid of standing up to-morrow and encountering in wedlock's ceremony the battery of bright eyes of the three Christinas. Now I realize that a friend should not only 'bear a friend's infirmities,' but that he should stand by him in the hour of danger; and so to-morrow, 'when fear comes down upon you like a house,' Estella and I have concluded to stand with you, in the imminent deadly breach, and share your fate; and if, when you get through, there are any of the Christinas left, I will—with Estella's permission— even marry them myself! For I am determined that such good material shall not go to waste."

There was a general rejoicing, and Max embraced me; and then he hugged Christina; and then I took advantage of the excuse—I was very happy in finding such excuses—to do likewise by my stately beauty; and then there was hand-shaking by the old folks all around, and kisses from the little folks.

Not long afterward there was much whispering and laughing between Christina and Estella; they were in the garden; they seemed to be reading some paper, which they held between them. And then that scamp, Max, crept quietly behind them, and, reaching over, snatched the paper out of their hands. And then Estella looked disturbed, and glanced at me and blushed; and Max began to dance and laugh, and cried out, "Ho! ho! we have a poet in the family!" And then I realized that some verses, which I had given Estella the day before, had fallen into the hands of that mocker. I would not give much for a man who does not grow poetical when he is making love. It is to man what song is to the bird. But to have one's weaknesses exposed—that is another matter! And so I ran after Max; but in vain. He climbed into a tree, and then began to recite my love poetry:

"Listen to this," he cried; "here are fourteen verses; each one begins and ends with the word '*thee.*' Here's a sample:

> "'All thought, all fear, all grief, all earth, all air,
>   Forgot shall be;
>   Knit unto each, to each kith, kind and kin,—
>   Life, like these rhyming verses, shall begin
>   And end in—*thee!*'

"And here," he cried, "is another long poem. Phœbus! what a name—'*Artesian Waters!*'

Here Christina, Estella and I pelted the rogue with apples.

"I know why they are called 'Artesian Waters,'" he cried; "it is because it took a great *bore* to produce them. Ha! ha! But listen to it:

> "'There is a depth at which perpetual springs
>   Fresh water, in all lands:
>   The which once reached, the buried torrent flings
>   Its treasures o'er the sands.'

"Ouch!" he cried, "that one hit me on the nose: I mean the apple, not the verse.

> "'One knows not how, beneath the dark, deep crust,
>   The clear flood there has come:
> One knows not why, amid eternal dust,
>   Slumbers that sea of foam.'

"Plain enough," he cried, dodging the apples; "the attraction of gravitation did the business for it.

> "'Dark-buried, sepulchred, entombed and deep,
>   Away from mortal ken,
> It lies, till, summoned from its silent sleep,
>   It leaps to light again.'

"Very good," he said, "and now here comes the application, the moral of the poem.

> "'So shall we find no intellect so dull,
>   No soul so cold to move,
> No heart of self or sinfulness so full,
>   But still hath power to love.'

"Of course," he said; "he knows how it is himself; the poet fills the bill exactly.

> "'It lives immortal, universal all,
>   The tenant of each breast;
> Locked in the silence of unbroken thrall,
>   And deep and pulseless rest;
> Till, at a touch, with burst of power and pride,
>   Its swollen torrents roll,
> Dash all the trappings of the mind aside,
>   And ride above the soul.'

"Hurrah!" he cried, "that's splendid! But here's some more: '*To Estella.*'"

But I could stand no more, and so began to climb the tree. It was an apple-tree, and not a very big one at that, and Max was forced to retreat out upon a limb, and then drop to the ground. But the young ladies were too quick for him; they pounced upon him as he fell; and very soon my precious verses were hidden in Estella's bosom, whence, in a burst of confidence and pride, they had been taken to exhibit to Christina.

"Yes," said Estella, it was nothing but mean jealousy, because he could not write such beautiful poetry to Christina.

"Exactly," said Christina, "and I think I will refuse to marry him until he produces some verses equally fine."

"Before I would write such poetry as that," said Max, "I would go and hang myself."

"No man ought to be allowed to marry," said Estella, "until he has written a poem."

"If you drive Max to that," I said, "other people will hang themselves rather than hear his verses."

And thus, with laugh and jest and badinage, the glorious hours passed away.

It was growing late; but we could not go until we had seen the cows milked, for that was a great event in the household; and "Bossy" especially was a wonderful cow. Never before in the world had there been such a cow as "Bossy." The children had tied some ribbons to her horns, and little Ole was astride of her broad back, his chubby legs pointing directly to the horizon, and the rest of the juveniles danced around her; while the gentle and patient animal stood chewing her cud, with a profound look upon her peaceful face, much like that of a chief-justice considering "the rule in Shelley's case," or some other equally solemn and momentous subject.

And I could not help but think how kindly we

should feel toward these good, serviceable ministers to man; for I remembered how many millions of our race had been nurtured through childhood and maturity upon their generous largess. I could see, in my imagination, the great bovine procession, lowing and moving, with their bleating calves trotting by their side, stretching away backward, farther and farther, through all the historic period; through all the conquests and bloody earth-staining battles, and all the sin and suffering of the race; and far beyond, even into the dim, pre-historic age, when the Aryan ancestors of all the European nations dwelt together under the same tents, and the blond-haired maidens took their name of "daughters" (the very word we now use) from their function of milk-maidens. And it seemed to me that we should love a creature so intimately blended with the history of our race, and which had done so much, indirectly, to give us the foundation on which to build civilization.

But we must away; and Carl, glad to do something in scenes in which he was not much fitted to shine, drove us to the station in his open spring wagon; Estella, once more the elderly, spectacled maiden, by my side; and the sunny little Christina beside Max's mother—going to the station to see us off; while that gentleman, on the front seat, talked learnedly with Carl about the pedigree of the famous horse "Lightning," which had just trotted its mile in less than two minutes.

And I thought, as I looked at Carl, how little it takes to make a happy household; and what a beautiful thing the human race is under favorable circumstances; and what a wicked and cruel and utterly abominable thing is the man who could oppress it, and drive it into the filth of sin and shame.

I will not trouble you, my dear brother, by giving you a detailed account of the double marriage the next day. The same person married us both—a Scandinavian preacher, a friend of the Jansen family. I was not very particular who tied the knot and signed the bill of sale of Estella, provided I was sure the title was good. But I do think that the union of man and wife should be something more than a mere civil contract. Marriage is not a partnership to sell dry goods—(sometimes, it is true, it is principally an obligation to buy them)—or to practice medicine or law together; it is, or should be, an intimate blending of two souls, and natures, and lives; and where the marriage is happy and perfect there is, undoubtedly, a growing-together, not only of spirit and character, but even in the physical appearance of man and wife. Now as these two souls came—we concede—out of heaven, it seems to me that the ceremony which thus destroys their individuality, and blends them into one, should have some touch and color of heaven in it also.

It was a very happy day.

As I look back upon it now it seems to me like one of those bright, wide rays of glorious light which we have sometimes seen bursting through a rift in the clouds, from the setting sun, and illuminating, for a brief space of time, the black, perturbed and convulsed sky. One of our poets has compared it to—

"A dead soldier's sword athwart his pall."

But it faded away, and the storm came down, at last, heavy and dark and deadly.

CHAPTER XXX.

A FEW days after our joint wedding Max came running in one day, and said:

"It is to be to-morrow."

He gave each of us a red cross to sew upon our clothes. He was very much excited, and hurried out again.

I had said to him, the morning of our marriage, that I desired to return home before the outbreak came, for I was now responsible for Estella's life and safety; and I feared that all communication of one part of the world with another would be cut off by the threatened revolution. He had begged me to remain. He said that at the interview with General Quincy it had been made a condition of the contract that each of the executive committee — Cæsar, the vice-president and himself — should have one of the flying air-ships placed at his disposal, after the outbreak, well manned and equipped with bombs and arms of all kinds. These "Demons" were to be subject to their order at any time, and to be guarded by the troops at their magazine in one of the suburbs until called for.

The committee had several reasons for making this arrangement: the outbreak might fail and they would have to fly; or the outbreak might succeed, but become ungovernable, and they would have to escape from the tempest they had themselves invoked. Max had always had a dream that after the Plutocracy was overthrown the insurgents would reconstruct a purer and better state of society; but of late my conversations with him, and his own observations, had begun to shake his faith in this particular.

He said to me that if I remained he would guarantee the safety of myself and wife, and after I had seen the outbreak he would send me home in his airship; and moreover, if he became satisfied that the revolution had passed beyond the control of himself and friends, he would, after rescuing his father from the prison where he was confined, accompany me with his whole family, and we would settle down together in my distant mountain home. He had, accordingly, turned all his large estate into gold and silver, which he had brought to the house; and I had likewise filled one large room full of a great library of books, which I had purchased to take with me— literature, science, art, encyclopedias, histories, philosophies, in fact all the treasures of the world's genius—together with type, printing presses, telescopes, phonographs, photographic instruments, electrical apparatus, eclesions, phemasticons, and all the other great inventions which the last hundred years have given us. For, I said to myself, if civilization utterly perishes in the rest of the world, there, in the mountains of Africa, shut out from attack by rocks and ice-topped mountains, and the cordon of tropical barbarians yet surrounding us, we will wait until exhausted and prostrate mankind is ready to listen to us and will help us reconstruct society upon a wise and just basis.

In the afternoon Max returned, bringing with him

Carl Jansen and all his family. A dozen men also came, bearing great boxes. They were old and trusted servants of his father's family; and the boxes contained magazine rifles and pistols and fixed ammunition, together with hand-grenades. These were taken out, and we were all armed. Even the women had pistols, and knives strapped to their girdles. The men went out and again returned, bearing quantities of food, sufficient to last us during a siege, and also during our flight to my home. Water was also collected in kegs and barrels, for the supply might be cut of. Then Max came, and under his orders, as soon as night fell, the lower windows, the cellar openings and the front door were covered with sheathings of thick oak plank, of three thicknesses, strongly nailed; then the second story windows were similarly protected, loop-holes being first bored, through which our rifles could be thrust, if necessary. Then the upper windows were also covered in the same way. The back door was left free for ingress and egress through the yard and back street, but powerful bars were arranged across it, and the oak plank left ready to board it up when required. The hand-grenades — there were a pile of them — were carried up to the flat roof. Then one of the men went out and painted red crosses on the doors and windows.

We ate our supper in silence. A feeling of awe was upon all of us. Every one was told to pack up his goods and valuables and be ready for instant flight when the word was given; and to each one were assigned the articles he or she was to carry.

About ten o'clock Max returned and told us all to come up to the roof. The house stood, as I have already said, upon a corner; it was in the older part of the city, and not far from where the first great battle would be fought. Max whispered to me that the blow would be struck at six o'clock in Europe and at twelve o'clock at night in America. The fighting therefore had already begun in the Old World. He further explained to me something of the plan of battle. The Brotherhood at twelve would barricade a group of streets in which were the Sub-Treasury of the United States, and all the principal banks, to-wit: Cedar, Pine, Wall, Nassau, William, Pearl and Water Streets. Two hundred thousand men would be assembled to guard these barricades. They would then burst open the great moneyed institutions and blow up the safes with giant powder and Hecla powder. At daybreak one of Quincy's air-ships would come and receive fifty millions of the spoils in gold, as their share of the plunder, and the price of their support. As soon as this was delivered, and carried to their armory, the whole fleet of air-vessels would come up and attack the troops of the Oligarchy. If, however, General Quincy should violate his agreement, and betray them, they had provided a large number of great cannon, mounted on high wheels, so that they could be fired vertically, and these were to be loaded with bombs of the most powerful explosives known to science, and so constructed with fulminating caps that, if they struck the air-ship at any point, they would explode and either destroy it or so disarrange its machinery as to render it useless. Thus they were provided, he thought, for every emergency.

At eleven he came to me and whispered that if anything happened to him he depended on me to take his wife and mother and his father, if possible, with me to Africa. I grasped his hand and assured him of my devotion. He then embraced Christina and his mother and left them, weeping bitterly, in each other's arms.

There was a parapet around the roof. I went to the corner of it, and, leaning over, looked down into the street. Estella came and stood beside me. She was very calm and quiet. The magnetic lights yet burned, and the streets below me were almost as bright as day. There were comparatively few persons moving about. Here and there a carriage, or a man on horseback, dashed furiously past, at full speed; and I thought to myself, "The Oligarchy have heard of the tremendous outbreak in Europe, and are making preparations for another here." It was a still, clear night; and the great solemn stars moved over the face of heaven unconscious or indifferent as to what was going forward on this clouded little orb.

I thought it must be nearly twelve. I drew out my watch to look at the time. It lacked one minute of that hour. Another instant, and the whole city was wrapped in profound darkness. Some of the workmen about the Magnetic Works were members of the Brotherhood, and, in pursuance of their orders, they had cut the connections of the works and blotted out the light.

CHAPTER XXXI.

"SHEOL."

I LOOKED down into the dark street. I could see nothing; but immediately a confused buzz and murmur, of motion everywhere, arose from the depths below me. As it grew louder and clearer I could hear the march of thousands of feet, moving rapidly; and then a number of wagons, heavily loaded, creaked and groaned over the pavements. I surmised that these wagons were loaded with stones, and were to be used in the construction of the barricades. There was no music, no shouting, not even the sound of voices; but tramp, tramp, tramp, in endless multitude, the heavy feet went by; and now and then, where the light yet streamed out of the window of some house, I could see the glitter of the steel barrels of rifles; and here and there I caught a glimpse of men on horseback, officers apparently, but dressed in the rough garb of workmen. Along the line of the houses near me, I could see, at opened, lighted windows, an array of pale faces, looking out with astonishment and terror at this dark and silent procession, which seemed to have arisen out of the earth, and was so vast that one might dream that the trumpet of the archangel had been blown, and all the dead of a thousand battle-fields had risen up for one last grand review. And not alone past our doors, but through all the streets near us, the same mighty, voiceless procession moved on; all converging to the quarter where the treasures of the great city lay, heaped up in safe and vault.

And then, several blocks away, but within the clear range of my vision, a light appeared in the street—it blazed—it rose higher and higher. I could see shadowy figures moving around it, heaping boxes, barrels and other combustibles upon the flame. It was a bonfire, kindled to light the work of building a barricade at that point. Across the street a line of wagons had been placed; the tail of each one touching the front of another, the horses having been withdrawn. And then hundreds of busy figures were to be seen at work, tearing up the pavements of the street and heaping the materials under the wagons; and then shovels flew, and the earth rose over it all; a deep ditch being excavated quite across the street, on the side near me. The men, lit by the red light, looked, at the distance, like hordes of busy black insects. Behind them swarmed, as far as I could see, thousands upon thousands of dark forms, mere masses, touched here and there by the light of the bonfire, gleaming on glittering steel. They were the men within the barricades. There was a confused noise in other quarters, which I supposed was caused by the erection of a number of similar barricades elsewhere. Then the tramp of the marching masses past our doors ceased; and for a time the silence was profound.

So far not a soldier or policeman had been visible. The Oligarchy were evidently carrying out the plan of the Prince of Cabano. They were permitting the insurgents to construct their "rat-trap" without interruption. Only a few stragglers were upon the street, drawn there doubtless by curiosity; and still the pale faces were at the windows; and some even talked from window to window, and wondered what it all meant.

Suddenly there was a terrific explosion that shook the house. I could see a shower of stones and brick and timbers and dust, rising like a smoke, seamed with fire, high in the air, within the lines of the barricades. Then came another, even louder; then another, and another, and another, until it sounded like a bombardment. Then these ceased, and after a little time came the sounds of smaller explosions, muffled as if under ground or within walls.

"They are blowing open the banks," I whispered to Estella.

Then all was quiet for a space. In a little while the bombardment began again, as if in another part of the territory inclosed in the barricades.

And still there was not a soldier to be seen in the deserted streets near me.

And again came other explosions.

At last I saw the red light beginning to touch the clouds along the eastern horizon with its crimson brush. The fateful day was dawning.

And then, in a little while, far away to the north, soft and dull at first, but swelling gradually into greater volume, a mighty sound arose; and through it I could hear bursts of splendid melody, rising and falling and fluttering, like pennons, above the tumult; and I recognized the notes of that grand old Scotch air, "The Campbells are Coming."

It was the defenders of society advancing with the swinging step of assured triumph.

Oh, it was a splendid sight! In all the bravery of banners, and uniforms, and shining decorations, and amidst the majestic and inspiriting outpouring of music, they swept along, the thousands moving as one. How they did contrast with that gloomy, dark, ragged, sullen multitude who had preceded them. And with them came, rattling along, multitudes of those dreadful machine guns—those cataracts of fire and death—drawn by prancing, well-fed, shining horses. And the lips of the gunners were set for carnage; for they had received orders *to take no prisoners!* The world was to be taught a lesson to-day—a bloody and an awful lesson. Ah! little did they think how it would be taught!

In the gray light of the breaking day they came —an endless multitude. And all the windows were white with waving handkerchiefs, and the air stormy with huzzas and cries of "God bless you." And at the head of every column, on exuberant steeds, that seemed as if they would leap out of their very skins with the mere delight of living, rode handsome officers, smiling and bowing to the ladies at the windows;—for was it not simply holiday work to slay the *canaille*—the insolent *canaille*—the unreasonable dogs—who demanded some share in the world's delights—who were not willing to toil and die that others might live and be happy? And the very music had a revengeful, triumphant ring and sting to it, as if every instrument cried out: "Ah, we will give it to them!"

But it was splendid! It was the very efflorescence of the art of war—the culmination of the evolution of destruction—the perfect flower of ten thousand years of battle and blood.

But I heard one officer cry out to another, as they passed below me:

"What's the matter with the Demons? Why are they not here?"

"I can't say," replied the one spoken to; "but they will be here in good time."

The grand and mighty stream of men poured on. They halted close to the high barricade. It was a formidable structure at least fifteen feet high and many feet in thickness. The gray of dawn had turned into red, and a pale, clear light spread over all nature. I heard some sparrows, just awakened, twittering and conversing in a tall tree near me. They, too, wondered, doubtless, what it all meant, and talked it over in their own language.

The troops deployed right and left, and soon the insurgent mass was closely surrounded in every direction and every outlet closed. The "rat-trap" was set. Where were the rat-killers? I could see many a neck craned, and many a face lifted up, looking toward the west, for their terrible allies of the air. But they came not.

There was a dead pause. It was the stillness before the thunder.

CHAPTER XXXII.

THE RAT-TRAP.

SOME of the troops advanced toward the barricade. Instantly the long line of its top bristled with
fire; the fire was returned; the rattle was continuous and terrible, mingled with the rapid, grinding
noise of the machine guns. The sound spread in
every direction. The barricades were all attacked.

Suddenly the noise began to decrease. It was as
if some noble orator had begun to speak in the
midst of a tumultuous assembly. Those nearest
him catch his utterances first, and become quiet; the
wave of silence spreads like a great ripple in the
water; until at last the whole audience is as hushed
as death. So something— some extraordinary
thing — had arrested the battle; down, down,
dropped the tumult; and at last there were only a
few scattering shots to be heard, here and there; and
then these, too, ceased.

I could see the soldiers looking to the west. I
swept the sky with my glass. Yes, something portentous had indeed happened! Instead of the whole
dark flight of thousands of air-ships for which the
soldiers had been looking, there came, athwart the
sky, like a great black bird, a single Demon.

As it approached it seemed to be signaling some
one. Little flags of different colors were run up and
taken down. I turned and looked to the barricaded
district. And there on the top of a very high build-

ing, in its midst, I could see a group of men. They, too, were raising and lowering little flags. Nearer and nearer swept the great bird; every eye and many a field-glass in all that great throng were fastened upon it, with awe-struck interest—the insurgents rejoicing; the soldiers perplexed. Nearer and nearer it comes.

Now it pauses right over the tall building; it begins to descend, like a sea-gull about to settle in the waves. Now it is but a short distance above the roof. I could see against the bright sky the gossamer traces of a rope ladder, falling down from the ship to the roof. The men below take hold of it and steady it. A man descends. Something about him glitters in the rising sun. He is probably an officer. He reaches the roof. They bow and shake hands. I can see him wave his hand to those above him. A line of men descend; they disappear in the building; they reappear; they mount the ladder; again and again they come and go.

"They are removing the treasure," I explain to our party, gathering around me.

Then the officer shakes hands again with the men on the roof; they bow to each other; he reascends the ladder; the air-ship rises in the air, higher and higher, like an eagle regaining its element; and away it sails, back into the west.

An age of bribery terminates in one colossal crime of corruption!

I can see the officers gathering in groups and taking counsel together. They are alarmed. Then they write. They must tell the Oligarchy of this singular scene, and their suspicions, and put them on their guard. There is danger in the air. In a moment orderlies dash down the street in headlong race, bearing dispatches. In a little while they come back, hurrying, agitated. I look to the north. I can see a black line across the street. It is a high barricade. It has been quietly constructed while the fight raged. And beyond, far as my eyes can penetrate, there are dark masses of armed men.

The orderlies report—there is movement—agitation. I can see the imperious motions of an officer. I can read the signs. He is saying, "Back—back— for your lives! Break out through the side streets!" They rush away; they divide; into every street they turn. Alas! in a few minutes, like wounded birds, they come trailing back. There is no outlet. Every street is blockaded, barricaded, and filled with huge masses of men. *The rat-trap has another rat-trap outside of it!*

The Oligarchy will wait long for those dispatches. They will never read them this side of eternity. The pear has ripened. The inevitable has come. The world is about to shake off its masters.

There is dead silence. Why should the military renew the fight in the midst of the awful doubt that rests upon their souls?

Ah! we will soon know the best or worst; for, far away to the west, dark, portentous as a thunder-cloud—spread out like the wings of mighty armies— moving like a Fate over the bright sky, comes on the vast array of the Demons.

"Will they be faithful to their bargain?" I ask myself; "or will old loyalty and faith to their masters rise up in their hearts?"

No, no, it is a rotten age. Corruption sticks faster than love.

On they come! Thousands of them. They swoop, they circle; they pause above the insurgents. The soldiers rejoice! Ah, no! No bomb falls, a meteor of death. They separate; they move north, south, east, west; they are above the streets packed full of the troops of the government!

May God have mercy on them now! The sight will haunt me to my dying day. I can see, like a great black rain of gigantic drops, the lines of the falling bombs against the clear blue sky.

And, oh, my God! what a scene below, in those close-packed streets, among those gaily dressed multitudes! The dreadful astonishment! The crash — the bang — the explosions; the uproar, the confusion; and, most horrible of all, the inevitable, invisible death by the poison.

The line of the barricade is alive with fire. With my glass I can almost see the dynamite bullets exploding in the soldiers, tearing them to pieces, like internal volcanoes.

An awful terror is upon them. They surge backward and forward; then they rush headlong down the streets. The farther barricades open upon them a hail of death; and the dark shadows above — so well named Demons — slide slowly after them; and drop, drop, drop, the deadly missiles fall again among them.

Back they surge. The poison is growing thicker. They scream for mercy; they throw away their guns; they are panic-stricken. They break open the doors of houses and hide themselves. But even here the devilish plan of Prince Cabano is followed out to the very letter. The triumphant mob pour in through the back yards; and they bayonet the soldiers under beds, or in closets, or in cellars; or toss them, alive and shrieking, from windows or roofs, down into the deadly gulf below.

And still the bombs drop and crash, and drop and crash; and the barricades are furnaces of living fire. The dead lie in heaps and layers in the invisible, pernicious poison.

But, lo! the fire slackens; the bombs cease to fall; only now and then a victim flies out of the houses, cast into death. There is nothing left to shoot at. The grand army of the Plutocracy is annihilated; it is not.

"The Demons" moved slowly off. They had earned their money. The Mamelukes of the Air had turned the tables upon the Sultan. They retired to their armory, doubtless to divide the fifty millions equitably between them.

The mob stood still for a few minutes. They could scarcely realize that they were at last masters of the city. But quickly a full sense of all that their tremendous victory signified dawned upon them. The city lay prostrate, chained, waiting to be seized upon.

CHAPTER XXXIII.

"THE OCEAN OVERPEERS ITS LIST."

AND then all avenues were open. And like a huge flood, long dammed up, turbulent, turbid, muddy, loaded with wrecks and debris, the gigantic mass broke loose, full of foam and terror, and flowed in every direction. A foul and brutal and ravenous multitude it was, dark with dust and sweat, armed with the weapons of civilization, but possessing only the instincts of wild beasts.

At first they were under the control of some species of discipline and moved toward the houses of the condemned, of whom printed catalogues had been furnished the officers. The shouts, the yells, the delight were appalling.

Now and then some poor wretch, whose sole offense was that he was well-dressed, would take fright and start to run, and then, like hounds after a rabbit, they would follow in full cry; and when he was caught a hundred men would struggle to strike him, and he would disappear in a vortex of arms, clubs and bayonets, literally torn to pieces.

A sullen roar filled the air as this human cyclone moved onward, leaving only wrecks behind it. Now it pauses at a house. The captain consults his catalogue. "This is it," he cries; and doors and windows give way before the thunderous mob; and then the scenes are terrible. Men are flung headlong, alive, out of the windows to the ravenous wretches below; now a dead body comes whirling down; then the terrified inhabitants fly to the roofs, and are pursued from house to house and butchered in sight of the delighted spectators. But when the condemned man—the head of the house—is at last found, hidden perhaps in some coal-hole or cellar, and is brought up, black with dust, and wild with terror, his clothes half torn from his back; and he is thrust forth, out of door or window, into the claws of the wild beasts, the very heavens ring with acclamations of delight; and happy is the man who can reach over his fellows and know that he has struck the victim.

Then up and away for another vengeance. Before them is solitude; shops and stores and residences are closed and barricaded; in the distance teams are seen flying and men scurrying to shelter; and through crevices in shutters the horrified people peer at the mob, as at an invasion of barbarians.

Behind them are dust, confusion, dead bodies, hammered and beaten out of all semblance of humanity; and, worse than all, the criminal classes—that wretched and inexplicable residuum, who have no grievance against the world except their own existence — the base, the cowardly, the cruel, the sneaking, the inhuman, the horrible! These flock like jackals in the track of the lions. They rob the dead bodies; they break into houses; they kill if they are resisted; they fill their pockets. Their joy is unbounded. Elysium has descended upon earth for them this day. Pickpockets, sneak-thieves, confidence-men, burglars, robbers, assassins, the refuse and outpouring of grog-shops and brothels, all are here. And women, too—or creatures that pass for such—having the bodies of women and the habits of ruffians;—harpies—all claws and teeth and greed—bold—desperate—shameless—incapable of good. They, too, are here. They dart hither and thither; they swarm—they dance—they howl—they chatter—they quarrel and battle, like carrion-vultures, over the spoils.

Civilization is gone, and all the devils are loose! No more courts, nor judges, nor constables, nor prisons! That which it took the world ten thousand years to create has gone in an hour.

And still the thunderous cyclones move on through a hundred streets. Occasionally a house is fired; but this is not part of the programme, for they have decided to keep all these fine residences for themselves! They will be rich. They will do no more work. The rich man's daughters shall be their handmaidens; they will wear his purple and fine linen.

But now and then the flames rise up—perhaps a thief kindles the blaze—and it burns and burns; for who would leave the glorious work to put it out? It burns until the streets stop it and the block is consumed. Fortunately, or unfortunately, there is no wind to breed a general conflagration. The storms to-day are all on earth; and the powers of the air are looking down with hushed breath, horrified at the exceeding wickedness of the little crawlers on the planet we call men.

They do not, as a rule, steal. Revenge—revenge—is all their thought. And why should they steal? Is it not all their own? Now and then a too audacious thief is caught and stuck full of bayonets; or he is flung out of a window, and dies at the hands

of the mob the death of the honest man for whom
he is mistaken; and thus, by a horrible travesty of
fate, he perishes for that which he never was nor
could be.

Think of the disgust of a thief who finds himself
being murdered for an honest man, an aristocrat,
and can get no one to believe his asseverations
that he is simply and truly a thief—and nothing
more! It is enough to make Death grin!

The rude and begrimed insurgents are raised by
their terrible purposes to a certain dignity. They
are the avengers of time—the God-sent—the righters
of the world's wrongs—the punishers of the ineffably
wicked. They do not mean to destroy the world;
they will reform it—redeem it. They will make it a
world where there shall be neither toil nor oppression. But, poor fellows! their arms are more potent for evil than their brains for good. They are
omnipotent to destroy; they are powerless to create.

But still the work of ruin and slaughter goes on.
The mighty city, with its ten million inhabitants, lies
prostrate, chained, helpless, at the mercy of the
enraged *canaille*. The dogs have become lions.

The people cannot comprehend it. They look
around for their defenders—the police, the soldiery.
"Where are they? Will not this dreadful nightmare
pass away?" No; no; never—never. This is the
culmination—this is the climax—"the century's
aloe flowers to-day." These are "the grapes of
wrath" which God has stored up for the day of his
vengeance; and now he is trampling them out, and
this is the red juice—look you!—that flows so thick
and fast in the very gutters.

You were blind, you were callous, you were indifferent to the sorrows of your kind. The cry of the poor did not touch you, and every pitiful appeal wrung from human souls, every groan and sob and shriek of men and women, and the little starving children— starving in body and starving in brain—rose up and gathered like a great cloud around the throne of God; and now, at last, in the fullness of time, it has burst and comes down upon your wretched heads, a storm of thunderbolts and blood.

You had money, you had power, you had leisure, you had intelligence, you possessed the earth; all things were possible unto you. Did you say to one another: "These poor souls are our brethren. For them Christ died on Calvary. What can we do to make their lives bright and happy?" No; no; you cried out, "'On with the dance!' Let them go down into the bottomless pit!"

And you smiled and said to one another, in the words of the first murderer, when he lied to God: "Am I my brother's keeper?" Nay, you said further to one another, "There is no God!" For you thought, if there was one, surely He would not permit the injustice manifest in the world. But, lo! He is here. Did you think to escape him? Did you think the great Father of Cause and Effect—the All-knowing, the universe-building God,—would pass you by?

As you sowed, so must you reap. Evil has but one child—Death! For hundreds of years you have nursed and nurtured Evil. Do you complain if her monstrous progeny is here now, with sword and torch? What else did you expect? Did you think she would breed angels?

Your ancestors, more than two centuries ago, established and permitted Slavery. What was the cry of the bondman to them? What the sobs of the mother torn from her child—the wife from her husband—on the auction block? Who among them cared for the lacerated bodies, the shameful and hopeless lives? They were merry; they sang and they danced; and they said, "God sleeps."

But a day came when there was a corpse at every fireside. And not the corpse of the black stranger— the African—the slave;—but the corpses of fair, bright-faced men; their cultured, their manly, their noble, their best-beloved. And, North and South, they sat, rocking themselves to and fro, in the midst of the shards and ashes of desolation, crying aloud for the lives that would come back to bless them never, nevermore.

God wipes out injustice with suffering; wrong with blood; sin with death. You can no more get beyond the reach of His hand than you can escape from the planet.

CHAPTER XXXIV.

THE PRINCE GIVES HIS LAST BRIBE.

BUT it was when the mob reached the wealthier parts of the city that the horrors of the devastation really began. Here almost every grand house was the abode of one of the condemned. True, many of them had fled. But the cunning cripple—the vice-president—had provided for this too. At the railroad stations, at the bridges and ferries, even on the yachts of the princes, men were stationed who would recognize and seize them; and if they even escaped the dangers of the suburbs, and reached the country, there they found armed bands of desperate peasants, ranging about, slaying every one who did not bear on his face and person the traces of the same wretchedness which they themselves had so long endured. Nearly every rich man had, in his own household and among his own servants, some bitter foe, who hated him, and who had waited for this terrible day and followed him to the death.

The Prince of Cabano, through his innumerable spies, had early received word of the turn affairs had taken. He had hurriedly filled a large satchel with diamonds and other jewels of great value, and, slinging it over his shoulders, and arming himself with sword, knife and pistols, he had called Frederika to him (he had really some little love for his handsome concubine), and loading her pockets and his own with gold pieces, and taking her by the hand, he had fled in great terror to the river side. His fine yacht lay off in the stream. He called and shouted until he was hoarse, but no one replied from the vessel. He looked around. The wharves were deserted; the few boats visible were chained and padlocked to their iron rings. The master of many servants was helpless. He shouted, screamed, tore his hair, stamped and swore viciously. The man who had coolly doomed ten million human beings to death was horribly afraid he would have to die himself. He ran back, still clinging to Frederika, to hide in the thick shrubbery of his own garden; there, perhaps, he might find a faithful servant who would get him a boat and take him off to the yacht in safety.

But then, like the advancing thunder of a hurricane, when it champs the earth and tears the trees to pieces with its teeth, came on the awful mob.

Now it is at his gates. He buries himself and companion in a thick grove of cedars, and they crouch to the very ground. Oh, how humble is the lord of millions! How all the endowments of the world fall off from a man in his last extremity! He shivers, he trembles—yea, he prays! Through his bloodshot eyes he catches some glimpses of a God — of a merciful God who loves *all* his creatures. Even Frederika, though she has neither love nor respect for him, pities him, as the bloated mass lies shivering beside her. Can this be the same lordly gentleman, every hair of whose mustache bespoke empire and dominion, who a few days since plotted the abasement of mankind?

But, hark! the awful tumult. The crashing of glass, the breaking of furniture, the beating in of doors with axes; the *canaille* have taken possession of the palace. They are looking for him everywhere. They find him not.

Out into the grounds and garden; here, there, everywhere, they turn and wind and quarter, like bloodhounds that have lost the scent.

And then the Prince hears, quite near him, the piping voice of a little ragged boy—a bare-footed urchin—saying: "They came back from the river; they went in here." (He is one of the cripple's spies, set upon him to watch him.) "This way, this way!" And the next instant, like a charge of wild cattle, the mob bursts through the cedars, led by a gigantic and ferocious figure, black with dust and mantled with blood—the blood of others.

The Prince rose from his lair as the yell of the pursuers told he was discovered; he turned as if to run; his trembling legs failed him; his eyes glared wildly; he tried to draw a weapon, but his hand shook so it was in vain. The next instant there was a crack of a pistol in the hands of one of the mob. The ball struck the Prince in the back of the neck, even in the same spot where, a century before, the avenging bullet smote the assassin of the good President Lincoln. With a terrible shriek he fell down, and moaned in the most exquisite torture. His suffering was so great that, coward as he was, he cried out: 'Kill me! kill me!" A workman, stirred by a humane sentiment, stepped forward and pointed his pistol, but the cripple struck the weapon up.

"No, no," he said; "let him suffer for a few hours something of the misery he and his have inflicted on mankind during centuries. A thousand years of torture would not balance the account. The wound is mortal—his body is now paralyzed—only the sense of pain remains. The damned in hell do not suffer more. Come away."

But Cæsar had seen a prize worth pursuing. Frederika had risen, and when the Prince was shot she fled. Cæsar pursued her, crashing through the shrubbery like an enraged mammoth; and soon the cripple laughed one of his dreadful laughs—for he saw the giant returning, dragging the fair girl after him, by the hair of her head, as we have seen, in the pictures, ogres hauling off captured children to destruction.

And still the Prince lay upon his back; and still he shrieked and moaned and screamed in agony, and begged for death.

An hour passed, and there was dead silence save for his cries; the mob had swept off to new scenes of slaughter.

The Prince heard the crackling of a stick, and then a stealthy step. A thief, hunting for plunder, was approaching. The Prince, by a great effort, hushed his outcries.

"Come here," said he, as the pale, mean face peered at him curiously through the shrubbery. "Come nearer."

The thief stood close to him.

"Would you kill a man for a hundred thousand dollars?" asked the Prince.

The thief grinned, and nodded his head; it signified that he would commit murder for the hundred thousandth part of that sum.

"I am mortally wounded and in dreadful pain," growled the Prince, the suppressed sobs interrupting his speech. "If I tell you where you can find a hundred thousand dollars, will you drive my knife through my heart?"

"Yes," said the thief.

"Then take the knife," he said.

The thief did so, eying it rapaciously—for it was diamond-studded and gold-mounted.

"But," said the Prince—villain himself and anticipating all villainy in others,—"if I tell you where the money is you will run away to seek it, and leave me here to die a slow and agonizing death."

"No," said the thief; "I promise you on my honor."

A thief's honor!

"I tell you what you must do," said the Prince, after thinking a moment. "Kneel down and lean over me; put your arms around me; I cannot hold you with my hands, for they are paralyzed; but put the lapel of your coat between my teeth. I will then tell you where the treasure is; but I will hold on to you by my teeth until you kill me. You will have to slay me to escape from me."

The thief did as he was directed; his arms were around the Prince; the lapel of his coat was between the Prince's teeth; and then through his shut teeth, tight clenched on the coat, the Prince muttered:

"It is in the satchel beneath me."

Without a word the thief raised his right hand and drove the knife sidewise clear through the Prince's heart.

The last of the accumulations of generations of wrong and robbery and extortion and cruelty had sufficed to purchase their heritor a miserable death,—in the embrace of a thief!

CHAPTER XXXV.

THE LIBERATED PRISONER.

ABOUT two o'clock that day Maximilian returned
home. He was covered with dust and powder-smoke,
but there was no blood upon him. I did not see him
return; but when I entered the drawing-room I
started back. There was a stranger present. I could
not long doubt as to who he was. He was locked in
the arms of Max's mother. He was a pitiful sight.
A tall, gaunt man; his short hair and stubby beard
white as snow. He was prematurely aged—his
back was stooped—his pallid complexion reminded
one of plants grown in cellars; he had a dejected,
timorous look, like one who had long been at the
mercy of brutal masters; his hands were seamed and
calloused with hard work; he was without a coat,
and his nether garments had curious, tiger-like
stripes upon them. He was sobbing like a child in
the arms of his wife. He seemed very weak in body
and mind. Maximilian gave him a chair, and his
mother sat down by him, weeping bitterly, and holding the poor calloused hands in her own, and pat-
ting them gently, while she murmured words of comfort and rejoicing. The poor man looked bewildered,
as if he could not quite collect his faculties; and
occasionally he would glance anxiously at the door,
as if he expected that, at any moment, his brutal
masters would enter and take him back to his tasks.

"Gabriel," said Maximilian,—and his face was flushed and working,—"this is — or was — my father."

I took the poor hand in my own and kissed it, and spoke encouragingly to him. And this, I thought, was once a wealthy, handsome, portly, learned gentleman; a scholar and a philanthropist; and his only crime was that he loved his fellow-men! And upon how many such men have the prison doors of the world closed — never to open again?

They took him away to the bath; they fed him; they put upon him the clothes of a gentleman. He smiled in a childish way, and smoothed the fine cloth with his hands; and then he seemed to realize, for the first time, that he was, indeed, no longer a prisoner — that his jailers had gone out of his life forever.

"I must go now," said Maximilian, hurriedly; "I will be back this evening. I have a duty to perform."

He returned at nightfall. There was a terrible light in his eyes.

"I have avenged my father," he said to me, in a hoarse whisper. "Come this way."

He took me into the library, for he would not have the women hear the dreadful story. I shut the door. He said:

"I had made all the necessary arrangements to prevent the escape of the Count and his accomplices. I knew that he would fly, at the first alarm, to his yacht, which lies out in the harbor. He had ruined my father by bribery; so I brought his own instrument to bear upon him, and bribed, with a large sum, his confidential friend, who was in command of his vessel, to deliver him up to me. As I had anticipated, the cunning wretch fled to the yacht; they took him on board. Then they made him prisoner. He was shackled and chained to the mast. He begged for his life and liberty. He had brought a fortune with him in gold and jewels. He offered the whole of it to his *friend*, as a bribe, for he surmised what was coming. The faithful officer replied, as I had instructed him, that the Count could not offer that treasure, for he himself had already appropriated it to his own purposes. The miscreant had always had a lively sense of the power of money for evil; he saw it now in a new light—for he was penniless. After taking my father from the prison and bringing him home, I arranged as to the other prisoners and then went to the yacht. I introduced myself to the Count. I told him that I had deceived his spies—that I had led a double life; that I had joined the Brotherhood and had become one of its leading spirits, with but two objects:—to punish him and his villainous associates and to rescue my father. That, as they had destroyed my father for money, the same instruments should now destroy him, through fear. That they were all prisoners, and should die together a fearful death; but if they had a hundred lives they could not atone for the suffering they had caused one good and great-hearted man. They had compelled him, for years, to work in the society of the basest of his species—at work too hard for even a young and strong man; they had separated him from his family; they had starved his mind and heart and body; they had beaten and scourged him for the slightest offenses. He had suffered a thousand deaths. It would be no equivalent to simply kill them. They should die in prolonged agony. And as he—the

Count—had always gone upon the principle that it was right to work upon the weaknesses of others to accomplish his purposes, I should imitate him. I should not touch him myself.

"I then ordered the captain and his men to put him in the boat and carry him ashore.

"He begged and pleaded and abased himself; he entreated and shrieked; but he addressed hearts as hard as his own.

"On the river-bank were a body of my men. In the midst of them they had the other prisoners—the corrupt judge, eight of the jurymen—four had died since the trial—and the four lying witnesses. They were all shackled together. A notary public was present, and they signed and acknowledged their confessions, that they had been bribed to swear against my father and to convict him; and they even acknowledged, in their terror, the precise sums which they had received for their dreadful acts.

"'Spare me! spare me!' shrieked the Count, groveling on the ground; 'only part of that money came from me. I was but the instrument of the government. I was commanded to do as I did.'

"'The others have already gone to their account,' I replied, 'every man of them. You will overtake them in a little while.'

"I ordered the prisoners to chain him to a stout post which stood in the middle of one of the wharves. They were unshackled and did so with alacrity; my men standing around ready to shoot them down if they attempted to fly. The Count writhed and shrieked for help, but in a little while he was securely fastened to the post. There was a ship loaded with lumber lying beside the next wharf. I ordered them to bring the lumber; they quickly piled it up in great walls around him, within about ten feet of him; and then more and more was heaped around these walls. The Count began to realize the death that awaited him, and his screams were appalling. But I said to him:

"'O Count, be calm. This is not as bad as a sentence of twenty years in the penitentiary for an honest and innocent man. And, remember, my dear Count, how you have enjoyed yourself all these years, while my poor father has been toiling in prison in a striped suit. Think of the roast beef you have eaten and the wine you have consumed! And, moreover, the death you are about to die, my dear Count, was once fashionable and popular in the world; and many a good and holy man went up to heaven from just such a death-bed as you shall have—a death-bed of fire and ashes. And see, my good Count, how willingly these honest men, whom you hired, with your damnable money, to destroy my father—see how willingly they work to prepare your funeral pile! What a supple and pliant thing, O Count, is human baseness. It has but one defect— it may be turned upon ourselves! And then, O my dear Count, it shocks us and hurts our feelings. But say your prayers, Count, say your prayers. Call upon God, for He is the only one likely to listen to you now.'

"'Here,' I said to the judge, 'put a match to the pile.'"

"The miserable wretch, trembling and hoping to save his own life by his superserviceable zeal, got down upon his knees, and lighted a match, and puffed and blew to make the fire catch. At last it started briskly, and in a few minutes the Count was screaming in the center of a roaring furnace.

"I gave a preconcerted signal to my men. In the twinkling of an eye each of the prisoners was manacled hand and foot, shrieking and roaring for mercy.

"'It was a splendid joke, gentlemen,' I said to them, 'that you played on my father. To send that good man to prison, and to go home with the price of his honor and his liberty jingling in your pockets. It was a capital joke; and you will now feel the finest point of the witticism. In with them!'

"And high above the walls of fire they were thrown, and the briber and the bribed — the villain and his instruments — all perished howling together."

I listened, awestruck, to the terrible story. There was a light in Max's eyes which showed that long brooding over the wrongs of his father and the sight of his emaciated and wretched form had "worked like madness in his brain," until he was, as I had feared, a monomaniac, with but one idea — *revenge*.

"Max, dear Max," I said, "for Heaven's sake never let Christina or your mother hear that dreadful story. It was a madman's act! Never think of it again. You have wiped out the crime in blood; there let it end. And leave these awful scenes, or you will become a maniac."

He did not answer me for a time, but looked down thoughtfully; and then he glanced at me, furtively, and said:

"Is not revenge right? Is it not simply justice?"

"Perhaps so, in some sense," I replied; "and if you had killed those base wretches with your own hand the world could not have much blamed you.

Remember, however, 'Vengeance is mine, saith the Lord, and I will repay.' But to send them out of life by such dreadful tortures! It is too terrible."

"But death," he said, "is nothing; it is the mere end of life—perhaps of consciousness; and that is no atonement for years of suffering, every day of which was full of more agony than death itself can wring from the human heart."

"I will not argue with you, Max," I replied, "for you are wrong, and I love you; but do you not see, when a heart, the kindest in the world, could conceive and execute such a terrible revenge, that the condition of the mind is abnormal? But let us change the gloomy subject. The dreadful time has put 'tricks of desperation' in your brain. And it is not the least of the crimes of the Oligarchy that it could thus pervert honest and gentle natures, and turn them into savages. And that is what it has done with millions. It has fought against goodness, and developed wickedness."

CHAPTER XXXVI.

CÆSAR ERECTS HIS MONUMENT.

"WHAT other news have you?" I asked.

"The strangest you ever heard," replied Max.

"What is it?"

"Cæsar," said Max, "has fallen upon a scheme of the most frenzied and extraordinary kind."

"Are the members of the Executive Committee all going crazy together?" I asked.

"Surely," replied Max, "the terrible events we are passing through would be our excuse if we did. But you shall hear. After I had avenged my father I proceeded to find Cæsar. I heard from members of the Brotherhood, whom I met on the streets, that he was at Prince Cabano's palace. I hurried there, as it was necessary I should confer with him on some matters. A crowd had reassembled around the building, which had become in some sort a headquarters; and, in fact, Cæsar has confiscated it to his own uses, and intends to keep it as his home hereafter. I found him in the council-chamber. You never saw such a sight. He was so black with dust and blood that he looked like a negro. He was hatless, and his mat of hair rose like a wild beast's mane. He had been drinking; his eyes were wild and rolling; the great sword he held in his right hand was caked with blood to the hilt. He was in a fearful state of excitement, and roared when he spoke. A king-devil, come fresh out of hell, could scarcely have looked more terrible. Behind him in one corner, crouching and crying together, were a bevy of young and handsome women. The Sultan had been collecting his harem. When he caught sight of me he rushed forward and seized my hand, and shouted out:

" 'Hurrah, old fellow! This is better than raising potatoes on the Saskatchewan, or hiding among the niggers in Louis—hic—iana. Down with the Oligarchy. To hell with them. Hurrah! This is my palace. I am a king! Look-a-there,' he said, with a roll and a leer, pointing over his shoulder at the shrinking and terrified women; 'ain't they beauties, —hic—all mine—every one of 'em.'

"Here one of his principal officers came up, and the following dialogue occurred:

" 'I came, General, to ask you what we are to do with the dead.'

" 'Kill 'em,' roared Cæsar, 'kill 'em, d——n 'em.'

" 'But, General, they are dead already,' replied the officer, who was a steady fellow and perfectly sober.

" 'Well, what's the matter with 'em, then?' replied Cæsar. 'Come, come, Bill, if they're dead, that's the end of them. Take a drink,' and he turned, unsteadily, toward the council-table, on which stood several bottles and demijohns.

" 'But some of us have talked it over,' said the officer. 'A number of the streets are impassable already with the dead. There must be a quarter of a million of soldiers and citizens lying about, and the number is being added to every minute. The weather is warm, and they will soon breed a pestilence that will revenge them on their slayers. Those killed by the poison are beginning to smell already. We couldn't take any action without your authority, and so I came to ask you for your orders.'

" 'Burn 'em up,' said Cæsar.

" 'We can't,' said the man; 'we would have to burn up the city to destroy them in that way; there are too many of them; and it would be an immense task to bury them.'

" 'Heap 'em all up in one big pile,' said Cæsar.

" 'That wouldn't do—the smell they would make in decaying would be unbearable, to say nothing of the sickness they would create.'

"Cæsar was standing unsteadily, looking at us with lack-luster eyes. Suddenly an idea seemed to dawn in his monstrous head—an idea as monstrous and uncouth as the head itself. His eyes lighted up.

" 'I have it!' he shouted. 'By G—d, I have it! Make a pyramid of them, and pour cement over them, and let it stand forever as a monument of this day's glorious work! Hoorrah!'

" 'That's a pretty good idea,' said the officer, and the others present, courtier-like—for King Cæsar already has his courtiers—applauded the idea vociferously.

" 'We'll have a monument that shall last while the earth stands,' cried Cæsar. 'And, hold on, Bill,' he continued, 'you shall build it;—and—I say—we won't make a pyramid of it—it shall be a column— *Cæsar's Column*—by G—d. It shall reach to the skies! And if there aren't enough dead to build it of, why, we'll kill some more; we've got plenty to kill. Old Thingumbob, who used to live here—in my palace—said he would kill ten million of us to-day. But he didn't. Not much! Max's friend—that d——d long-legged fellow, from Africa—he dished him, for he told old Quincy all about it. And now I've got old Thingumbob's best girl in the corner yonder. Oh, it's jolly. But build the column, Bill—build it high and strong. I remember—hic—how they used to build houses on the Saskatchewan, when I was grubbing for potatoes there. They had a board frame the length of a wall, and three or four feet high. They would throw in stones, bowlders, pebbles, dirt, anything, and, when it was full, they would pour cement over it all; and when it hardened—hic— which it did in a few minutes, they lifted up the frame and made another course. I say, Bill, that's the way you must build Cæsar's column. And get Charley Carpenter to help you; he's an engineer. And, hold on, Bill, put a lot of dynamite—Jim has just told me they had found tons of it—put a lot of dynamite—hic—in the middle of it, and if they try to tear down my monument, it will blow them to the d——l. And, I say, Max, that long-legged, preaching son-of-thunder—that friend of yours—he must write an inscription for it. Do you hear? He's the man to do it. Something fine. By G—d, we will build a monument that will beat the pyramids of all the other Cæsars. Cæsar's Column! Hoorrah!'

"And the great brute fairly jumped and danced with delight over his extraordinary conception.

"Bill hurried out. They have sixty thousand prisoners—men who had not been among the condemned —but merchants, professional men, etc. They were debating, when I came up, whether they would kill them, but I suggested that they be set to work on the construction of Cæsar's Column, and if they worked well, that their lives be spared. This was

agreed to. They are now building the monument on
Union Square. Thousands of wagons are at work
bringing in the dead. Other wagons are hauling
cement, sand, etc. Bill and his friend Carpenter are
at work. They have constructed great wooden
boxes, about forty feet from front to rear, about
four feet high and fifty feet long. The dead are to be
laid in rows—the feet of the one row of men near
the center of the monument, and the feet of the next
row touching the heads of the first, and so on. In
the middle of the column there is to be a cavity,
about five feet square, running from the top to the
bottom of the monument, in which the dynamite is
to be placed; while wires will lead out from it among
the bodies, so arranged, with fulminating charges,
that any attempt to destroy the monument or
remove the bodies will inevitably result in a dreadful explosion. But we will go up after dinner and
look at the work," he said, "for they are to labor
night and day until it is finished. The members of
the Brotherhood have entered with great spirit into
the idea of such a monument, as a symbol and
memorial of their own glory and triumph."

"I remember," said I, "reading somewhere that,
some centuries ago, an army of white men invaded
one of the Barbary states. They were defeated by
the natives, and were every one slain. The Moors
took their bodies and piled them up in a great monument, and there the white bones and grinning skulls
remain to this day, a pyramid of skeletons; a ghastly
warning to others who might think to make a like
attempt at invasion of the country. Cæsar must
have read of that terrible trophy of victory."

"Perhaps so," said Maximilian; "but the idea
21

may have been original with him; for there is no telling what such a monstrous brain as his, fired by whisky and battle, might or might not produce."

At dinner poor Mr. Phillips was looking somewhat better. He had a great many questions to ask his son about the insurrection.

"Arthur," he said, "if the bad man and his accomplices, who so cruelly used me, should be made prisoners, I beg you, as a favor to me, not to punish them. Leave them to God and their own consciences."

"I shall," said Max, quietly.

Mrs. Phillips heartily approved of this sentiment. I looked down at my plate, but before my eyes there came a dreadful picture of that fortress of flame, with the chained man in the midst, and high above it I could see, swung through the air by powerful arms, manacled figures, who descended, shrieking, into the vortex of fire.

After many injunctions to his guards, to look well after the house, Max and I, well armed and wearing our red crosses, and accompanied by two of our most trusted men, sallied forth through the back gate.

What a scene! Chaos had come. There were no cars or carriages. Thieves and murderers were around us; scenes of rapine and death on every hand. We moved together in a body; our magazine rifles ready for instant use.

Our red crosses protected us from the members of the Brotherhood; and the thieves gave our guns a wide berth. At a street crossing we encountered a wagon-load of dead bodies; they were being hauled to the monument. The driver, one of the Brotherhood, recognized Max, and invited us to seats beside

him. Familiarity makes death as natural as life.
We accepted his offer—one of our men sitting on the
tail-board of the wagon; and in this gory chariot
we rode slowly through Broadway, deserted now by
everything but crime. The shops had all been broken
open; dead bodies lay here and there; and occasionally a burned block lifted its black arms appealingly
to heaven. As we drew near to Union Square a wonderful sight—such as the world had never before beheld—expanded before us. Great blazing bonfires
lighted the work; hundreds of thousands had gathered to behold the ghastly structure, the report of
which had already spread everywhere. These men
nearly all belonged to the Brotherhood, or were members of the lower orders, who felt that they had nothing to fear from insurrection. There were many
women among them, and not a few thieves, who,
drawn by curiosity, for awhile forgot their opportunities and their instincts. Within the great outer
circle of dark and passionate and exultant faces, there
was another assemblage of a very different appearance. These were the prisoners at work upon the
monument. Many of them were gray-haired; some
were bloody from wounds upon their heads or bodies; they were all pale and terrified; not a few were
in rags, or half naked, their clothes having been
literally torn from their backs. They were dejected,
and yet moved with alacrity, in fear of the whips or
clubs in the hands of their masters, who passed
among them, filling the air with oaths. Max pointed
out to me prominent merchants, lawyers and clergy-
men. They were all dazed-looking, like men after a
terrific earthquake, who had lost confidence in the
stability of everything. It was Anarchy personified:

— the men of intellect were doing the work; the men of muscle were giving the orders. The under-rail had come on top. It reminded me of Swift's story of the country where the men were servants to the horses.

The wagons rolled up, half a dozen at a time, and dumped their dreadful burdens on the stones, with no more respect or ceremony than if they had been cord-wood. Then the poor trembling prisoners seized them by the head and feet, and carried them to other prisoners, who stood inside the boxes, and who arranged them like double lines from a central point:— it was the many-rayed sun of death that had set upon civilization. Then, when the box was full and closely packed, they poured the liquid cement, which had been mixed close at hand, over them. It hardened at once, and the dead were entombed forever. Then the box was lifted and the work of sepulture went on.

While I stood watching the scene I heard a thrilling, ear-piercing shriek—a dreadful cry! A young man, who was helping to carry a corpse, let go his hold and fell down on the pavement. I went over to him. He was writhing and moaning. He had observed something familiar about the form he was bearing—it was the body of a woman. He had peered through the disheveled hair at the poor, agonized, blood-stained features, and recognized—*his wife!*"

One of the guards raised his whip to strike him, and shouted:

"Here! Get up! None of this humbugging."

I caught the ruffian's arm. The poor wretch was embracing the dead body, and moaning pitiful expressions of love and tenderness into the ears that would never hear him more. The ruffian threatened me. But the mob was moved to mercy, and took my part; and even permitted the poor creature to carry off his dead in his arms, out into the outer darkness. God only knows where he could have borne it.

I grew sick at heart. The whole scene was awful.

I advanced toward the column. It was already several feet high, and ladders were being made, up which the dead might be borne. Coffee and bread and meat were served out to the workers.

I noticed a sneaking, ruffianly fellow, going about among the prisoners, peering into every face. Not far from me a ragged, hatless, gray-haired man, of over seventy, was helping another, equally old, to bear a heavy body to the ladders. The ruffian looked first into the face of the man at the feet of the corpse; then he came to the man at the head. He uttered an exclamation of delight.

"Ha! you old scoundrel," he cried, drawing his pistol. "So I've found you. You're the man that turned my sick wife out of your house, because she couldn't pay the rent. I've got you now."

The old man fell on his knees, and held up his hands, and begged for mercy. I heard an explosion — a red spot suddenly appeared on his forehead, and he fell forward, over the corpse he had been carrying — dead.

"Come! move lively!" cried one of the guards, snapping his whip; "carry them both to the workmen."

I grew dizzy. Maximilian came up.

"How pale you are," he said.

"Take me away!" I exclaimed, "or I shall faint."

We rode back in another chariot of revolution — a death-cart.

CHAPTER XXXVII.

THE SECOND DAY.

IT WAS a dreadful night. Crowds of farmers from the surrounding country kept pouring into the city. They were no longer the honest yeomanry who had filled, in the old time, the armies of Washington, and Jackson, and Grant, and Sherman, with brave and patriotic soldiers; but their brutalized descendants — fierce serfs — cruel and bloodthirsty peasants. Every man who owned anything was their enemy and their victim. They invaded the houses of friend and foe alike, and murdered men, women and children. Plunder! plunder! They had no other thought.

One of our men came to me at midnight, and said:

"Do you hear those shrieks?"

"Yes," I replied.

"They are murdering the family next door."

These were pleasant, kindly people, who had never harmed any one. But this maelström swallows good and bad alike.

Another came running to me, and cried:

"They are attacking the house!"

"Where?" I asked.

"At the front door."

"Throw over a hand-grenade," I said.

There was a loud crash, and a scurrying of flying feet. The cowardly miscreants had fled. They were murderers, not warriors.

All night long the awful Bedlam raged. The dark
streets swarmed. Three times we had to have recourse to the hand-grenades. Fires sprang up all
over the city, licking the darkness with their hideous
tongues of flame, and revealing by their crimson
glare the awful sights of that unparalleled time. The
dread came upon me: What if some wretch should
fire a house in our block? How should we choose
between the conflagration and those terrible streets?
Would it not be better to be ashes and cinders, than
to fall into the hands of that demoniacal mob?

No one slept. Max sat apart and thought. Was
he considering—too late!—whether it was right to
have helped produce this terrible catastrophe? Early
in the morning, accompanied by three of his men,
he went out.

We ate breakfast in silence. It seemed to me we
had no right to eat in the midst of so much death
and destruction.

There was an alarm, and the firing of guns above
us. Some miscreants had tried to reach the roof of
our house from the adjoining buildings. We rushed
up. A lively fusillade followed. Our magazine rifles
and hand-grenades were too much for them; some
fell dead and the rest beat a hasty retreat. They
were peasants, searching for plunder.

After awhile there came a loud, rapping at the
front door. I leaned over the parapet and asked who
was there. A rough-looking man replied:

"I have a letter for you."

Fearing some trick, to break into the house, I
lowered a long cord and told him to tie the letter to
it. He did so. I pulled up a large sheet of dirty
wrapping-paper. There were some lines scrawled

upon it, in lead-pencil, in the large hand of a school-boy—almost undecipherable. With some study I made out these words:

MISTER GABRIEL, MAX'S FRIEND:—Cæsar wants that thing to put on the front of the column.   BILL.

It took me a few minutes to understand it. At last I realized that Cæsar's officer—Bill—had sent for the inscription for the monument, about which Cæsar had spoken to Max. I called down to the messenger to wait, and that I would give it to him.

I sat down, and, after some thought, wrote, on the back of the wrapping-paper, these words:

THIS GREAT MONUMENT

IS

ERECTED BY

CÆSAR LOMELLINI,

COMMANDING GENERAL OF

THE BROTHERHOOD OF DESTRUCTION,

IN

COMMEMORATION OF

THE DEATH AND BURIAL OF

MODERN CIVILIZATION.

It is composed of the bodies of a quarter of a million of human beings, who were once the rulers, or the instruments of the rulers, of this mighty, but, alas! this ruined city.

They were dominated by leaders who were altogether evil.

They corrupted the courts, the juries, the newspapers, the legis-latures, the congresses, the ballot-boxes and the hearts and souls of the people.

They formed gigantic combinations to plunder the poor; to make the miserable more miserable; to take from those who had least and give it to those who had most.

They used the machinery of free government to effect oppression; they made liberty a mockery, and its traditions a jest; they drove justice from the land and installed cruelty, ignorance, despair and vice in its place.

Their hearts were harder than the nether mill-stone; they degraded humanity and outraged God.

At length indignation stirred in the vasty courts of heaven; and overburdened human nature rose in universal revolt on earth.

By the very instruments which their own wickedness had created they perished; and here they lie, sepulchred in stone, and heaped around explosives as destructive as their own lives. We execrate their vices, while we weep for their misfortunes. They were the culmination of centuries of misgovernment; and they paid an awful penalty for the sins of generations of short-sighted and selfish ancestors, as well as for their own cruelty and wickedness.

Let this monument, O man! stand forever.

Should civilization ever revive on earth, let the human race come hither and look upon this towering shaft, and learn to restrain selfishness and live righteously. From this ghastly pile let it derive the great lesson, that no earthly government can endure which is not built on mercy, justice, truth and love.

I tied the paper to the cord and lowered it down to the waiting messenger.

At noon Max returned. His clothes were torn, his face pale, his eyes wild-looking, and around his head he wore a white bandage, stained with his own blood. Christina screamed and his mother fainted.

"What is the matter, Max?" I asked.

"It is all in vain," he replied despairingly; "I thought I would be able to create order out of chaos and reconstruct society. But that dream is past."

"What has happened?" I asked.

"I went this morning to Prince Cabano's palace to get Cæsar to help me. He had held high carnival all night and was beastly drunk, in bed. Then I went out to counsel with the mob. But another calamity had happened. Last night the vice-president—the Jew—fled, in one of the Demons, carrying away one hundred million dollars that had been left in his charge."

"Where did he go?" I asked.

"No one knows. He took several of his trusted followers, of his own nation, with him. It is rumored that he has gone to Judea; that he proposes to make himself king in Jerusalem, and, with his vast wealth, re-establish the glories of Solomon, and revive the ancient splendors of the Jewish race, in the midst of the ruins of the world."

"What effect has his flight had on the mob?" I asked.

"A terrible effect. They are wild with suspicions and full of rumors. They gathered, in a vast concourse, around the Cabano palace, to prevent Cæsar leaving them, like the cripple. They believe that he, too, has another hundred millions hidden in the cellars of the palace. They clamored for him to appear. The tumult of the mob was frightful.

"I rose to address them from the steps of the palace. I told them they need not fear that Cæsar would leave them—he was dead drunk, asleep in bed. If they feared treachery, let them appoint a committee to search the palace for treasure. But— I went on—there was a great danger before them which they had not thought of. They must establish some kind of government that they would all obey. If they did not they would soon be starving. I explained to them that this vast city, of ten million inhabitants, had been fed by thousands of carloads of food which were brought in, every day, from the outside world. Now the cars had ceased to run. The mob had eaten up all the food in the shops, and to-morrow they would begin to feel the pangs of starvation. And I tried to make them understand what it meant for ten million people to be starving together.

"They became very quiet. One man cried out:

"'What would you have us do?'

"'You must establish a provisional government. You must select one man to whose orders you will all submit. Then you must appoint a board of counselors to assist him. Then the men among you who are engineers and conductors of trains of cars and of air-lines must reassume their old places; and they must go forth into the country and exchange the spoils you have gathered for cattle and flour and vegetables, and all other things necessary for life.'

"'He wants to make himself a king,' growled one ruffian.

"'Yes,' said another, 'and set us all at work again.'

"'He's a d——d aristocrat, anyhow,' cried a third.

"But there were some who had sense enough to see that I was right, and the mob at once divided into two clamorous factions. Words led to blows. A number were killed. Three wretches rushed at me. I shot one dead, and wounded another; the third gave me a flesh wound on the head with a sword; my hat broke the force of the blow, or it would have made an end of me. As he raised his weapon for a second stroke, I shot him dead. My friends forced me through the door of the palace, in front of which I had been standing; we double-locked it to keep out the surging wild beasts; I fled through the back door, and reached here.

"All hope is gone," he added sadly; "I can do nothing now but provide for our own safety."

CHAPTER XXXVIII.

THE FLIGHT.

"Yes," I replied, "we cannot remain here another night. Think what would be the effect if a fire broke out anywhere in this block!"

He looked at me in a startled way.

"True," he said; "we must fly. I would cheerfully give my life if its sacrifice would arrest these horrors; but it would not."

Christina came and stood beside him. He wrote a letter to General Quincy. He made three copies of it. Selecting three of his best men, he gave each a copy, and told them to make their way together, well armed, to the armory of the air-ships. It was a perilous journey, but if either of them reached his destination, he was to deliver his copy of the letter to the general. In it Max asked General Quincy to send him one of the "Demons," as promised, that night at eight o'clock; and he also requested, as a signal that the messengers had reached him and that the air-ship would come, that he would send up a single Demon, high in the air, at once on receiving the letter.

We went to the roof with our field-glasses. In two hours, we thought, the messengers, walking rapidly, would reach the armory. Two hours passed. Nothing was visible in the heavens in the direction of the armory, although we swept the whole region with our glasses. What if our messengers had all been slain?

What if General Quincy refused to do as he had agreed, for no promises were likely to bind a man in such a dreadful period of anarchy? Two hours and a quarter—two hours and a half passed, and no signal. We began to despair. Could we survive another night of horrors? At last Estella, who had been quietly looking to the west with her glass, cried out:

"See! there is something rising in the air."

We looked. Yes, thank heaven! it was the signal. The Demon rose like a great hawk to a considerable height, floated around for awhile in space, and then slowly descended.

It would come!

All hands were set at work. A line was formed from the roof to the rooms below; and everything of value that we desired to carry with us was passed from hand to hand along the line and placed in heaps, ready for removal. Even the women joined eagerly in the work. We did not look for our messengers; they were to return to us in the air-ship.

The afternoon was comparatively quiet. The mobs on the street seemed to be looking for food rather than treasure. They were, however, generally resting, worn out; they were sleeping—preparing for the evening. With nightfall the saturnalia of death would begin again with redoubled force.

We ate our dinner at six; and then Mr. Phillips suggested that we should all join in family prayers. We might never have another opportunity to do so, he said. He prayed long and earnestly to God to save the world and protect his dear ones; and we all joined fervently in his supplications to the throne of grace.

At half past seven, equipped for the journey, we

were all upon the roof, looking out in the direction of the west for the coming of the Demon. A little before eight we saw it rise through the twilight above the armory. Quincy, then, was true to his pledge. It came rapidly toward us, high in the air; it circled around, and at last began to descend just over our heads. It paused about ten feet above the roof, and two ladders were let down. The ladies and Mr. Phillips were first helped up to the deck of the vessel; and the men began to carry up the boxes, bales, trunks, money, books and instruments we had collected together.

Just at this moment a greater burst of tumult reached my ears. I went to the parapet and looked down. Up the street, to the north, came a vast concourse of people. It stretched far back for many blocks. My first notion was that they were all drunk, their outcries were so vociferous. They shouted, yelled and screamed. Some of them bore torches, and at their head marched a ragged fellow with a long pole, which he carried upright before him. At the top of it was a black mass, which I could not make out in the twilight. At this instant they caught sight of the Demon, and the uproar redoubled; they danced like madmen, and I could hear Max's name shouted from a hundred lips.

"What does it mean?" I asked him.

"It means that they are after me. Hurry up, men," he continued, "hurry up."

We all sprang to work; the women stood at the top and received the smaller articles as a line of men passed them up.

Then came a thunderous voice from below:

"Open the door, or we will break it down."

Max replied by casting a bomb over the parapet. It exploded, killing half a dozen men. But this mob was not to be intimidated like the thieves. The bullets began to fly; fortunately the gathering darkness protected us. The crowd grew blacker, and more dense and turbulent. Then a number of stalwart fellows appeared, bearing a long beam, which they proposed to use as a battering-ram, to burst open the door, which had resisted all previous attacks.

"Bring down one of the death bombs," said Max to the men in the Demon.

Two stout fellows, belonging to the air-ship, carried down, carefully, between them, a great black sphere of iron.

"Over with it!" cried Max.

There was a crash, an explosion; the insurgents caught a whiff of the poisoned air; the men dropped the beam; there was a rush backward amid cries of terror, and the street was clear for a considerable space around the house.

"Hurry, men, hurry!" cried Max.

I peeped over the parapet. A number of the insurgents were rushing into a house three doors distant. In a few moments they poured out again, looking behind them as they ran.

"I fear they have fired that house," I said to Max.

"I expected as much," he replied, quietly .

"Hurry, men, hurry," he again cried.

The piles on the roof were diminishing rapidly. I turned to pass up bundles of my precious books. Another sound broke on my ears; a roaring noise that rapidly increased—it was the fire. The mob cheered. Then bursts of smoke poured out of the windows of the doomed house; then great arms and

22

hands of flame reached out and snapped and clutched at the darkness, as if they would drag down ancient Night itself, with all its crown of stars, upon the palpitating breast of the passionate conflagration. Then the roof smoked; then it seemed to burst open, and vast volumes of flame and smoke and showers of sparks spouted forth. The blaze brought the mob into fearful relief, but fortunately it was between us and the great bulk of our enemies.

"My God," said Max, "it is Cæsar's head!"

I looked, and there, sure enough, upon the top of the long pole I had before noticed, was the head of the redoubtable giant. It stood out as if it had been painted in gory characters by the light of the burning house upon that background of darkness. I could see the glazed and dusty eyes; the protruding tongue; the great lower jaw hanging down in hideous fashion; and from the thick, bull-like neck were suspended huge gouts of dried and blackened blood.

"It is the first instinct of such mobs," said Max, quietly, "to suspect their leaders and slay them. They killed Cæsar, and then came after me. When they saw the air-ship they were confirmed in their suspicions; they believe that I am carrying away their treasure."

I could not turn my eyes from that ferocious head. It fascinated me. It waved and reeled with the surging of the mob. It seemed to me to be executing a hideous dance in mid-air, in the midst of that terrible scene; it floated over it like a presiding demon. The protruding tongue leered at the blazing house and the unspeakable horrors of that assemblage, lit up, as it was, in all its awful features, by the towering conflagration.

The crowd yelled and the fire roared. The next house was blazing now, and the roof of the one nearest us was smoking. The mob, perceiving that we did not move, concluded that the machinery of the air-ship was broken, and screamed with joy as the flames approached us.

Up, up, went bundle and package and box; faster, and faster, and faster. We were not to be intimidated by fire or mobs! The roof of the house next us was now blazing, and we could hear the fire, like a furnace, roaring within it.

The work is finished; every parcel is safe.

"Up, up, men!"

Max and I were the last to leave the roof; it had become insufferably hot. We stood on the deck; the engineer touched the lever of the electric engine; the great bird swayed for an instant, and then began to rise, like a veritable Phœnix from its nest of flame, surrounded by cataracts of sparks. As the mob saw us ascend, veiled dimly, at first, by that screen of conflagration, they groaned with dismay and disappointment. The bullets flew and hissed around us, but our metallic sides laughed them to scorn. Up, up, straight and swift as an arrow we rose. The mighty city lay unrolled below us, like a great map, starred here and there with burning houses. Above the trees of Union Square, my glass showed me a white line, lighted by the bon-fires, where Cæsar's Column was towering to the skies, bearing the epitaph of the world.

I said to Max:

"What will those millions do to-morrow?"

"Starve," he said.

"What will they do next week?"

"Devour each other," he replied.

There was silence for a time.

"Will not civil government rise again out of this ruin?" I asked.

"Not for a long time," he replied. "Ignorance, passion, suspicion, brutality, criminality, will be the lions in the path. Men who have such dreadful memories of labor can scarcely be forced back into it. And who is to employ them? After about three-fourths of the human family have died of hunger, or been killed, the remainder, constituting, by the law of the survival of the fittest, the most powerful and brutal, will find it necessary, for self-defense against each other, to form squads or gangs. The greatest fighter in each of these will become chief, as among all savages. Then the history of the world will be slowly repeated. A bold ruffian will conquer a number of the adjacent squads, and become a king. Gradually, and in its rudest forms, labor will begin again; at first exercised principally by slaves. Men will exchange liberty for protection. After a century or two a kind of commerce may arise. Then will follow other centuries of wars, between provinces or nations. A new aristocracy will spring up. Culture will lift its head. A great power, like Rome in the old world, may arise. Some vast superstition may take possession of the world; and Alfred, Victoria and Washington may be worshiped, as Saturn, Juno and Hercules were in the past; with perhaps dreadful and bloody rites like those of the Carthaginians and ancient Mexicans. And so, step by step, mankind will re-enact the great human drama, which begins always with a tragedy, runs through a comedy, and terminates in a catastrophe."

The city was disappearing—we were over the ocean—the cool salt breeze was refreshing. We both looked back.

"Think," I said, "what is going on yonder."

Max shuddered. There was a sullen light in his eyes. He looked at his father, who was on his knees praying.

"I would destroy the world," he said, "to save *him* from a living death."

He was justifying himself unto himself.

"Gabriel," he said, after a pause, "if this outbreak had not occurred now, yet would it certainly have come to pass. It was but a question of time. The breaking-strain on humanity was too great. The world could not have gone on; neither could it have turned back. The crash was inevitable. It may be God's way of wiping off the blackboard. It may be that the ancient legends of the destruction of our race by flood and fire are but dim remembrances of events like that which is now happening."

"It may be so, Max," I replied; and we were silent.

Even the sea bore testimony to the ruin of man. The light-houses no longer held up their fingers of flame to warn the mariner from the treacherous rocks. No air-ship, brilliant with many lights shining like innumerable eyes, and heavy with passengers, streamed past us with fierce swiftness, splitting the astonished and complaining air. Here and there a sailing vessel, or a steamer, toiled laboriously along, little dreaming that, at their journey's end, starving creatures would swarm up their sides to kill and devour.

How still and peaceful was the night—the great,

solemn, patient night! How sweet and pure the air!
How delightful the silence to ears that had rung so
lately with the clamors of that infuriated mob!
How pleasant the darkness to eyeballs seared so
long by fire and flame and sights of murder! Estella and Christina came and sat down near us.
Their faces showed the torture they had endured,—
not so much from fear as from the shock and agony
with which goodness contemplates terrific and triumphant evil.

I looked into the grand depths of the stars
above us; at that endless procession of shining
worlds; at that illimitable expanse of silence. And I
thought of those vast gaps and lapses of manless
time, when all these starry hosts unrolled and marshaled themselves before the attentive eyes of God,
and it had not yet entered into his heart to create
that swarming, writhing, crawling, contentious mass
we call humanity. And I said to myself, "Why
should a God condescend to such a work as man?"

And yet, again, I felt that one grateful heart,
that darted out the living line of its love and adoration from this dark and perturbed earth, up to the
shining throne of the Great Intelligence, must be
of more moment and esteem in the universe than
millions of tons of mountains—yea, than a wilderness
of stars. For matter is but the substance with
which God works; while thought, love, conscience
and consciousness are parts of God himself. We
think; therefore we are divine: we pray; therefore we
are immortal.

Part of God! The awful, the inexpressible, the in-
comprehensible God. His terrible hand swirls, with
unresting power, yonder innumerable congregation

of suns in their mighty orbits, and yet stoops, with tender touch, to build up the petals of the anemone, and paint with rainbow hues the mealy wings of the butterfly.

I could have wept over man; but I remembered that God lives beyond the stars.

CHAPTER XXXIX.

EUROPE.

THE next day we were flying over the ocean. The fluctuous and changeable waves were beneath us, with their multitudinous hues and colors, as light and foam and billows mingled. Far as the eye could reach, they seemed to be climbing over each other forever, like the endless competitions of men in the arena of life. Above us was the panorama of the clouds — so often the harbingers of terror; for even in their gentlest forms they foretell the tempest, which is ever gathering the mists around it like a garment, and, however slow-paced, is still advancing.

A whale spouted. Happy nature! How cunningly were the wet, sliding waves accommodated to that smooth skin and those nerves which rioted in the play of the tumbling waters. A school of dolphins leaped and gamboled, showing their curved backs to the sun in sudden glimpses; a vast family; merry, social, jocund, abandoned to happiness. The gulls flew about us as if our ship was indeed a larger bird; and I thought of the poet's lines wherein he describes —

"The gray gull, balanced on its bow-like wings,
Between two black waves, seeking where to dive."

And here were more kindly adjustments. How the birds took advantage of the wind and made it lift them or sink them, or propel them forward;

tacking, with infinite skill, right in the eye of the gale, like a sailing-vessel. It was not toil—it was delight, rapture—the very glory and ecstasy of living. Everywhere the benevolence of God was manifest: light, sound, air, sea, clouds, beast, fish and bird; we were in the midst of all; we were a part of all; we rejoiced in all.

And then my thoughts reverted to the great city; to that congregation of houses; to those streets swarming with murderers; to that hungry, moaning multitude.

Why did they not listen to me? Why did rich and poor alike mock me? If they had not done so, this dreadful cup might have been averted from their lips. But it would seem as if faith and civilization were incompatible. Christ was only possible in a bare-footed world; and the few who wore shoes murdered him. What dark perversity was it in the blood of the race that made it wrap itself in misery, like a garment, while all nature was happy?

Max told me that we had had a narrow escape. Of the three messengers we had sent forth to General Quincy, but one reached him; the others had been slain on the streets. And when that solitary man fought his way through to the armory he found the Mamelukes of the Air full of preparations for a flight that night to the mountain regions of South America. Had we delayed our departure for another day, or had all three of our messengers been killed by the marauders, we must all have perished in the midst of the flames of the burning building. We joined Mr. Phillips, therefore, with unwonted heartiness in the morning prayers.

The next day we came in sight of the shores of

Europe. As we drew near, we passed over multitudes of open boats, river steamers and ships of all kinds, crowded with people. Many of these vessels were unfitted for a sea voyage, but the horrors they fled from were greater than those the great deep could conjure up. Their occupants shouted to us, through speaking-trumpets, to turn back; that all Europe was in ruins. And we, in reply, warned them of the condition of things in America, and advised them to seek out uncivilized lands, where no men dwelt but barbarians.

As we neared the shore we could see that the beaches, wharves and tongues of sand were everywhere black with people, who struggled like madmen to secure the few boats or ships that remained. With such weapons as they had hurriedly collected they fought back the better-armed masses of wild and desperate men who hung upon their skirts, plying the dreadful trade of murder. Some of the agonized multitude shrieked to us for help. Our hearts bled for them, but we could do nothing. Their despairing hands were held up to us in supplication as the air-ship darted over them.

But why dilate upon the dreadful picture that unrolled beneath us? Hamlets, villages, towns, cities, blackened and smoking masses of ruin. The conflicts were yet raging on every country road and city street; we could hear the shrieks of the flying, the rattle of rifles and pistols in the hands of the pursuers. Desolation was everywhere. Some even rushed out and fired their guns viciously at us, as if furious to see anything they could not destroy. Never before did I think mankind was so base. I realized how much of the evil in human nature had been for ages suppressed and kept in subjection by the iron force of law and its terrors. Was man the joint product of an angel and a devil? Certainly in this paroxysm of fate he seemed to be demoniacal.

We turned southward over the trampled gardens and vineyards of France. A great volcanic lava field of flame and ashes — burning, smoking — many miles in extent — showed where Paris had been. Around it ragged creatures were prowling, looking for something to eat, digging up roots in the fields. At one place, in the open country, I observed, ahead of us, a tall and solitary tree in a field; near it were the smouldering ruins of a great house. I saw something white moving in the midst of the foliage, near the top of the tree. I turned my glass upon it. It was a woman, holding something in her arms.

"Can we not take her up?" I asked the captain of the air-ship.

"We cannot stop the vessel in that distance — but we might return to it," he replied.

"Then do so, for God's sake," I said.

We swooped downward. We passed near the tree. The woman screamed to us to stop, and held up an infant. Christina and Estella and all the other women wept. We passed the tree — the despairing cries of the woman were dreadful to listen to. But she takes courage; sees us sweep about; we come slowly back; we stop; a rope ladder falls; I descend; I grasp the child's clothes between my teeth; I help the woman up the ladder. She falls upon the deck of the ship, and cries out in French: "Spare my child!" Dreadful period! when every human being is looked upon as a murderer. The women comfort her. Her clothes are in rags, but upon her fingers are costly jewels. Her babe is restored to her arms; she faints with hunger and exhaustion. For three days, she tells us, she has been hidden in that tree, without food or drink; and has seen all dear to her perish—all but her little François. And with what delight Estella and Christina and the rest cuddle and feed the pretty, chubby, hungry little stranger!

Thank God for the angel that dwells in human nature. And woe unto him who bids the devil rise to cast it out!

Max, during all this day, is buried in profound thought. He looks out at the desolated world and sighs. Even Christina fails to attract his attention. Why should he be happy when there is so much misery? Did he not help to cause it?

But, after a time, we catch sight of the blue and laughing waters of the Mediterranean, with its pleasant, bosky islands.

This is gone, and in a little while the yellow sands of the great desert stretch beneath us, and extend ahead of us, far as the eye can reach. We pass a toiling caravan, with its awkward, shuffling, patient camels, and its dark attendants. They have heard nothing, in these solitudes, of the convulsions that rend the world. They pray to Allah and Mahomet and are happy. The hot, blue, cloudless sky rises in a great dome above their heads; their food is scant and rude, but in their veins there burn not those wild fevers of ambition which have driven mankind to such frenzies and horrors. They live and die as their ancestors did, ten thousand years ago—unchangeable as the stars above their heads; and these are even as they shone clear and bright when the Chaldean shepherds first studied the outlines of the constellations, and marked the pathways of the wandering planets.

Before us, at last, rise great blue masses, towering high in air, like clouds, and extending from east to west; and these, in a little while, as we rush on, resolve themselves into a mighty mountain range, snow-capped, with the yellow desert at its feet, stretching out like a Persian rug.

I direct the pilot, and in another hour the great ship begins to abate its pace; it sweeps in great circles. I see the sheep flying terrified by our shadow; then the large, roomy, white-walled house, with its broad verandas, comes into view; and before it, looking up at us in surprise, are my dear mother and brothers, and our servants.

The ship settles down from its long voyage. We are at home. We are at peace.

CHAPTER XL.

THE GARDEN IN THE MOUNTAINS.

[These concluding lines are from the journal of Gabriel Weltstein.]

SINCE my return home I have not been idle. In the first place, I collected and put together the letters I had written to my brother Heinrich, from New York. I did this because I thought they were important, as a picture of the destruction of civilization, and of the events which led up to it. I furthermore had them printed on our printing-press, believing that every succeeding century would make them more valuable to posterity; and that in time they would be treasured as we now treasure the glimpses of the world before the Deluge, contained in the Book of Genesis.

And I have concluded to still further preserve, in the pages of this journal, a record of events as they transpire.

As soon as I had explained to my family the causes of our return—for which they were in part prepared by my letters to Heinrich—and had made them acquainted with my wife and friends, I summoned a meeting of the inhabitants of our colony—there are about five thousand of them, men, women and children.

They all came, bringing baskets of provisions with them, as to a picnic. We met in an ancient grove upon a hillside. I spoke to them and told them the dreadful tale of the destruction of the world. I need not say that they were inexpressibly shocked by the awful narrative. Many of them wept bitterly, and some even cried out aloud—for they had left behind them, in Switzerland, many dear friends and relatives. I comforted them as best I could, by reminding them that the Helvetian Republic had survived a great many dynasties and revolutions; that they were not given to the luxuries and excesses that had wrecked the world, but were a primitive people, among whom labor had always remained honorable. Moreover, they were a warlike race, and their mountains were their fortifications; and they would, therefore, probably, be able to defend themselves against the invasion of the hungry and starving hordes who would range and ravage the earth.

The first question for us, I said, was to ascertain how to best protect ourselves from like dangers. We then proceeded to discuss the physical conformation of our country. It is a vast table-land, situated at a great height far above the tropical and miasmatic plains, and surrounded by mountains still higher, in which dwell the remnants of that curious white race first described by Stanley. The only access to our region from the lower country is by means of the ordinary wagon road which winds upward through a vast defile or gorge in the mountains. At one point the precipitous walls of this gorge approach so closely together that there is room for only two wagons to pass abreast. We determined to assemble all our men the next day at this place, and build up a high wall that would completely cut off communication with the external world, making the wall so thick and strong that it would be impossible for any force that was likely to come against us to batter it down.

This was successfully accomplished; and a smooth, straight wall, thirty feet high and about fifty broad at its widest point, now rises up between our colony and the external world. It was a melancholy reflection that we—human beings—were thus compelled to exclude our fellow-men.

We also stationed a guard at a high point near the wall, and commanding a view of its approaches for many miles; and we agreed upon a system of bale-fires (*Bael* fires), or signal beacons, to warn the whole settlement, in case of the approach of an enemy.

We next established a workshop, under the charge of Carl Jansen, in which he trained some of our young men in metal-working, and they proceeded to make a large supply of magazine rifles, so that every man in the settlement might be well armed. Carl is one of those quiet, unpretending men whose performance is always better than their promise; and he is a skillful worker in the metals. The iron and coal we found in abundance in our mountains. We also cast a number of powerful cannon, placed on very high wheels, and which could be fired vertically in case we were attacked by air-ships;—although I thought it probable that the secret of their manufacture would be lost to the world in the destruction of civilization. We, however, carefully housed the Demon under a shed, built for the purpose, intending, when we had time, to make other air-ships like it, with which to communicate with the external world, should we desire to do so.

Having taken all steps necessary to protect ourselves from others, we then began to devise means by which we might *protect ourselves from ourselves;* for the worst enemies of a people are always found in their own midst, in their passions and vanities. And the most dangerous foes of a nation do not advance with drums beating and colors flying, but creep upon it insidiously, with the noiseless feet of a fatal malady.

In this work I received great help from Max, and especially from his father. The latter had quite recovered the tone of his mind. He was familiar with all the philosophies of government, and he continued to be filled with an ardent desire to benefit mankind. Max had seemed, for some days after our arrival, to be seriously depressed, brooding over his own thoughts; and he seized eagerly upon the work I gave him to do, as if he would make up by service to our people for any injuries he had done the world. We held many consultations. For good purposes and honest instincts we may trust to the multitude; but for long-sighted thoughts of philanthropy, of statesmanship and statecraft, we must look to a few superior intellects. It is, however, rarely that the capacity to do good and the desire to do good are found united in one man.

When we had formulated our scheme of government we called the people together again; and after several days of debate it was substantially agreed upon.

In our constitution we first of all acknowledged our dependence on Almighty God; believing that all good impulses on earth spring from his heart, and that no government can prosper which does not possess his blessing.

23

We decreed, secondly, a republican form of government. Every adult man and woman of sound mind is permitted to vote. We adopted a system of voting that we believed would insure perfect secrecy and prevent bribery—something like that which had already been in vogue, in some countries, before the revolution of the Proletariat.

The highest offense known to our laws is treason against the state, and this consists not only in levying war against the government, but in corrupting the voter or the office-holder; or in the voter or office-holder selling his vote or his services. For these crimes the penalty is death. But, as they are in their very nature secret offenses, we provide, in these cases only, for three forms of verdict: *"guilty," "not guilty"* and *"suspected."* This latter verdict applies to cases where the jury are morally satisfied, from the surrounding circumstances, that the man is guilty, although there is not enough direct and positive testimony to convict him. The jury then have the power—not as a punishment to the man, but for the safety of the community—to declare him incapable of voting or holding office for a period of not less than one nor more than five years. We rank bribery and corruption as high treason; because experience has demonstrated that they are more deadly in their consequences to a people than open war against the government, and many times more so than murder.

We decreed, next, universal and compulsory education. No one can vote who cannot read and write. We believe that one man's ignorance should not countervail the just influence of another man's intelligence. Ignorance is not only ruinous to the individual, but destructive to society. It is an epidemic which scatters death everywhere.

We abolish all private schools, except the higher institutions and colleges. We believe it to be essential to the peace and safety of the commonwealth that the children of all the people, rich and poor, should, during the period of growth, associate together. In this way, race, sectarian and caste prejudices are obliterated, and the whole community grow up together as brethren. Otherwise, in a generation or two, we shall have the people split up into hostile factions, fenced in by doctrinal bigotries, suspicious of one another, and antagonizing one another in politics, business and everything else.

But, as we believe that it is not right to cultivate the heads of the young to the exclusion of their hearts, we mingle with abstract knowledge a cult of morality and religion, to be agreed upon by the different churches; for there are a hundred points wherein they agree to one wherein they differ. And, as to the points peculiar to each creed, we require the children to attend school but five days in the week, thus leaving one day for the parents or pastors to take charge of their religious training in addition to the care given them on Sundays.

We abolish all interest on money, and punish with imprisonment the man who receives it.

The state owns all roads, streets, telegraph or telephone lines, railroads and mines, and takes exclusive control of the mails and express matter.

As these departments will in time furnish employment for a great many officials, who might be massed together by the party in power, and wielded for political purposes, we decree that any man who accepts office relinquishes, for the time being, his right of suffrage. The servants of the people have no right to help rule them; and he who thinks more of his right to vote than of an office is at liberty to refuse an appointment.

As we have not an hereditary nobility, as in England, or great geographical subdivisions, as in America, we are constrained, in forming our Congress or Parliament, to fall back upon a new device.

Our governing body, called *The People*, is divided into three branches. The first is elected exclusively by the producers, to-wit: the workmen in the towns and the farmers and mechanics in the country; and those they elect must belong to their own class. As these constitute the great bulk of the people, the body that represents them stands for the House of Commons in England, or the House of Representatives in America. The second branch is elected exclusively by and from the merchants and manufacturers, and all who are engaged in trade, or as employers of labor. The third branch, which is the smallest of the three, is selected by the authors, newspaper writers, artists, scientists, philosophers and literary people generally. This branch is expected to hold the balance of power, where the other two bodies cannot agree. It may be expected that they will be distinguished by broad and philanthropic views and new and generous conceptions. Where a question arises as to which of these three groups or subdivisions a voter belongs to, the matter is to be decided by the president of the Republic.

No law can be passed, in the first instance, unless it receives a majority vote in each of the three branches, or a two-thirds vote in two of them. Where a difference of opinion arises upon any point of legislation, the three branches are to assemble together and discuss the matter at issue, and try to reach an agreement. As, however, the experience of the world has shown that there is more danger of the upper classes combining to oppress the producers than there is of the producers conspiring to govern them,—except in the last desperate extremity, as shown recently,—it is therefore decreed that if the Commons, by a three-fourths vote, pass any measure, it becomes a law, notwithstanding the veto of the other two branches.

The executive is elected by the Congress for a period of four years, and is not eligible for re-election. He has no veto and no control of any patronage. In the election of president a two-thirds vote of each branch is necessary.

Whenever it can be shown, in the future, that in any foreign country the wages of labor and the prosperity of the people are as high as in our own, then free trade with that people is decreed. But whenever the people of another country are in greater poverty, or working at a lower rate of wages than our own, then all commercial intercourse with them shall be totally interdicted. For impoverished labor on one side of a line, unless walled out, must inevitably drag down labor on the other side of the line to a like condition. Neither is the device of a tariff sufficient; for, although it is better than free trade, yet, while it tends to keep up the price of goods, it lets in the products of foreign labor; this diminishes the wages of our own laborers by decreasing the demand for their productions to the extent of the goods imported; and thus, while the price of

commodities is held up for the benefit of the manufacturers, the price of labor falls. There can be no
equitable commerce between two peoples representing
two different stages of civilization, and both engaged
in producing the same commodities. Thus the freest
nations are constantly pulled down to ruin by the
most oppressed. What would happen to heaven if
you took down the fence between it and hell? We
are resolved that our republic shall be of itself, by
itself—"in a great pool, a swan's nest."

As a corollary to these propositions, we decree
that our Congress shall have the right to fix the
rate of compensation for all forms of labor, so that
wages shall never fall below a rate that will afford the
laborer a comfortable living, with a margin that will
enable him to provide for his old age. It is simply a
question of the adjustment of values. This experi-
ment has been tried before by different countries, but
it was always tried in the interest of the employers;
the laborers had no voice in the matter; and it was
the interest of the upper class to cheapen labor; and
hence *Muscle* became a drug and *Cunning* invaluable
and masterful; and the process was continued indefinitely until the catastrophe came. Now labor
has its own branch of our Congress, and can defend
its rights and explain its necessities.

In the comparison of views between the three
classes some reasonable ground of compromise will
generally be found; and if error is committed we prefer that it should enure to the benefit of the many,
instead of, as heretofore, to the benefit of the few.

We declare in the preamble to our constitution
that "this government is intended to be merely a
plain and simple instrument, to insure to every in-

dustrious citizen not only liberty, but an educated mind, a comfortable home, an abundant supply of food and clothing, and a pleasant, happy life."

Are not these the highest objects for which governments can exist? And if government, on the old lines, did not yield these results, should it not have been so reformed as to do so?

We shall not seek to produce uniformity of recompense for all kinds of work; for we know that skilled labor is intrinsically worth more than unskilled; and there are some forms of intellectual toil that are more valuable to the world than any muscular exertion. The object will be not to drag down, but to lift up; and, above all, to prevent the masses from falling into that awful slough of wretchedness which has just culminated in world-wide disaster.

The government will also regulate the number of apprentices who shall enter any given trade or pursuit. For instance, there may be too many shoemakers and not enough farmers; if, now, more shoemakers crowd into that trade, they will simply help starve those already there; but if they are distributed to farming, and other employments, where there is a lack, then there is more work for the shoemakers, and in time a necessity for more shoemakers.

There is no reason why the ingenuity of man should not be applied to these great questions. It has conquered the forces of steam and electricity, but it has neglected the great adjustments of society, on which the happiness of millions depends. If the same intelligence which has been bestowed on perfecting the steam-engine had been directed to a consideration of the correlations of man to man, and pursuit to pursuit, supply and demand would have precisely matched each other, and there need have been no pauperism in the world—save that of the sick and imbecile. And the very mendicants would begin to rise when the superincumbent pressure of those who live on the edge of pauperism had been withdrawn.

We deny gold and silver any function as money except for small amounts—such as five dollars or less. We know of no supplies of those metals in our mountains, and if we tied our prosperity to their chariot, the little, comparatively, there is among us, would gradually gravitate into a few hands, and these men would become the masters of the country. We issue, therefore, a legal-tender paper money, receivable for all indebtedness, public and private, and not to be increased beyond a certain *per capita* of population.

We decree a limitation upon the amount of land or money any one man can possess. All above that must be used, either by the owner or the government, in works of public usefulness.

There is but one town in our colony—it is indeed not much more than a village—called Stanley. The republic has taken possession of all the land in and contiguous to it, not already built on—paying the owners the present price of the same; and hereafter no lots will be sold except to persons who buy to build homes for themselves; and these lots will be sold at the original cost price. Thus the opportunity for the poor to secure homes will never be diminished.

We further decree that when hereafter any towns or cities or villages are to be established, it shall only be by the nation itself. Whenever one hundred persons or more petition the government, expressing their desire to build a town, the government shall then take possession of a sufficient tract of land, paying the intrinsic, not the artificial, price therefor. It shall then lay the land out in lots, and shall give the petitioners and others the right to take the lots at the original cost price, provided they make their homes upon them. We shut out all speculators.

No towns started in any other way shall have railroad or mail facilities.

When once a municipality is created in the way I have described, it shall provide, in the plat of the town, parks for recreation; no lot shall contain less than half an acre; the streets shall be very wide and planted with fruit trees in double and treble rows. In the center of the town shall be erected a town hall, with an assembly chamber, arranged like a theater, and large enough to seat all the inhabitants. The building shall also contain free public baths, a library, a reading-room, public offices, etc. The municipality shall divide the people into groups of five hundred families each, and for each group they shall furnish a physician, to be paid for out of the general taxes. They shall also provide in the same way concerts and dramatic representations and lectures, free of charge. The hours of labor are limited to eight each day; and there are to be two holidays in the week, Wednesdays and Sundays. Just as the state is able to carry the mails for less than each man could carry them for himself, so the cost of physicians and entertainments procured by the municipality will be much less than under the old system.

We do not give any encouragement to labor-saving inventions, although we do not discard them. We think the end of government should be—not cheap goods or cheap men, but happy families. If any man makes a serviceable invention the state purchases it at a reasonable price for the benefit of the people.

Men are elected to whom all disputes are referred; each of the contestants selects a man, and the three act together as arbitrators. Where a jury is demanded the defeated party pays all the expenses. We hold that it is not right that all the peaceable citizens should be taxed to enable two litigious fellows to quarrel. Where a man is convicted of crime he is compelled to work out all the cost of his trial and conviction, and the cost of his support as a prisoner, before he can be discharged. If vice will exist, it must be made self-supporting.

[*An extract from Gabriel's journal—five years later.*]

I have just left a very happy group upon the veranda—Estella and our two darling little children; Christina and her three flaxen-haired beauties. Max is away on his sheep farm. My mother and Mrs. and Mr. Phillips are reading, or playing with the children. The sun is shining brightly, and the birds are singing. I enter my library to make this entry in my journal.

God has greatly blessed us and all our people. There were a few conservatives who strenuously objected at first to our reforms; but we mildly suggested to them that if they were not happy—and desired it—we would transfer them to the outside world, where they could enjoy the fruits of the time-hallowed systems they praised so much. They are now the most vigorous supporters of the new order of things. And this is one of the merits of your true conservative: if you can once get him into the right course he will cling to it as tenaciously as he formerly clung to the wrong. They are not naturally bad men; their brains are simply incapable of suddenly adjusting themselves to new conceptions.

The Demon returned yesterday from a trip to the outside world. Max's forebodings have been terribly realized. Three-fourths of the human race, in the civilized lands, have been swept away. In France and Italy and Russia the slaughter has been most appalling. In many places the Demon sailed for hundreds of miles without seeing a human being. The wild beasts—wolves and bears—are reassuming possession of the country. In Scandinavia and in northern America, where the severity of the climate somewhat mitigated the ferocity of man, some sort of government is springing up again; and the peasants have formed themselves into troops to defend their cattle and their homes against the marauders.

But civility, culture, seem to have disappeared. There are no newspapers, no books, no schools, no teachers. The next generation will be simply barbarians, possessing only a few dim legends of the refinement and wonderful powers of their ancestors. Fortunate it is, indeed, that here, in these mountains, we have preserved all the instrumentalities with which to restore, when the world is ready to receive it, the civilization of the former ages.

Our constitution has worked admirably. Not far

from here has arisen the beautiful village of Lincoln. It is a joy to visit it, as I do very often.

The wide streets are planted with trees; not shade trees, but fruit trees, the abundance of which is free to all. Around each modest house there is a garden, blooming with flowers and growing food for the household. There are no lordly palaces to cast a chill shadow over humble industry; and no resplendent vehicles to arouse envy and jealousy in the hearts of the beholders. Instead of these shallow vanities a sentiment of brotherly love dwells in all hearts. The poor man is not worked to death, driven to an early grave by hopeless and incessant toil. No; he sings while he works, and his heart is merry. No dread shadow of hunger hangs over him. We are breeding men, not millionaires.

And the good wife sings also while she prepares the evening meal, for she remembers that this is the night of the play; and yonder, on that chair, lies the unfinished dress which her handsome daughter is to wear, next Saturday night, to the weekly ball. And her sons are greatly interested in the lectures on chemistry and history.

Let us look in upon them at their supper. The merry, rosy faces of young and old; the cheerful converse; the plain and abundant food. Here are vegetables from their own garden, and fruit from the trees that line the wide streets.

Listen to their talk! The father is telling how the municipality bought, some three years ago, a large number of female calves, at a small cost; and now they are milch cows; and the town authorities are about to give one of them to every poor family that is without one.

And they praise this work; they love mankind, and the good, kindly government—their own government—which so cares for humanity and strives to lift it up. And then the father explains that each person who now receives a free gift of a milch cow is to bring to the municipal government the first female calf raised by that cow, and the city will care for that, too, for two or three years, and then bestow it upon some other poor family; and so, in endless rotation, the organized benevolence does its work, perennial as seed-time and harvest; and none are the poorer for it, and all are the happier.

But come; they have finished their supper, amid much merriment, and are preparing to go to the play. Let us follow them. How the streets swarm! Not with the dark and terrible throngs that dwell so vividly in my memory; but a joyous crowd—laughing, talking, loving one another—each with a merry smile and a kindly word for his neighbor. And here we are at the door of the play-house.

There is no fumbling to find the coins that can perhaps be but poorly spared; but free as the streets the great doors stand open. What hurry, what confusion, what chatter, what a rustle of dresses, as they seek their seats.

But hush! The curtain rises. The actors are their own townspeople — young men and women who have shown an aptitude for the art; they have been trained at the cost of the town, and are paid a small stipend for their services once a week. How the lights shine! How sweet is the music! What a beautiful scene! And what lovely figures are these, clad in the picturesque garb of some far-away country or some past age. And listen! They are telling the old,

old story; old as the wooing of Eve in Eden; the story of human love, always so dear, so precious to the human heart.

But see! the scene has changed—here is a merry-making; a crowd of flower-wreathed lads and lasses enter, and the harmonious dance, instinct with life and motion,—the poetry of human limbs,—unrolls itself before our eyes.

And so the pretty drama goes forward. An idyl of the golden age; of that glorious epoch when virtue was always triumphant, and vice was always exposed and crushed.

But the play is over; and the audience stream back, laughing and chatting, under the stars, down the long, fruit-embowered streets, to their flower-bedecked, humble homes.

And how little it costs to make mankind happy!

And what do we miss in all this joyous scene? Why, where are the wolves, that used to prowl through the towns and cities of the world that has passed away? The slinking, sullen, bloody-mouthed miscreants, who, under one crafty device or another, would spring upon, and tear, and destroy the poor, shrieking, innocent people—where are they?

Ah! this is the difference: The government which formerly fed and housed these monsters, under cunning kennels of perverted law, and broke open holes in the palisades of society, that they might crawl through and devastate the community, now shuts up every crevice through which they could enter; stops every hole of opportunity; crushes down every uprising instinct of cruelty and selfishness. And the wolves have disappeared; and our little world is a garden of peace and beauty, musical with laughter.

And so mankind moves with linked hands through happy lives to happy deaths; and God smiles down upon them from his throne beyond the stars.